Gardening
through the **Year**

Arthur Hellyer

Cover photograph by Paul Williams

This book is based on
Your Garden Week by Week first published 1936
by W. H. & L. Collingridge Limited.

First published 1981 in this completely revised form
by The Hamlyn Publishing Group Limited

First published 1983 as a Hamlyn Gondola Book by
The Hamlyn Publishing Group Limited
London · New York · Sydney · Toronto
Astronaut House, Feltham, Middlesex, England.

ISBN 0 600 30550 3

Phototypeset in 11 pt Monophoto Sabon by
Tameside Filmsetting Ltd., Ashton-under-Lyne, Lancashire

Printed in Hong Kong

Gardening through the Year

LONDON · NEW YORK · SYDNEY · TORONTO

Contents

Introduction

ANYONE attempting to write a comprehensive account of garden management has the choice of two quite different approaches to the task. The more usual is to deal with the matter subject by subject. To have, maybe, a section on vegetables, another on fruits, a third on ornamental plants and so on, any one of which may be further subdivided as each individual subject warrants and the finances of the publisher, who has to pay for it all to be printed, permits. This is, in fact, the standard encyclopedic approach and provided it is well thought out and carefully put together it works very well.

Yet it does suffer from one major drawback. It puts the onus on the reader to remember what has been read and when each task ought to be done. That, for example, there are some seeds to be sown as early as January and some as late as September with all the rest strung out at various dates between; that planting is equally fragmented – some plants needing to be moved early, some mid-season and some late. Pruning, spraying, plant feeding and many other tasks are also tied strictly to seasons and so there is much to be said in favour of writing a book based on time rather than on plants. In this way, provided the reader scans the appropriate pages a week or so ahead, there should be no need ever to be caught napping; to be saying to oneself, 'Oh yes, of course I did read that bit about transplanting bearded irises directly the flowers fade but it was so long ago that I quite forgot to do it when the right time came round'.

So *Gardening through the Year* is an attempt to deal with the whole subject of gardening, with the exception of orchids and some other exotic plants, in precisely this way. Inevitably it is a method that brings problems of its own. It is not so easy to sit down and read about the complete culture of any one crop or plant since it is most unlikely to appear all on one page, or even on several consecutive pages. One must search for the various mentions of it through the book, but I have tried to make this easy by copious and clear cross referencing as well as by a comprehensive index which tells the enquirer which particular aspect of culture or management will be found on this or that page.

However, there is a second difficulty about the calendar approach to gardening that some experts consider to be so insurmountable as to rule it out altogether. Plants, they say, do not grow according to the calendar but according to the weather – and everyone knows how unpredictable British weather can be. And even if, in some years the weather does behave in a more or less expected way, there is still a vast difference in the time at which things happen in one part of the country and another. Is it not a fact that the north is very much colder than the south and doesn't this make a nonsense of any attempt to suggest correct times for doing particular jobs, especially very seasonal work such as sowing, planting and pruning?

It would be foolish to say that there is nothing in this objection but it is far less serious than it might at first appear; there is, in fact, far more of a west-east peoblem than a south-north problem. This is because the biggest effect on the climate in various parts of the British Isles is not due to the difference in latitude, which is not very great since these are rather small islands, but to the relatively warm water drifting across the Atlantic Ocean from the Caribbean and washing on all the western and some of the southern shores. The result of this is to keep these coastal areas warmer than inland or east-coast regions. However, it is mainly a winter and early spring effect and during the summer all the coastal regions may actually be less warm than the inland areas because of the cooling influence of the sea. Altitude, too, has a considerable bearing on climate and so does proximity to the continental land mass. This is why Kent can often be the coldest county in the British Isles when north-easterly winds sweep in after travelling thousands of miles across northern Europe or even Asia.

In Britain, spring (using that term to mean the time at which grass begins to grow again and seeds start to germinate outdoors) usually comes first in the extreme south-west and then slowly sweeps across the country in a mainly north-easterly direction. The difference which this can make to the timing of garden jobs occurs chiefly in the period from January to March when, in any case, most seed sowing is being done under cover in an environment that can be artificially controlled. By summer climatic differences are tending to level out and by autumn there is not really a great deal in it, since it is the shortening

Metric conversion table

heights and lengths				weights		liquids	
in	*cm (approx)*	*ft*	*m (approx)*	*oz*	*g*	*pt*	*litres*
$\frac{1}{2}$	1	3	1	$\frac{1}{2}$	14	$\frac{1}{2}$	285 ml
1	2.5	5	1.5	1	25	1	570 ml
2	5	6	2	2	55	$1\frac{3}{4}$	1
4	10	8	2.5	5	140	2	1.2
6	16	10	3	8	225	3	1.75
8	20	16	5	12	340	4	2.5
10	25	20	6	16 (1 lb)	450	8 (1 gal)	4.5
12 (1 ft)	30	30	9				
18	45	50	15				
24 (2 ft)	60	100	30				

days more than the lower temperature which warn plants that winter is near and they must prepare for it in whatever way is appropriate for them.

So, taking all these things into account, I think that it is possible to suggest correct times for doing most garden work. Obviously these recommendations must be applied with commonsense. If the book says 'sow in mid-March', and in mid-March the garden is covered in snow or is a morass, clearly it is necessary to wait a while until conditions improve. However, it must be remembered that there are limits to the length of time over which a job can be postponed since each plant has its own rhythm of growth and needs sufficient time in which to complete it. These are more exacting for some plants than for others and so it is more important to keep as near as possible to the optimum date – provided other conditions make this possible. That is why most months in this book are divided into four sections. The first concerns tasks that can be done at any time during that month – and some of which may actually have to be continued in other months – whereas the other three sections are for work that I regard as more highly seasonal. Each of these three sections covers a period of about ten days, though again commonsense must be used since a good deal of overlap can be can be allowed from one section to another without anything very disastrous happening.

Having said all this I would still urge readers to acquire as much local information as possible. Good gardeners quickly discover that there are such things as micro-climates which can affect the behaviour of plants that are growing only a few hundred yards apart. A south-facing wall can create a warm, dry micro-climate of its own which may make it possible to sow, plant or harvest days ahead of a cooler spot in the same garden.

A similar effect can sometimes be seen when plants growing on a hillside appear to be hardier than when they are situated in a hollow. This is partly because, being so fully exposed, they really are kept cold in winter and so are discouraged from starting into growth prematurely and then having their tender young shoots killed by late frosts.

Hollows and valleys that appear very sheltered can, in fact, be misleading and may act as death traps for some plants when radiation frosts occur in spring or early summer. These are frosts caused by loss of heat from the soil to the sky on cloudless nights. Cold air is heavier than warm air and so runs downhill, collecting in valleys and hollows and often destroying the blossom of fruit and ornamental trees and shrivelling the young growth of even normally hardy plants. In order to counteract this effect, commercial fruit growers sometimes use powerful fans to stir up the air and in particular to draw down the warmer air that has risen out of their orchards. Such measures are scarcely practicable in gardens but it is surprising how light a protection, perhaps no more than a screen of polythene or fine mesh plastic-coated wire netting, placed around the plants will make sufficient difference to check this source of damage. It can also be useful either to remove altogether or cut holes in hedges, fences and walls placed across the natural fall of the land since these may be causing cold air to pile up which would otherwise go on flowing harmlessly by. In fact if one can learn to think of the movement of cold air as being very much like that of water, it is possible to devise all manner of ways of getting rid of it.

In some gardens, especially in autumn and spring, work is frequently delayed because the soil is too wet. It is difficult to plant and impossible to sow successfully if the soil is so wet that it clings to tools and feet. In very severe cases of badly draining soil it may be necessary to consider the possibility of getting rid of the surplus water with land drain pipes laid in gravel or hard core 1 ft to 18 in below the surface. However, in town and suburban gardens it is usually a problem to know how to dispose of the water that collects in these surface drains. It is illegal to divert it into public sewers and probably difficult to connect the garden drains with any major surface water drainage system. Still inquiries can be made and it is possible that some solution will be found.

The usual suggestion is to dig a soakaway at the lowest point of the garden and run the water into this. A soakaway is simply a large hole filled with hard rubble and covered with soil or turf so that it is not unsightly.

However, before one goes to all the labour and expense of land drains and soakaways, it is worth trying the effect of surface improvement of the soil texture. It is often quite remarkable how much difference this can make. If you can get the topmost 4 to 6 in of soil into really good working condition, a lot of the rain that previously collected on top, making work impossible, will simply drain away almost as fast as it falls. Anything that makes the soil more porous will help but the materials most likely to be available at not too outrageous a cost are leafmould (swept up leaves from the roads stacked and allowed to rot for two or three months will do), peat, spent mushroom compost, pulverised or shredded bark, garden compost, rotted straw and any bulky animal manure – that from a stable being best of all. Grit is also useful, the sharper and coarser the better because

fine sand will tend to bind the soil particles together and that will only make matters worse.

The way to use any of these materials is to spread them thickly over the surface and then fork them in. As a rule it is not necessary to dig them in deeply since what one is endeavouring to do is to improve the texture of the top few inches of soil. The trouble with many soils is that they are so lacking in humus and grit, and maybe also contain so much clay, that they become puddled on the surface almost as soon as it rains hard, and certainly if they are then walked on. As a result water collects in pools, runs about all over the place and in a very short while completes the destruction of the natural soil texture; prevent that from happening and you are halfway towards solving the problem.

Dry soil can also make it impossible to sow or plant at the right time but as a rule this is much easier to correct. Again the first step must be to improve the porosity of the top soil, for this will allow rain to seep in when it falls and not run uselessly off the surface. But, in addition, it is usually possible to add extra water – even if it means carrying a few bucketfuls to where it is most needed. However, sprinklers of many types are available and portable water pumps to feed them if no mains supply is at hand. The most important thing about watering dry ground prior to sowing or planting is to do it slowly, otherwise one will be back with the old problems of run off and puddling. Sprinklers that deliver water at the rate of about $\frac{1}{2}$ in per hour are ideal and if the soil is really dry it may be necessary to continue watering for several hours and then allow a few more hours further for the surface to drain adequately.

By one means or another, therefore, it will usually be found possible to do garden work around the optimum time and when, in some favourable places, experience suggests that it could, with advantage, be done earlier, by all means experiment and see what happens. But do not trust all your seeds or your plants to this out-of-season treatment. Try only a few and keep plenty in reserve until you know for certain precisely what liberties you can take in your own garden.

January

General Work

In the Garden

EVEN WHEN the ground is frozen hard there are still jobs to be done out of doors. It is an ideal time for wheeling out manure and placing it about in handy heaps ready for spreading and digging in as soon as conditions improve. It is not wise to dig soil immediately after a thaw nor during or immediately after a heavy fall of snow, for it is then too wet on the surface to break up properly. The clods will lie in the bottom of the trenches and gradually harden into brickbats, especially if the ground is of a clayey nature. But whenever the soil is soft enough to be dug, and yet not so wet that it sticks to the spade badly, digging can proceed.

FLOWERS AND SHRUBS

Take root cuttings Many plants can be raised more readily from root cuttings taken during January than in any other way. Well-known examples are oriental poppies, perennial statices, anchusas, perennial verbascums, *Romneya coulteri*, *Perovskia atriplicifolia*, *Phlox decussata* and gaillardias. The roots are cut up into pieces about 1 to 2 in in length. In all except the last four these cuttings are pushed vertically, right end up, into a sandy compost in well-drained pots or boxes. The tops of the cuttings should be just level with the soil. Romneya, phlox and gaillardia cuttings are simply strewn thinly over the surface of the soil and covered with a further $\frac{1}{4}$ in of compost. Place in a frame or greenhouse either slightly heated or unheated and water moderately. Shoots will form slowly and in late spring, after proper hardening off, the small plants can be established outdoors.

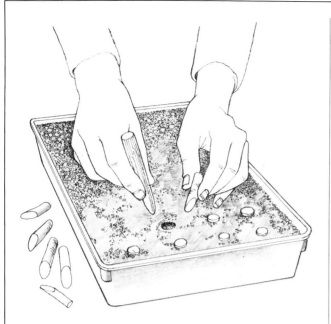

Take root cuttings at this time of year. Cut the roots into lengths and insert them, right way up, in sandy compost

Prune roses Continue to prune bush and standard roses (see page 192).

VEGETABLES AND FRUIT

Protect cauliflowers The curds of cauliflowers will require protection as they start to form (see page 165).

Collect scions for grafting This is a good time to collect suitable shoots for grafting if you intend to do any later on. Ordinary prunings will do quite well. Select strong, well-ripened shoots formed the previous summer. Label them carefully and then heel them in a trench about 10 cm (4 in) deep prepared in a cool, shady place, preferably under a north-facing wall or fence. The object is to keep them dormant until grafting time (see page 51). Old trees that are to be reworked should also be headed back now; that is the main branches should be sawn off about a couple of feet from the trunk. Apples and pears stand this treatment best. Plums, cherries and other stone fruits resent the hard cutting back.

Complete fruit tree pruning Fruit tree pruning should really be done in November and December but if it is delayed for one reason or another, it can be completed in January but the sooner the better. Work on the peaches, nectarines and apricots first,

then do the gooseberries and red and white currants, leaving the pears and apples till the last. Very soon the sap will be on the move once more and the wise gardener will always get his trees pruned while they are quite dormant (see page 196).

Spray fruit trees with tar oil When the weather is favourable spray all outdoor fruit trees and bushes with tar oil wash. This is to kill any insect eggs which may be left in the crevices of the bark and to clean the trees of green, scummy growth and pests such as scale insects. It is at this time of the year that really powerful insecticides can be used without fear of damaging the trees and the gardener who neglects this opportunity must not be surprised if his trees in the summer are more freely attacked by pests and diseases than those of his more alert neighbour.

Tar oil washes are sold under several different trade names and can be purchased from any dealer in horticultural sundries. They are prepared by diluting with water, the usual strength being six parts of the neat tar oil to a hundred parts of water, for instance 6 pints in 100 pints ($12\frac{1}{2}$ gallons) of water. Instructions are always given on the container, and you should consult these in case the purchased brand is not of standard strength.

The important thing in tar oil spraying is to employ a machine that will give a fine but driving spray capable of penetrating well down into the crevices of the bark. A powerful coarse spray is efficient but wasteful. It is also wasteful to attempt to spray trees when the weather is windy, and it is not effective to spray while it is freezing; so choose a calm and comparatively mild day for the work, and not one when it is raining, or the dilution will be upset.

Under Glass

General greenhouse management The well-managed greenhouse should be full of plants during January, many of them in flower and all wanting careful watering. Greenhouse calceolarias are particularly susceptible to bad watering and may collapse quite suddenly if given too much; yet dryness is equally bad. Winter-flowering primulas, greenhouse calceolarias and some other plants are apt to suffer severely if water is allowed to collect at the base of the leaves and in the heart of the plant. Do not forget the golden rule of all watering – namely that when water is given it must be supplied in sufficient quantity to moisten the soil in pot or box right through. There is nothing worse than keeping the surface wet and letting the lower soil remain dry.

Ventilation is also bound to be a tricky matter, especially in a small house or one that is not too well heated. The ideal is a constant circulation of air without draughts or sudden variations of temperature. Only the top ventilators will be needed during January, and even these must be closed at night. Open them a little during the day provided it is not freezing or foggy, but, if there is any choice in the matter, be sure to open them on the side away from the wind and be equally sure to get them closed well before the sun goes down, for a little sun heat trapped late in the afternoon will go a long way towards keeping up the night temperature. Watch carefully for decaying leaves as this is a sure sign of a stuffy atmosphere (see page 185).

The ideal average temperature to be aimed at for the common winter-flowering plants such as primulas, cinerarias, calceolarias and cyclamen is 13 to 16°C (55 to 60°F) by day and 7 to 10°C (45 to 50°F) at night. If winter-flowering begonias are grown, it will be all to the good to have 2 or 3°C more, but most plants are able to stand quite a wide variation in temperature. A good deal of nonsense is talked upon this subject and one is sometimes left with the impression that there are many plants which cannot be grown in anything but a thermostatically controlled atmosphere. A thermostat is certainly an immense help, but it is by no means a necessity. The great thing to avoid is any very sudden fluctuations, especially in the early morning or evening.

FLOWERS AND SHRUBS

Bring bulbs into the greenhouse Successive small batches of tulips, narcissi of all types, including trumpet daffodils and hyacinths should be brought into the greenhouse from plunge bed or frame to maintain a continuity of flowers later on.

Ventilate plants in frames Violets and other hardy or nearly hardy plants in frames, such as violas, pansies, anemones, penstemons, bedding calceolarias, antirrhinums from late-summer seeds and cuttings, sweet peas, cauliflowers, bulbs and alpines in pots must be ventilated just as freely as the weather permits. On all mild, sunny days remove the lights altogether for a few hours. If there is a cold wind blowing, tilt the lights with blocks of wood placed on the leeward side. At night the frames should be closed and if the weather is very cold it is advisable to throw a few sacks over them into the bargain. An occasional stirring of the soil between the plants with a pointed stick does a lot of good.

Pot rooted carnation and chrysanthemum cuttings During the month keep a careful watch on carnation cuttings taken during December, and if these are in pure sand get them potted up singly in 2-in pots as soon as they are well rooted (which means that roots ½ in long have been formed). It is quite easy to tell when a cutting is rooted, because it will start to grow at once. Until then it will remain at a standstill. There is not the same urgency with carnation cuttings that are in soil and sand, nor with chrysanthemum cuttings, which are almost always rooted in soil and sand, but even with these it is a good plan to get them singly into pots before the roots get tangled together. Use 3-in pots for the chrysanthemums, for these grow more rapidly. Propagating frames must be ventilated freely as soon as cuttings start to grow. Use a compost such as John Innes potting compost No. 1 or a soilless equivalent for both carnations and chrysanthemums at this early stage. Shade the plants from direct sunlight for a few days and then start to harden them off by placing on a shelf near the glass and ventilating more freely.

VEGETABLES AND FRUIT

Lift and blanch chicory Roots can be lifted as required from the open ground and blanched in a warm place (see page 184).

Force seakale and rhubarb You should also bring in at least two batches of seakale and rhubarb to force in heat if you wish to maintain an unbroken succession. These, of course, are forced in complete darkness (see page 194).

Fruit trees and vines under glass Greenhouses in which vines or fruit trees are grown should still be ventilated as freely as possible. No heat must be used, and ventilators should be opened widely whenever it is not actually freezing hard. Light frost will do no harm but rather good, preparing the trees for very rapid growth when the house is closed later on.

Early January

In the Garden

Order seeds The very first task for January should be to compile a complete list of all seeds that will be required during the following two or three months and to get these ordered without delay. It is true that a good many of the seeds cannot be sown before March or even April, but later on seedsmen become inundated with orders and even with the best of organizations there may be delay in execution. There is no sense in risking that, because the seeds can be kept quite as well at home as in the seedsmen's store, and they will then be at hand at the very moment that the most favourable opportunity arrives. Order seed potatoes at the same time and as soon as they arrive set them up in shallow trays, eyed (rose) ends uppermost, and place them in a light but frost-proof room, shed or greenhouse to form sprouts. This is particularly important with early varieties, but is worth doing with all kinds.

Under Glass

FLOWERS AND SHRUBS

Sow exhibition sweet peas This is the time for the exhibition grower to sow sweet peas in pots if this was not done in a frame in September. A warm greenhouse will be needed for germination, but a great amount of heat is not desirable; 10 to 13°C (50 to 55°F) will be ample. Sow four or five seeds in each 3-in pot of John Innes seed compost or an equivalent mixture.

Pot and plant lilies There is no doubt that early autumn is the best time to pot and plant most lilies, but it is sometimes impossible to get certain varieties then, especially if they have to be imported from America or Japan. These should be dealt with as soon as they are available and this often adds quite appreciably to the extent of one's January tasks. Bulbs that have travelled a long distance may have become rather soft or shrivelled and it is wise to plump them up before potting or planting them. This is done by placing them in seed trays, partly surrounding them with moist moss peat keeping this damp by daily spraying with water. As soon as the bulbs get plump and firm, plant or pot without further delay.

A frame fitted with soil-warming cables should also have thermostats to control the air and soil temperatures

Bring shrubs in pots into green-house The first week in January is a good time to bring into the greenhouse any bush roses you may have well established in pots. Give them a light, airy place preferably on the staging, not too far from the glass. Water the soil moderately and spray with slightly warm water every morning. Maintain a temperature of about 13 to 16°C (55 to 60°F). All the roses must be pruned, previous year's growth being shortened to within an inch or so of the older wood. You could also bring in deutzias, Indian azaleas, lilacs or viburnums for forcing. One or two flowering shrubs would provide a succession of colour later in the house or greenhouse. A start may also be made with hydrangeas and astilbes, both of which require rather liberal watering once they have started into growth.

Prune climbers in the greenhouse Several of the permanent climbers

Colour in the greenhouse, even in
January

that can be grown in greenhouses
should be pruned now. These
include *Plumbago capensis* and
the passion flower (passiflora).
The plumbago is pruned by
cutting each of last year's
growths back to 9 in or thereabouts. This applies to fully
developed specimens. With young
plants which have not yet filled
their space, some shoots may be
left unpruned. Passion flowers
are pruned by cutting out weak
shoots altogether and reducing
the remainder of the previous
year's growths to about two buds
each.

VEGETABLES AND FRUIT

Sow shorthorn carrots in a frame
If a frame with soil-warming
cables is available, you can make
a first sowing of shorthorn
carrots. Sow these directly in the
soil in the frame and not in
boxes. The rows should be about
6 in apart. If the seedlings are
thinned to a couple of inches
apart later on, there will be a
nice supply of tender young roots
in the early spring.

Sow onions for exhibition If you
aspire to great successes on the
vegetable show bench later in the
year, you must make a sowing of
exhibition onions in a heated
greenhouse. It is no use to sow
onion seed as yet outdoors or in
an unheated frame. But if sown
thinly in John Innes seed compost
in well-drained seed trays and
placed in a greenhouse with an
average temperature of 13°C
(55°F) the seed will soon germinate and provide sturdy seedlings
for transferring to the open
ground in the spring. The best
method is to sow the seeds singly

1 in apart; then the seedlings
need not be pricked off.

Start early peaches With the aid
of a heated greenhouse it is
possible to have ripe peaches,
nectarines and apricots at any
time during the summer. If you
wish to eat ripe fruits in June,
this is the time to start the trees
into growth. Close doors and
ventilators and maintain an
average temperature of 8°C
(45°F) at night, rising to about
13°C (55°F) by day. Spray the
trees every morning with slightly
warm water and damp the floor
of the house to maintain the
moisture in the atmosphere.

Prune late vines Late-fruiting
vines such as Alicante and Gros
Colmar should be pruned.
Details of this are the same as for
the pruning of early vines (see
page 195).

Mid January

In the Garden

FLOWERS AND SHRUBS

Prick over bulb beds During the month tulips, daffodils and hyacinths will appear through the soil. As soon as the green sprouts can be seen clearly, go over the beds carefully with a small border fork, pricking up the soil between the bulbs, but only to a depth of about an inch. This will improve aeration and kill moss, green scummy growth and weeds. At the same time give the soil a dusting of a good and balanced fertilizer. If you wish to make your own mixture, do so with seven parts of superphosphate of lime, five parts of sulphate of ammonia, two parts of either sulphate or muriate of potash and one of bonemeal (all parts by weight). Use this at 4 oz per square yard. Of course, you must choose a fine day for this work and one when the soil is neither very wet nor frozen.

VEGETABLES AND FRUIT

Mulch asparagus beds If possible, get some well-rotted

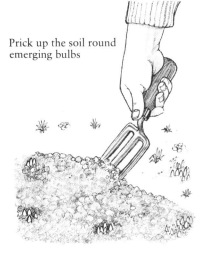

Prick up the soil round emerging bulbs

manure (farmyard manure is best, though stable manure will serve), break it up well and spread it a couple of inches thick over the asparagus beds. This will have a marked effect upon the quality of the shoots later on. The only condition when this may be inadvisable occurs when the soil is heavy, cold and inclined to be waterlogged. In these circumstances a light dressing of hop manure will be more suitable.

Under Glass

FLOWERS AND SHRUBS

Start begonia and gloxinia tubers If you own a well-heated greenhouse, you may start tuberous-rooted begonias and gloxinias into growth. The begonias can be managed quite satisfactorily in a temperature of 13°C (55°F), but a little more heat is advisable for the gloxinias. If the two have to be grown in the same house, the extra warmth will not do the begonias any harm. Prepare some rather deep seed trays with good drainage in the bottom and then a layer of moss peat. Set the tubers almost shoulder to shoulder in this and just cover them with more peat. Be careful to moisten the peat thoroughly some while before it is actually required. When peat is quite dry it is very difficult to make it take up water, which runs off the granules instead of soaking into them, but once they have become moistened they go on soaking up water like a sponge. If the peat is well wetted a few days before the begonia and gloxinia tubers are

to be boxed, no further watering will be needed at first, but do not let it dry out. Keep it just nicely moist until growth appears and then give more water.

Take chrysanthemum cuttings A task which can be carried out when opportunity permits is that of taking late-flowering chrysanthemum cuttings. It is rather early yet to start on the outdoor-flowering chrysanthemums, though even with these I would not hesitate to have a few cuttings, if there are any good ones showing, of a variety that is known to be shy in producing them. Later on, when the proper time arrives, there may be no suitable shoots to be had – and a cutting in the pot is certainly worth two in the bush.

Nevertheless, in the main, it is the late-flowering kinds that are to be propagated in January and particularly the incurves and exhibition Japanese kinds. Full particulars are given in the notes for December (page 204).

Take carnation cuttings Perpetual-flowering carnations should be propagated as opportunity occurs. They are best prepared from side shoots produced a little way up the flowering stems. Avoid those right at the base and right at the top. Shoots about 3 in in length are ideal and can be obtained by pulling gently away and down from the plant. The heel or small strip of skin that comes away from the old stem should be trimmed off close to the base of the cutting, which is then ready for insertion. Alternative methods are to cut the shoot just below a joint and not pull it away at the heel, or to pull it upwards so that it slips out of the joint. This last method is known as taking a piping. These cuttings are ready for insertion without further fuss. They should be inserted firmly 1 in deep in either pure silver sand or in equal parts of good loam and silver sand. They root more quickly and reliably in pure sand but need considerably more attention as to watering which is a nuisance if one has to be away from home most of the day. Carnation cuttings are rooted in a greenhouse maintained at a temperature of about 10°C (50°F), but it is an advantage to keep them in a propagating box and to warm the soil to about 16°C (60°F).

VEGETABLES AND FRUIT
Sow small salads under glass
Various small salad crops may be sown during the month in a slightly-heated greenhouse or a frame with soil-warming cables.

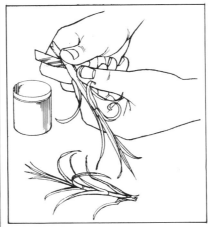

Trim the ends of carnation cuttings immediately below a leaf

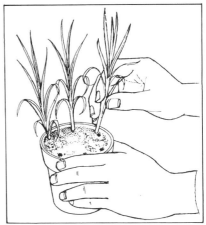

Dip in rooting powder and insert around the edge of a pot of sandy compost

Mustard and cress can be grown very readily in this manner or in shallow boxes in a warm greenhouse. Sow the mustard every week and the cress about once a fortnight, as it lasts longer. A couple of small sowings of radishes and lettuces made at fortnightly intervals under similar conditions in a frame or in deeper boxes or beds in the greenhouse will provide useful saladings later on.

Plant potatoes in frames and pots
These are not difficult to grow, but they do take up valuable space. However, if you want them, this is the time to start, with one well-sprouted tuber in each 8-in pot of John Innes potting compost No. 2 or with tubers planted 8 in apart in rows 1 ft apart directly in a bed of good soil mixed with some garden compost and a sprinkling of general fertilizer.

Sowing indoors

Seeds vary greatly in size and the very tiny ones like those of begonia and gloxinia, can get lost in crevices if the surface soil is not made smooth and level. Sieve the soil over the surface if necessary and then press it gently with a smooth wooden block. The larger seeds can be spaced out singly $\frac{1}{4}$ in or so apart but small seeds are best sprinkled over the surface very carefully and sparingly so that they do not germinate as a dense carpet. Cover with another light sifting of soil or, for the tiniest seeds, simply place a sheet of glass over the pan or seed tray and a single thickness of newspaper over this.

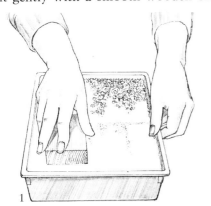

Plants for January

There are not many flowers in bloom outdoors in January but their very scarcity makes them all the more precious. One watches eagerly for the first fat buds of *Iris histrioides* to come spearing through the soil, soon to need the protection of a cloche or sheet of glass supported on notched sticks, not because this plant is in the least tender but because its fragile blue flowers are easily spoiled by wind, rain or frost. The same is true of *Crocus imperati*, always one of the first flowers to greet the new year and a ravishing beauty if it is not spoiled by the kind of weather a British winter can produce. Snowdrops, by contrast, need no protection and, though hard frost may throw them prostrate to the ground, when the thaw comes they will stand up again apparently none the worse for that experience.

It is astonishing how many winter flowers are scented. Both hamamelis and chimonanthus, the witch hazel and the winter sweet, can fill the air for many yards with their sweet perfume and though *Viburnum farreri (fragrans)* does not cast its fragrance quite so far, it is just as richly scented when one approaches close to it. The same is true of the winter-flowering bush honeysuckles and of *Azara microphylla* with flowers so small that they are almost hidden by the leaves until one is made aware of their presence by the strong scent of vanilla. It is a little puzzling to know what benefit plants gain from this sweetness since there are no insects around to be attracted by it so early in the year, at any rate not in Britain.

Under glass, or even in a well-lighted room, the picture can be quite the reverse. There are numerous exotic plants which flower in mid-winter provided a comfortable temperature can be maintained and some of them, including the free flowering greenhouse evergreen azaleas and the several races of winter-flowering primulas, are very easy to grow. There are plenty of bulbs, too, that will flower in winter without much heat and many of them can be planted outdoors in spring to make an annual display in the garden in subsequent years.

Top: Hamamelis mollis, commonly known as witch hazel
Centre: Azalea indica provides a lovely display indoors
Bottom: The delicate and perfumed *Viburnum farreri (fragrans)*

Herbaceous plants *Helleborus abchasicus, H. atrorubens, H. corsicus, H. foetidus, H. macranthus, H. niger, Iris unguicularis, Petasites fragrans, P. japonicus,* winter-flowering pansies.

Hardy bulbs, corms and tubers *Crocus ancyrensis, C. aureus, C. imperati, C. korolkowii, C. laevigatus, C. tomasinianus, Cyclamen coum, Eranthis cilicica, E. hyemalis, E. tubergeniana, Galanthus byzantinus, G. caucasicus, G. elwesii whittallii, G. nivalis, Iris bakeriana, I. danfordiae, I. histrio, I. histrioides, I. persica, I. reticulata.*

Evergreen shrubs *Azara integrifolia, A. microphylla, Camellia sasanqua, Daphne bholua, D. laureola, D. odora, Erica carnea, E. darleyensis, Garrya elliptica, Mahonia acanthifolia* (mild places only), *M. bealei, M. japonica, M. lomariifolia, M. media* vars. (Charity, Buckland and Lionel Fortescue in particular), *Rhododendron mucronulatum, R. nobleanum, Sarcococca confusa, S. hookeriana, S.h. digyna, S. humilis, S. ruscifolia chinensis, Viburnum tinus.*

Deciduous shrubs *Chimonanthus praecox, Corylus avellana, Daphne mezereum* Autumnalis, *Hamamelis intermedia, H. japonica, H. mollis, H. virginiana, Lonicera fragrantissima, L. purpusii, L. standishii, Prunus incisa praecox, Viburnum bodnantense, V. foetens, V. farreri (fragrans).*

Deciduous trees *Crataegus monogyna biflora, Prunus davidiana, P. subhirtella autumnalis, Salix aegyptiaca.*

Hardy climbers *Clematis cirrhosa, Jasminum nudiflorum.*

Sweetly-scented *Chimonanthus praecox*, the winter sweet, is best grown against a sunny wall

Late January

In the Garden

VEGETABLES AND FRUIT

Force rhubarb and seakale out of doors This is a good time to start forcing rhubarb outdoors. There is not much point in starting earlier, as it will be well-nigh impossible to generate sufficient heat to start any growth. The essentials for successful forcing are complete darkness and a mild, even temperature. First of all, the roots must be covered with something; either special earthenware forcing pots which are not unlike chimney pots with a lid on the top, but are difficult to obtain nowadays, or with old barrels, large boxes, plastic drums or buckets. It is convenient, but not essential, to have a removable lid on top so that the sticks of rhubarb can be gathered without

Rhubarb can be forced by placing dry leaves around the crowns. Then cover them with a box and some sacking to keep them warm and dark

having to move the whole contraption. Place the cover in position either before or after heaping up dead leaves around the crowns, the more the better since the leaves will keep the rhubarb crowns at a nice even temperature and encourage steady and early growth. Never attempt to force newly-planted or semi-established crowns. Only really strong roots should be covered, preferably those three or four years old.

Seakale can also be forced outdoors where it is growing by covering each strong crown with a large plant pot inverted and placing a piece of turf to block up the drainage hole in the bottom of the pot. Complete darkness is essential.

Protect fruit trees from birds From now onwards birds are very liable to attack the buds of fruit trees, particularly pears, plums and gooseberries. The best protection for small bush fruits is obviously a properly-constructed fruit cage covering the whole plantation. Pear and

plum trees can be protected by passing black thread from twig to twig, but it is a laborious job. A good protection against birds is by netting the trees or using Scaraweb, which consists of strands of nylon fibre stretched over the branches. This disintegrates gradually within about eight weeks. Various chemical deterrents are available and these should be used in accordance with the manufacturers' instructions.

Under Glass

FLOWERS AND SHRUBS

Sow begonias, gloxinias and other plants Sowings should be made now in propagating frames with heat or in the warm greenhouse of begonia, gloxinia, streptocarpus, canna, verbena, antirrhinium, pelargoniums (if required to bloom well the first summer) and scarlet salvia. With the exception of cannas and pelargoniums, all can be managed in an average temperature of 18°C (65°F). The antirrhinums will even do with rather less, but ideally the gloxinias should have a little more to germinate more rapidly and grow more sturdily. Cannas need 24°C (75°F), and even then germinate very irregularly and pelargoniums need at least 20°C (68°F) preferably a little more at this time of year. Do not forget that plants from these early sowings will be quite big by May, the time when many plants accommodated under glass during winter can be put outside once more. If your greenhouse is

A well designed fruit cage provides the very best protection from birds. If possible choose one with a door to allow for easy access

already rather full and you plan to sow half-hardy annuals in February and take a lot of cuttings, it may be wise to omit these first sowings. But if space is available you can take advantage of an early start. It will be reflected in the abundance and quality of the flowers.

Start early hippeastrums You can start hippeastrums by bringing the bulbs in the pots in which they flowered the previous year into a temperature of 16°C (60°F) or thereabouts and giving them a gradually increasing quantity of water. This can be done in the house if your green-house temperature is low. If any of the bulbs that have been resting since October show signs of starting, select these.

Pot on greenhouse calceolarias It is time to give greenhouse calceolarias their final move into the pots in which they will flower. These should be 7 to 8 in in diameter. Use John Innes potting compost No. 1. Stand the plants in a light, airy place on the staging, water very carefully, and maintain an average temperature of 13°C (55°F).

VEGETABLES AND FRUIT

Sow French beans for forcing You can obtain a May crop of French beans by sowing five or six in each 8-in pot filled to within a couple of inches of the rim with John Innes potting compost No. 1 or an equivalent mixture. Cover with a further inch of soil, water freely, and place in the greenhouse in a heated propagator kept at a temperature of from 16 to 21°C (60 to 70°F).

Sow leeks This is a good time to make a first sowing of leeks if large stems are required. Sow the seeds singly 1 in apart in well-drained seed boxes, using ordinary John Innes seed compost. Germinate in a greenhouse or frame with an average temperature of 13°C (55°F).

Sow tomatoes for an early crop Sow tomatoes now if you want a crop in June, but do not forget that this means plants 3 to 4 ft high by the beginning of May. They will take quite a lot of space and the June crop may not be worth it if it means ruining your bedding plants. If you sow now, do so very thinly in well-drained seed boxes, using John Innes seed compost. Germinate in a heated propagating case at a temperature of 16 to 18°C (60 to 65°F). Tomatoes love warmth, and will get hard and blue in the cold, obstinately refusing to grow and becoming more miserable every week. Germination will be more rapid if each box is covered with a sheet of glass and brown paper. Keep the soil well moistened, but not sodden.

Crops in Season

In the garden Jerusalem artichoke, broccoli, Brussels sprouts, cauliflower, celery, endive, kale, leeks, parsnips, savoys, spinach, turnips.

Under glass Chicory, endive, lettuce, mustard and cress, radish, rhubarb, seakale.

February

'February which gives snow promises us a fine summer'

General Work

In the Garden

THE GOOD gardener should have completed all his digging and trenching by this time, but if not, the quicker it is finished the better. Ground that was turned over earlier in the winter and left rough should be broken down to a fine surface some time during February. It is essential to choose a day when the surface is fairly dry; you will do more harm than good if you walk about on beds that are soaking wet. Still, the right day often turns up several times during this month, and may be looked for after a period of steady east winds. Lawn sites that are to be sown or turfed later should also be prepared now.

FLOWERS AND SHRUBS

Complete planting of lilies There is still time to plant lilies outdoors and also to transplant established lilies from one part of the garden to another. The latter will be in growth and must be handled in the same way as herbaceous plants; that is to say, they must be lifted carefully and with a good ball of soil, which should be kept around the roots while replanting.

Prune roses Continue to prune bush and standard roses (see page 192).

Finish planting trees and shrubs There is still just time to plant fruit trees, and also deciduous ornamental trees and shrubs, including roses, but the earlier this can be done in February the better, provided soil conditions are good. There is considerable controversy about the pruning of fruit trees transplanted as late as this, some experts urging that

it is unwise to give the tree two shocks at once, root disturbance and a curtailment of the branches. This group argues that it is better to leave the late-planted trees unpruned until the following November and then, if they have not made much new growth, to cut them hard back into the older wood; in other words, to prune them to just about the point where they would have been cut had the work been done at planting time. My own view is that this is a waste of time, and that in any case the idea that proper pruning is a shock is a fallacy. I would not hesitate to prune late-planted fruit trees immediately before planting. Ornamental shrubs and trees should certainly be cut back fairly drastically to encourage vigorous growth later on. February-planted roses are better left unpruned until the end of March.

VEGETABLES AND FRUIT

Start sowing outside Towards the end of the month it should be possible to start sowing vegetables in the open.

Continue to protect cauliflowers The curds are still liable to be damaged by frost and must be protected as they form (see page 165).

Under Glass

General greenhouse management Plants in flower or coming into flower in the greenhouse are very much the same as those for January. If there are any bright, warm days, seize the opportunity to give more top ventilation, but beware of cold winds. An occasional thorough airing, so long as it does not involve a drop in temperature or the admission of cold draughts, does the greenhouse a lot of good. Most plants will require rather more water, but winter-flowering begonias of the Optima type should have less.

Seedlings from January sowings of begonias, tomatoes, leeks and onions should now be appearing. At any rate, it is essential to examine the seed trays and boxes very carefully every day so that covering materials can be removed before seedlings get thin and drawn. Give water if the soil appears to be dry. The best method is to hold each receptacle almost to its rim in a pail of water for a few moments and let the water soak up from below, but if there are a number to be done and this method takes too long, water from an ordinary watering can fitted with a very fine rose. Be sure to go over the surface several times, because the fine spray of water tends to collect on the top and not soak in immediately.

Ventilate frames according to the weather There is little to add to my remarks on this subject in the General Work for January. As the days get a little longer you will be able to ventilate more freely, but run no unnecessary risks with frost.

FLOWERS AND SHRUBS

Take chrysanthemum and carnation cuttings As opportunity occurs during the month continue to take chrysanthemum and perpetual carnation cuttings. It is getting late for exhibition Japanese chrysanthemums in full-size pots, but decorative varieties can still be propagated with advantage, and February is the ideal month to start on the hardy border varieties.

Continue to pot rooted cuttings Throughout the month you must keep a sharp eye on chrysanthemum and perpetual-flowering carnation cuttings, and pot them singly as soon as they start to grow freely.

VEGETABLES AND FRUIT

Harden off autumn-sown cauliflowers Cauliflower seedlings growing in frames from late summer sowings must be gradually hardened off during February in readiness for planting out next month. Take the lights right off during the daytime if the weather is not frosty and the wind is not very cold. Even at night a little ventilation can be given on the leeward side if conditions are at all reasonable.

Sow small salads for succession To maintain a supply of mustard and cress and radishes, make further small sowings as advised on page 17.

Continue to force seakale Continue to pot and force seakale roots for succession (see page 194). There is not much point in bringing in any further supplies of rhubarb, however, as successional supplies will be obtained from the roots covered outdoors in Late January.

Pollinate and disbud early fruit Peaches, nectarines and apricots in heated greenhouses may be in flower during the month, and as there will certainly not be enough insects about to effect pollination it is necessary to do this by hand. The best method is to have a camel-hair brush and scatter the dry pollen from

Using a soft camel-hair brush or a rabbit's tail scatter pollen from flower to flower to assist fruit setting

bloom to bloom with this, the most favourable time being towards midday when the sun is shining. While the fruit trees are in bloom it is necessary to discontinue spraying with water and to raise the temperature by about 5°C (10°F) night and day and keep the atmosphere dry by judicious ventilation. When the fruit is set spray the trees freely again once every morning.

As shoots grow you must start the process known as disbudding on peaches and nectarines. The small side shoots that form on the fruiting laterals are gradually pinched off, a few at a time, until only two are left to each lateral, one at its base and the other at its extremity. Then in the winter the old fruiting lateral is cut right out and the young basal shoot is trained in its place. The object of leaving the terminal shoot is simply to encourage the flow of sap through the branch and so help the fruits to swell. This method of disbudding is only fully practised on established trees that have filled their space. Small young trees may be allowed to form new laterals wherever there is room for these to be trained in as branches.

Apricots bear on old as well as new wood, and with these, only shoots that are awkwardly placed are removed. Other side growths are cut back to four or five well-developed leaves each as soon as they start to get hard and woody at the base.

Outdoor sowing

Seeds can either be sown broadcast or in drills. Broadcasting means scattering them as evenly as possible all over the area in which the seedlings are to grow. They are then covered, either by raking the soil gently, so stirring the seeds into the soil, or by scattering or sifting soil over them. Broadcasting is economical of space and is specially useful where plants are to grow on undisturbed, though properly thinned, in natural looking groups.

Drilling means sowing in shallow furrows which can be made with a pointed stick, the corner of a hoe or rake or any other convenient implement. Seeds are then sprinkled evenly in this furrow, or 'drill', and are covered by drawing the dis-placed soil back over them. It is ideal for plants that are to be grown in straight lines, but a series of drills can also be used to form a clump, much as in broadcasting.

One advantage of drilling is that the sown seeds will germinate in rows whereas any weed seedlings will be distributed at random. It is, therefore, much easier to distinguish at an early stage the garden plant seedlings from the weeds.

Draw out a drill with the corner of a hoe held against a garden line

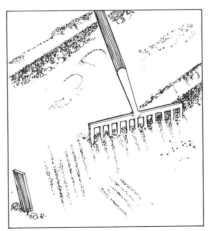

After sowing rake the soil lightly over the seed in the drill

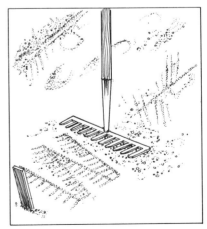

Tamp the soil firm using the back of a rake

Early February

In the Garden

FLOWERS AND SHRUBS

Prune flowering shrubs Flowering shrubs which should be pruned now include *Hydrangea paniculata*, *Spiraea japonica* (and varieties or hybrids such as Anthony Waterer), *S. douglasii*, *S. menziesii*, *S. salicifolia*, *Holodiscus discolor ariaefolius*, *Sorbaria aitchisonii*, *S. arborea*, *S. sorbifolia* and *S. tomentosa*, *Tamarix pentandra*, *Hypericum moserianum*, all kinds of willows, unless grown principally for bark effects, also varieties of *Cornus alba* grown for leaf but not those grown primarily for bark colour. In all these, stems made last year should be cut hard back to within one or two joints of the older wood. With the bigger shrubs you can, if you wish, allow some strong branches to remain at three-quarter length to build up a main framework of

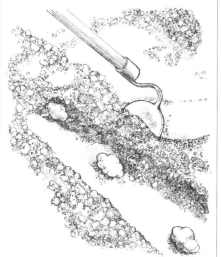

Plant Jerusalem artichokes in narrow trenches 4 in deep and 2½ ft apart. Space the tubers 15 in apart in the rows. This vegetable will grow well even in poor soil

Prune autumn-fruiting raspberries by cutting them right back to within 6 in of the ground

growth and so lay the foundation of larger specimens than could be obtained by constant hard pruning.

VEGETABLES AND FRUIT

Plant Jerusalem artichokes These should be planted at the earliest opportunity. These are amongst the hardiest of all vegetables, and as they make a lot of tall, sunflower-like growth they may well be used as a windbreak in exposed gardens. They will grow almost anywhere, and good crops are to be had from soil that would be far too poor to produce potatoes. Simply plant the tubers 15 in apart in rows 2½ ft apart. Cover with 3 in of soil.

Sow peas in a sheltered spot If you happen to live in a very mild part of the country or have an unusually sheltered garden you may even make an outside sowing of peas on a border with a southerly aspect, but you must certainly choose a really hardy variety, such as Foremost or Meteor.

Prune autumn-fruiting raspberries September-fruiting raspberries must now be cut right back to within 6 in of the ground. These varieties fruit on the young growth produced after pruning. The variety Lloyd George can also be pruned in this way for autumn fruiting but is really more profitable as a summer-fruiting variety, when it is pruned in Mid August.

Under Glass

FLOWERS AND SHRUBS

Pot annuals for the greenhouse If you were able to sow various annuals in Early September for flowering in the greenhouse during the spring, you should get the plants potted singly into 5- to 6-in pots, according to the growth they have made. Use John Innes potting compost No. 1 or an equivalent mixture. Stand the plants on the staging or a shelf quite close to the glass to encourage sturdy growth. Schizanthus sown in Late August must also be potted on in the same way. If you want very bushy plants pinch out the tips of the shoots.

Start achimenes Space tubers thinly in shallow boxes half-filled with a light sandy compost and just cover them with the same mixture. Water very moderately and place on the staging in a temperature of about 16°C (60°F). Very soon shoots will appear, and when these are a couple of inches in length the plants should be transferred to pots or pans. Five or six roots can be grown in a pot 5 in in diameter. An alternative method is to grow them in hanging baskets, but in any case the initial starting process is the same. Do not start all the tubers at once. Successional starting will give a longer display.

Force flowering shrubs You can still bring any bush roses, azaleas, deutzias, lilacs or astilbes you have well established in pots into the greenhouse to provide a succession of flowers after those introduced in Early January.

VEGETABLES AND FRUIT
Continue to blanch chicory Further roots can be dug up and blanched as required (see page 184).

Sow broad beans You can make a sowing of broad beans in boxes or pots during this week. Do not scatter the seeds haphazardly, but set them out at regular intervals 2 in apart each way, and cover them with about ¾ in of soil. Germinate in a slightly-heated greenhouse or even a frame, provided the latter is well covered with sacks or mats on frosty nights. This method of sowing early in boxes gives far more reliable results, at any rate on all but the lightest of soils, than the old-fashioned scheme of sowing out of doors in the autumn.

Sow lettuces, peas and cauliflowers If you want a really early outdoor supply of lettuces make a small sowing of a cabbage variety in seed boxes and place in a warm greenhouse to germinate. An average tempera-

Rhubarb can be forced under the traditional terracotta pots, alternatively use a box and some dry leaves

ture of 13°C (55°F) will be sufficient to ensure this. Seedlings from this indoor sowing will be planted out later, after proper hardening.

It is also an excellent plan to make a sowing of an early variety of pea in boxes and germinate in the same way as the lettuces. These seedlings will also be planted outdoors later.

Cauliflowers require a long and steady season of growth if they are to be a real success and if you have a warm greenhouse you should certainly make a first sowing now. A temperature of 13 to 16°C (55 to 60°F) in a

propagating case will be quite adequate for germination. It is even possible to germinate them satisfactorily in a frame with soil-warming cables. Sow the seeds as thinly as possible, either in deep seed trays or, if in a frame, directly in the soil in shallow drills.

Continue to force seakale and rhubarb More roots can be treated as described (see page 194).

Strawberries under glass If some strawberries have been grown in pots in Late July, bring a few into the greenhouse now and maintain a temperature of 10 to 16°C (50 to 60°F).

In the Garden

FLOWERS AND SHRUBS

Plant anemones and ranunculuses
This is an excellent time to make a planting of anemones of the St Brigid, de Caen and fulgens types, and also of turban ranunculuses for a summer display. The anemones should be $2\frac{1}{2}$ to 3 in deep and the ranunculuses about $1\frac{1}{2}$ to 2 in deep. The latter are queer-looking things, like dried-up claws, and the claws should be planted pointing downwards. Space both subjects about 6 in apart each way.

VEGETABLES AND FRUIT

Lift and store parsnips Parsnips that have been left in the ground all the winter will soon be starting to grow again, and it is best to lift them without delay and store in some cold place. A position alongside a north wall will do very well. It is only necessary to place the roots in a heap and cover them with a little soil; they are quite hardy and will not be injured by frost.

Sow parsnips If the weather is at all favourable do not hesitate to sow parsnips out of doors, for the longer and more steadily they can grow the better. However, there is no sense in sowing if the ground is sodden or frozen; it is better to wait two or three weeks than have all the seeds rot away. Sow in drills 1 in deep and about 15 in apart, scattering the seeds as thinly as possible, for later on the seedlings must be thinned to at least 9 in apart in the rows. Those who grow for exhibition

very often make a hole for each parsnip with a large iron crowbar. This is driven in to a depth of about 2 ft, the hole is then almost filled with fine potting soil, two seeds are sown, and a little more fine soil placed on top. The object of this is to encourage the tap root to grow straight down into the soft potting soil, and so obtain specimens of perfect shape. If both seeds germinate, the weaker seedling is pulled out.

Plant out spring cabbages
Cabbages for a spring supply are sown in July or August and are usually planted out in early autumn in the beds in which they are to mature. But sometimes one cannot find sufficient room for all the seedlings and if there are some still left in the seed beds, now is the time to get them planted – always provided the weather is reasonably good. These late plants are not likely to make such big hearts as the earlier ones, so it will be sufficient to plant them 10 in to 1 ft apart in rows 18 in apart.

Plant shallots There used to be an old-time idea that shallots should be planted on the shortest day of the year. There are, no doubt, some gardeners who follow this still, but my own opinion is that, at any rate around London and on heavy soils generally, it is much better to wait until Mid February. Indeed, even then, I would not plant unless the surface of the bed can be broken down reasonably fine. The method of planting is simply to push good

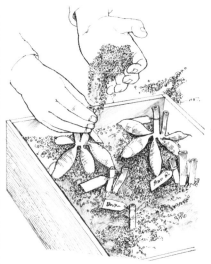

Dahlia tubers can now be boxed up in old compost or peat. Water and keep in a warm place to encourage shoots for use as cuttings

bulbs firmly into the soil until only the top third can be seen. Plant 9 in apart in rows 1 ft apart. Choose an open position and, for preference, ground that is well drained and has been adequately manured earlier in the winter.

Under Glass

FLOWERS AND SHRUBS

Prune and start greenhouse plants
Several well-known greenhouse plants require pruning now. Bougainvilleas should have last year's growth cut hard back unless you wish to retain some growths for extension. Bouvardias, gardenias, fuchsias, zonal and ivy-leaved pelargoniums should be cut sufficiently to give them a solid foundation for the coming season's growth and so prevent the least suspicion of untidiness. You can give all these plants water in gradually increasing

quantity from now onwards as growth starts. A slightly higher temperature will also be all to the good, though it is not essential. All need as much light as they can get.

Clivias and vallotas may also be brought into growth now, but as they are never dried off completely this simply means increasing the water supply a little and standing in a warmer part of the house. A temperature of 13°C (55°F) will be ample unless very early flowers are required.

Start dahlia tubers for cuttings
If you wish to increase your stock of dahlias take the old dahlia tubers out of store and place them in boxes in the greenhouse to start into growth. Old apple boxes serve very well for this purpose, orange boxes can be used or indeed, anything that is deep enough to take a dahlia tuber. Place a little old potting compost or moist peat in the

bottom of the box, then stand the tubers on it, as many in a box as can be accommodated comfortably, and place more soil around them until the fleshy tubers themselves are just covered, but the stumps of last year's stems are exposed. Water the tubers in and place the boxes in any light or semi-light place. They can go under the greenhouse staging for the time being, but as soon as growth starts they must be brought out into full light or the shoots will be leggy and useless. Give more water as necessary, sparingly at first but

Wait until the surface is dry enough to be raked down to a fine tilth before planting shallots. Then push each bulb into the soil leaving about one third exposed

much more freely when growth appears. Any temperature over 13°C (55°F) will be sufficient to start growth.

Growing bags

Growing bags were developed originally for commercial growers, mainly for tomatoes and cucumbers, but have found ready acceptance and many applications in home gardens and greenhouses. Basically they are polythene sacks, usually 3 to 4 ft long and 14 to 15 in wide, filled with peat to which sufficient fertiliser has been added to sustain plants for from four to eight weeks. The bags are laid flat on any firm, level surface, slits are made in the upper side and one plant is placed in each slit. Alternatively the bag can be slit from end to end to accommodate a row of plants. The plants are watered sufficiently to keep the peat constantly moist right through. After four or five weeks it is usually necessary to add to the water a small quantity of a compound fertiliser, either liquid or readily soluble, to supplement the diminishing supply of plant food in the peat.

The advantages of growing bags are that the peat is free of weed seeds and disease-causing organisms and is protected from infection by the bag. This also retains the water. If it does so excessively it will be necessary to make a few small slits low down in the sides to allow surplus to drain out. Crops and ornamental plants can be grown on balconies, roofs, in terraces and yards, as well as in conservatories and greenhouses. At the end of the season the spent peat can be used outdoors as a soil conditioner.

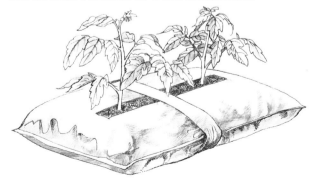

Plants for February

This is the month when the snowdrops really take charge, ably abetted by the winter aconites (eranthis) with their cheerful yellow flowers, each wearing a little green ruff. As the month wears on more and more crocuses will join the outdoor display and *Iris histrioides* will be replaced by the numerous varieties of *Iris reticulata* all of them delicately scented like violets. Some dainty rock plants, too, will begin to put in an appearance.

That fine old evergreen shrub, the laurustinus (*Viburnum tinus*) which in some mild places can commence to flower in the autumn, will be encouraged by the lengthening days to open many more of its purplish pink buds. Numerous trees and shrubs will also be producing catkins, the hazels, willows and alders among them. The evergreen *Garrya elliptica* produces male and female catkins on separate plants, the males being far more effective in flower because their catkins are long and grey-green.

However, if one or two females are planted not too far away for pollination to take place, one will be rewarded later on with trails of decidedly decorative purplish-black fruits. This also applies to some varieties of *Skimmia japonica* which need both male and female plants to ensure a good show of red berries.

Mahonia Charity is the best known of the hybrids made by crossing *M. japonica* with *M. lomariifolia* but, fine evergreen though it undoubtedly is, it can be rivalled or even surpassed in beauty by several others, most notably Buckland and Lionel Fortescue which have even larger flower clusters and have retained some of the violet perfume of *M. japonica*. The yellow winter jasmine, *Jasminum nudiflorum*, is always one of the first wall-trained shrubs to open but it is quickly joined by the scarlet, crimson, pink or white flowers of the cydonias or Japanese quinces (chaenomeles).

There will also be an increasing number of hellebores. The early Lenten roses, varieties of *H. orientalis*, will be joined by delightful green-flowered Corsican hellebore and the ill-named stinking hellebore, *H. foetidus*, which in many ways is the most decorative and only smells slightly unpleasant when bruised.

Mahonia Charity, one of the showiest winter-flowering plants

Herbaceous plants Adonis, hellebores, *Iris unguicularis*, petasites, pulmonaria, polyanthus, *Ranunculus ficaria* vars., violets, winter-flowering violas.

Hardy bulbs, corms and tubers *Anemone blanda*, spring-flowering crocuses, *Cyclamen coum*, *C. libanoticum*, eranthis, erythronium, galanthus, *Iris aucheri*, *I. bakeriana*, *I. danfordiae*, *I. histrioides*, *I. persica*, *I. reticulata*, *Leucojum vernum*, species narcissus, scilla.

Evergreen shrubs Azara, camellias, daphnes, ericas, *Garrya elliptica*, mahonias, pieris, rhododendrons, *Ribes* , *Viburnum*

...nas, *Corylus*
Edgeworthia
...era fragran-
...ronia cerasi-
...us praecox,
...diflorum.
...na, *Corylus*
...ng prunuses.
...sa, *Jasminum*

n right,

hrub
liptica

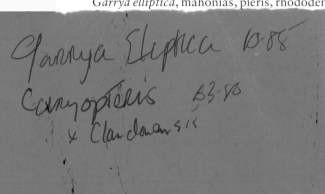

Garrya Eliptica 10.88
Caryopteris B3.50
x Clandonensis

Late February

In the Garden

VEGETABLES AND FRUIT

Plant chives Chives are not a very important vegetable crop, but a couple of clumps come in very useful for flavourings. This is the time of year to plant and to divide old clumps that have got overcrowded. Simply lift the plants and pull them apart, replanting small tufts about 10 in apart. Any ordinary soil and reasonably open position will do.

Plant out autumn-sown onions Directly the soil is in good condition – that is to say, as soon as you can walk on it without it sticking to your boots – plant out seedling onions from the Late August sowing. The method is to plant with a small dibber, just dropping the seedlings into holes about 2 in deep. Plant 6 in apart in rows 1 ft apart. The position chosen should be fully open and

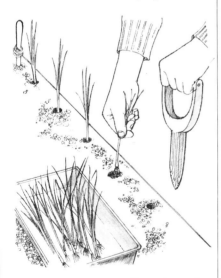

Autumn-sown onions will now be ready for planting outside. Drop them into 2-in deep holes, spaced 6 in apart, and water them in

the soil must have been well cultivated earlier in the winter with plenty of manure in the bottom spit and any wood ashes you may have mixed with the surface soil. Onions growing in rough, hard soil are almost certain to be misshapen.

Plant potatoes in a sheltered border If you have a very sheltered border, preferably one with a south aspect, and you are not afraid to take a small risk, you can now make a first planting of early potatoes. They will need watching later on and you will probably have to protect the young shoots with dry straw or bracken, but if you are successful there is no reason why you should not be digging new potatoes early in June. Of course, for this first planting it is essential to choose a quick-growing variety such as Arran Pilot or Sharpe's Express. Also you should use only well-sprouted sets. Reduce the number of sprouts to two or three sturdy ones on each tuber. Plant in trenches about 5 in deep and 2 ft apart, setting the tubers 9 in apart with the eyes pointing upwards. Surround each tuber with a couple of handfuls of leafmould or moss peat and sprinkle a little compound fertilizer in the bottom of each trench; about 2 oz per yard run. Then refill the trenches but do not firm the soil much. Plenty of good compound fertilizers suitable for potatoes can be bought ready to use, but if you prefer you can make your own with eight parts of superphosphate of lime, five parts of sulphate of

ammonia and three parts of sulphate of potash. This mixture will keep for quite a long time in a dry place. If it sets hard after a few days, break it up thoroughly with the back of a spade.

Sow parsley in a sheltered place Make a small sowing of parsley in a warm, sheltered place. It is much too early yet for the main sowing, but plants raised now will be useful in early summer before the main crop is ready. Parsley seed is quite cheap, so there is no great loss even if the sowing does not prove a success.

Sow turnips Make a first sowing of turnips outdoors in a warm, sheltered place. Sow the seeds thinly in drills $\frac{1}{2}$ in deep and 10 in apart. You should only sow a few seeds now and subsequently make small successional sowings every fortnight or so until the end of July, as by this method you will have a constant supply of young roots instead of a lot of old, tough and strongly-flavoured ones.

Prune cobnuts and filberts These must be pruned as soon as the small red female flowers can be seen. These are rather insignificant and you must look closely to find them. It is the male catkins that make the show. The leading shoots of established bushes which fill their space are shortened to a couple of buds each. If there is still room for the bushes to extend there is no need to prune these leaders at all, or at the most only to remove their tips. Side shoots are cut back to the first catkin, reckoning from

Crops in Season

In the garden Jerusalem artichoke, broccoli, Brussels sprouts, cauliflower, celery, endive, kale, leeks, spring onions, parsnips, savoys.

Under glass Chicory, endive, lettuce, mustard and cress.

the tip, or, if there are no catkins, to the first female flower. Some shoots may have catkins only. These should be left unpruned until the catkins fade and then be cut right back to two buds. There is no point in keeping them, as they will not produce any nuts. Badly-placed branches which crowd up the centre of the bush should be removed altogether, even if this means using a saw. The ideal nut bush is roughly in the form of a goblet, with a short main trunk and branches radiating from it at regular intervals.

Spray peaches and nectarines If your outdoor peaches or nectarines were attacked by red spider mites the previous summer, spray them now with lime-sulphur wash at the usual winter strength advised by the manufacturers. This treatment will also check the leaf-curl disease.

Under Glass

FLOWERS AND SHRUBS

Sow half-hardy annuals and greenhouse plants I usually make this time of the month a busy one in the greenhouse, reserving it for sowing a great number of half-hardy annuals and greenhouse plants. The half-hardy annuals

are principally required for summer bedding, but some of them may also come in useful for potting later on and growing as greenhouse plants during the summer.

The principal half-hardy annuals to be sown now are ageratum, amaranthus, anagallis, antirrhinum, *Begonia semper-florens*, brachycome, cobaea, cosmea, *Dianthus heddewigii*, eccremocarpus, kochia, limonium (statice), lobelia, marigolds of both French and African types, annual carnation, nicotiana, nemesia, *Phlox drummondii*, petunia, scarlet salvia, salpiglossis, schizanthus, ten-week stock and verbena. The greenhouse plants include balsam, begonia, celosia (including cockscomb), celsia, *Clerodendrum speciosissimum*, gloxinia, *Impatiens sultani*, ipomoea, mimulus, streptocarpus and trachelium. You may have sown some of these already, but even so plants from this later sowing will prove very useful for succession. Dahlias also do very well from a sowing made at this time, and make good strong plants for putting out early in June. They will all germinate in a temperature of 16 to 18°C (60 to 65°F).

For all these use either John Innes or a peat-based seed compost. Before filling trays or pots be sure to make them thoroughly clean by scrubbing them out with a stiff brush. Prepare the trays a day before you actually intend to sow the seeds and give the soil a thorough watering; then stand them on the staging to drain. Never fill a seed receptacle right to the rim; leave at least $\frac{1}{4}$ in for watering. The day after watering sow the seeds very thinly and evenly, cover lightly with soil (a good general

Early-sown seedlings should be ready for pricking out into trays. Use a forked stick and ease up the roots gently

rule is to cover a seed with twice its own depth of soil) and then place a sheet of glass over each pot or tray and a large piece of brown paper over the top. Any more water that may be needed must be given either from a can fitted with a very fine rose or else by holding the pan or tray almost to its rim in a tub of water.

Prick off early seedlings It should now be possible to prick off some of the early seedlings such as begonias, gloxinias and streptocarpus which were sown in Late January. They will be very small and it may be necessary to use a small forked stick to lift them, but early pricking out before roots become matted together is amply repaid. Fill rather deep seed trays or big earthenware pans with the same kind of compost as that used for seed raising, and dibble the seedlings in about 2 in apart each way. Water freely and keep rather warm and shaded for a few days until they recover from the shift, after which they may be placed on the ordinary greenhouse staging in a temperature of about 16°C (60°F).

Pot early begonias and gloxinia tubers If you were able to start begonia and gloxinia tubers into growth during January they will almost certainly need potting up by this time. It is not wise to leave them until their roots become matted together in the trays. Get them out when they have two or three leaves each and place them separately in the smallest sized pots that will accommodate them comfortably using John Innes potting compost No. 1 or a peat-based equivalent. The tubers should only just be covered with soil. Make them moderately firm, give them a thorough watering, and keep them in a temperature of 16 to 18°C (60 to 65°F), either in the house or heated greenhouse, for a few days. Syringe every morning with slightly warm water to prevent flagging, and shade for a few days from strong direct sunlight.

Start begonias, gloxinias and hippeastrums A further batch of begonias, gloxinias and hippeastrums may be started into growth to provide a succession after those started in January (see pages 16 and 21). Even if you were unable to start any then you may be safe in doing so now, for it will be easier to maintain the requisite temperatures.

VEGETABLES AND FRUIT

Sow early celery This is the time to make the earliest sowing of celery to give fully blanched stems by the end of August. I do not advise you to attempt this first sowing unless you have plenty of frame space available and are fairly accustomed to handling plants under glass. It is much easier to grow celery from

a March sowing, and from this you should have good sticks by the end of September. However, if you intend to exhibit in some August shows a few sticks of celery may make all the difference. A temperature of 16°C (60°F) will be necessary for germination. The seeds should be sown as thinly as possible in John Innes seed compost. It is an advantage to cover each box with a sheet of glass and to place a sheet of newspaper or brown paper on top of this. Of course, an early variety should be chosen for this sowing.

Sow French beans for succession Sow some more French beans in 8-in pots if you wish to keep up a successional supply under glass during the spring (see page 21).

Prick off lettuce and cauliflower seedlings These seedlings from the sowings made early in the month should now be ready for pricking off into deeper seed boxes filled with the same kind of compost as used in the seed trays. Lift the seedlings very carefully with a sharpened wooden label and dibble them in 2 in apart each way. Water freely and keep shaded for a day or so until they start to grow again.

Pot tomato seedlings Tomato seedlings from the Late-January sowing should be potted separately in 3-in pots as soon as they have made two or three leaves each beyond the first pair of plain seed leaves. Transfer them carefully to these pots, using John Innes potting compost. Water freely and keep shaded from direct sunshine for a day or so until they get over the move. Later sowings may be pricked off into deeper boxes before potting, but I find that for the earliest

crop it is better to pot separately as soon as possible.

Sow maincrop tomatoes A second sowing of tomatoes will provide you with good sturdy plants for planting in the greenhouse in May as soon as you have cleared it of bedding and early-flowering plants. Details of sowing are as before (see page 21).

Sow cucumbers for an early crop Sow a few cucumber seeds for an early crop if you have a well-heated greenhouse. Place the seeds singly in 3-in pots filled with John Innes or a peat seed compost and place in a heated propagating case to germinate at a temperature of 24°C (75°F). It is an excellent plan to half-fill the propagator with peat and plunge the pots to their rims in this. Cucumbers need more warmth than tomatoes in the early stages, as they must be kept in rapid growth.

Sow melons This is a good time to sow melon seeds. Sow them singly, $\frac{1}{2}$ in deep, in small pots (those $2\frac{1}{2}$-in in diameter will be admirable) and start them into growth in a temperature of 16 to 21°C (60 to 70°F) in a propagating case with bottom heat. It is a good plan to plunge the pots to their rims in moist peat in a warm propagating case.

Start fruit in the unheated greenhouse Give considerably less ventilation to the unheated greenhouses containing peaches, nectarines and apricots. By day the top ventilators may be opened a little if the weather is fine, but early in the afternoon the house should be closed completely. This will encourage the trees to start into growth.

Flowering plants including calceolaria, *Primula obconica*, lachenalia, cineraria, and cyclamen raised for the house

Start early vines into growth

You may also start early vines such as Black Hamburgh, Foster's Seedling and Buckland's Sweetwater into growth, provided you have a heating apparatus installed in the vinery adequate to maintain a temperature of 13°C (55°F) at night during the rest of February and March. A temperature rising to 16°C (60°F) by day, will do for the present. Higher temperatures are only necessary when growth actually starts. Spray the vines several times daily to keep the atmosphere moist, and give a little top ventilation by day whenever outside conditions permit this without lowering the temperature or causing cold draughts. Soak the border thoroughly with clear water and fill any evaporating trays over the pipes. Spread a 2-in thick layer of well-rotted manure or compost all over the border to feed the roots.

Indoor plants

The air in rooms is often a great deal drier than in greenhouses and the light intensity can be deceptively lower. Atmospheric moisture can be increased immediately around the plants, which is where it matters, by standing pots in plant holders sufficiently large to allow plenty of moss, vermiculite, leca (particles of heat-expanded clay) or other absorbent material to be packed around them and kept moist. Climbers can be trained around wire mesh cylinders also packed with damp moss and this will bring the moisture even closer to the leaves.

Light can be improved with reflectors of various kinds. Even white cardboard placed where it will reflect light on to the plant will help. It may also be possible to move plants nearer to windows but care must be taken that this does not increase the risk of chilling, especially at night.

Plant cabinets can provide the ideal conditions since the air inside them is isolated from the air in the room and can be just as humid and as warm as is best for the particular plants being grown. Artificial lighting can also be installed and used to intensify the natural light or to extend the length of the 'day'.

Bottle gardens provide similar conditions to plant cabinets though with less range of control. They are almost self maintaining since roots take moisture from the compost but return it as vapour through the leaves and it then condenses on the glass and trickles back into the soil. The

Philodendrons and monsteras can be trained round a cylinder of damp moss to keep the air near the leaves moist

leaves both use and give off oxygen and carbon dioxide so that a rough balance is maintained between the two and ventilation is almost non-existent.

In winter it may be necessary to move bottle gardens to lighter places or to improve existing lighting with reflectors or artificial lighting but to be effective this needs to be fluorescent and within a few feet of the bottle.

It is unlikely that bottle gardens will require much extra water during the winter. Hygiene must be scrupulous, all withering or decaying leaves or stems being removed as soon as noticed. Fungi can spread rapidly in the damp close air and low light intensity of the bottle garden.

Some of the greatest problems are presented by plants purchased for Christmas decoration since these are usually flowering plants which, in general, are less satisfactory for continuous cultivation indoors than plants grown mainly for their foliage. Nearly all require more light than can be obtained in rooms, except very close to windows, and in summer many will actually be happier standing outdoors provided they are not neglected.

Chrysanthemums are barely worth retaining once they have finished flowering since the dwarf ones will almost certainly have been chemically treated to keep them short and will become much taller the following year. However they can be cut back after flowering, kept in the lightest place available, watered moderately and planted outdoors in April or May. If they flower by October, well and good, if not they must be lifted, repotted and brought back indoors.

Cyclamens are handsome foliage plants even when out of flower but they die down naturally in late spring when the water supply should be reduced considerably. From late May until late September they are best outdoors in a partially shady place.

Evergreen azaleas suffer most from dry air and may be sprayed daily with water to counteract this. They, too, are best outdoors from May to October, also in a rather shady place but with plenty of water as they will be growing and forming their flower buds during that time.

Poinsettias are difficult since, like chrysanthemums, they are usually chemically treated to keep them short. When the coloured bracts fade plants should be cut down to about 4 in and the soil kept only just moist

for a few weeks. Repot in May and renew normal watering plus a feed every ten to fourteen days. From late September until late November cover plants each afternoon at about 5 p.m. with a blackout (black polythene will do) and do not remove it before 7 a.m. the following morning since fourteen hours darkness daily is required to enable the plants to initiate their flower buds without which there will be no coloured bracts.

Cinerarias and winter-flowering primulas are not worth

keeping when their flowers fade but, with care, *Primula obconica* can be kept flowering for many months. Winter-flowering heaths are difficult to retain in good health as they require good light and very careful watering. They need sufficient to keep the peat compost always moist but never sodden and certainly never allowed to become dry.

Gently slide in some pebbles for drainage and then pour in compost through a paper funnel

To plant up a bottle garden first drop in a plant and then firm it in position with a cotton reel fixed on a stick

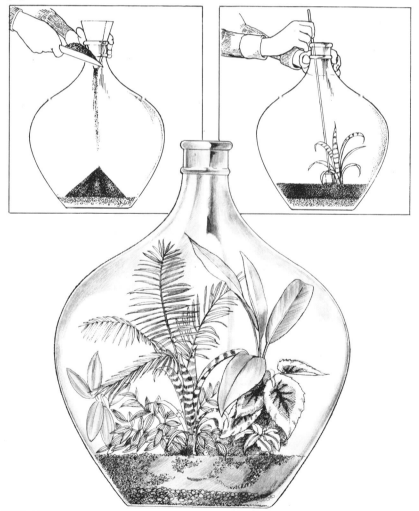

March

'A windy March forecasts a fine May'

General Work

In the Garden

THERE IS much more to do in the garden now the weather is improving and growth is getting underway. Sowing and planting of vegetables and flowers can begin in earnest and March is usually the best month during which to transplant the majority of herbaceous plants. There are a few exceptions, but they are not very important. Flag or German irises are usually planted by experts at the end of June because they will then give a full display of flowers the following year, but they can be transplanted with equal safety in March, the only drawback being that there will be a few flowers the following summer. Similar remarks apply to pyrethrums, which are also moved by experts immediately after flowering. Peonies and eremuruses are often quoted as examples of plants that benefit greatly by autumn transplanting. My own opinion is that this is well enough on properly drained soil, but that even with these plants it is better to wait until March if one has to contend with heavy clay.

Try to get the job done on any good days early in the month or you may find that later on persistent rain holds you up.

When transplanting old clumps always break them up into smaller pieces and, if you have plenty of stock, throw away the hard central portions and keep only the young outside pieces. This is particularly important with vigorous spreading plants such as Michaelmas daisies, heleniums, rudbeckias, and solidagos. Split up by hand where possible, but for very tough clumps use a couple of small border forks thrust back to back through the middle of the mass and then levered apart. Only use a knife with

Particularly tough clumps of herbaceous perennials can be divided by thrusting two forks, back to back, through the centre of the clump and forcing them apart

plants that make a solid crown, for example, peonies, delphiniums and Caucasian scabious. Even then be careful only to cut the crowns and not the roots; always pull these apart.

Always replant with a spade or trowel and not a dibber. Prepare good wide holes and spread the roots out well. Work some fine dry soil around them (it is an excellent plan to prepare a barrow-load in advance) and thoroughly firm in the plants. If you have no facilities for handling cuttings you can still get quite good results by treating the border chrysanthemums like ordinary herbaceous perennials, lifting the roots now and splitting them up into small pieces. Throw away the hard, woody stumps of last year's growth and keep only the young outer shoots. Plant these 18 in apart in the border or, if in rows 1 ft apart in lines 2 to 3 ft apart. Propagation of the main stock of late-flowering chrysanthemums should now be almost completed, but towards the end of the month you may take a few more cuttings to be flowered in pots.

Plant snowdrops This is also a good month for transplanting snowdrops, moving them while in growth just like herbaceous plants and not waiting for bulbs to ripen and dry off as is the usual commercial method. A few specialist bulb nurseries will supply snowdrops at this time of the year.

Prune roses Continue to prune bush and standard roses (see page 192).

THE LAWN

Lay turves This is a good month for turf laying, and also for repairing bare places in lawns. So, if you have any of this work to do, choose any day during March when the surface is dry enough to be walked on without it sticking to your boots and it can be broken down reasonably well with the fork or rake. Beat the turves down on to the soil with a special wooden turf beater or roll them with a light roller, first in one direction and then transversely (see page 147 for full details on laying turves).

Under Glass

General greenhouse management The greenhouse will now be filling with many more seedlings of vegetables, half-hardy annuals and greenhouse plants needing pricking out and young rooted cuttings. These must have plenty of light and air if they are to be kept short-jointed and sturdy and are not to be attacked by the deadly damping-off fungus. In consequence it may not be possible to do with much less artificial heat in a general-purpose greenhouse than in January or February because, although the days may be a little warmer, more ventilation must be given, and yet the temperature inside the greenhouse must be still kept at an average of 13 to 16°C (55 to 60°F) for the majority of popular greenhouse plants. If you have a heated propagating case or a section of a house that can be devoted to seed germination, starting bulbs and tubers and rooting soft cuttings, this can be ventilated less and the necessary temperature of 16 to 21°C (60 to 70°F) maintained with considerably less artificial heat.

In a greenhouse where you have flowering and foliage plants, seedlings, and cuttings that have been removed from the propagating case and are being hardened off, avoid sudden large rises of temperature caused by direct sun heat. On a bright, still day the thermometer may rise rapidly in an hour or so if you are not on the watch. Give increased top ventilation to counteract this, so avoiding rises of more than 3 or 4°C (10°F) and preventing serious scorching of both foliage and flowers.

Roses in pots started in the greenhouse during January or February will benefit from an occasional spraying with a greenfly killer like malathion or bio-resmethrin. On warm, bright days many plants not in bloom will benefit from spraying with tepid water. It should be done in the morning, but not too early. Plants must not be sprayed while they are in bloom.

FLOWERS AND SHRUBS

Take cuttings of bedding and greenhouse plants In a moderately heated greenhouse such popular bedding plants as heliotrope, marguerite, fuchsia and pelargonium will be making suitable growth to provide cuttings. Secure these as soon as they are long enough. The actual length of the cutting will depend on the type of plant – for example, with pelargoniums, which have comparatively thick stems, cuttings 3 in in length are ideal, but 2-in cuttings will do for the thinner fuchsias and heliotropes. Prepare all by severing them cleanly immediately below a joint and then insert them in well-drained boxes or 4-in pots filled with a sandy compost, dropping them in just sufficiently deep to keep them erect. They can be rooted on the greenhouse staging if they are shaded during the day, but better results with all except pelargoniums are obtained by placing them in a propagating case, especially if this is over the heating apparatus or has its own built-in soil-warming cable.

You can propagate quite a number of popular greenhouse plants in precisely the same way. It is

Select sturdy growths of pelargoniums for cuttings. Remove the lower leaves and make a clean cut below a leaf joint to give a 3-in cutting. Insert in sandy compost

worth trying a few shoots of any perennial that is just making new growth, such as abutilon, bouvardia, coleus, datura, eupatorium, gardenia, jacobinia, lantana, berried solanums, the double-flowered tropaeolums and petunia. All these should be kept as close as possible in a heated propagating case until they are rooted. Winter-flowering begonias of the Gloire de Lorraine type make basal growths at this time of the year, and these can be secured as cuttings when 2 in in length. The base of each cutting can be treated with a root-forming hormone before insertion.

Stop early carnations Complete the propagation of perpetual-flowering carnations from cuttings as soon

Thermostatically controlled propagating cases are invaluable in the greenhouse for raising tender plants and germinating seeds that need high temperatures

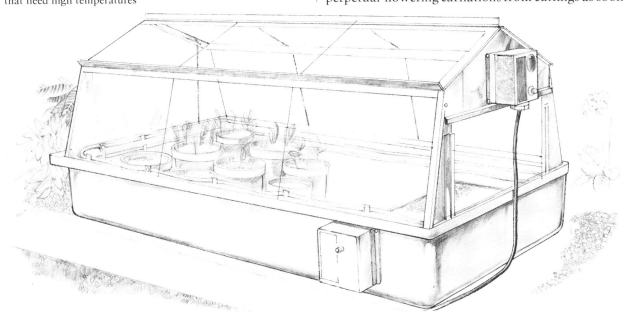

as possible. Cuttings that were rooted in December and January will be ready for stopping some time during the month. This simply means that the top of each cutting is broken off with a sideways movement. The effect of this is to make the plants produce side shoots. The right stage of growth for stopping is when the plant has made about seven joints; one complete joint is broken out.

Pot chrysanthemum and carnation cuttings You must continue to pot chrysanthemum and perpetual-flowering carnation cuttings as soon as they are well rooted (see page 13).

Perpetual-flowering carnations that were potted into 2-in pots in January and early February will also need a move on into 3- or 3½-in pots some time during the month, using the same compost as before. Do not place the plants in a frame in the same way as the chrysanthemums, but stand them on the staging or a shelf in the greenhouse with an average temperature of 13°C (55°F), and as much ventilation as possible without cold draughts.

Chrysanthemum cuttings that were rooted during December and January should be ready for the second potting into 5-in pots quite early in the month. Use John Innes potting compost No. 2 or an equivalent mixture and pot a little more firmly. After potting place the plants in a frame but keep the lights on at first and have plenty of thick sacks or mats at hand to cover them on cold nights.

This is also a good time to purchase rooted cuttings of all kinds of chrysanthemums. Pot the cuttings up singly directly they arrive, and place them in the greenhouse, keeping them shaded from direct sunshine for a few days and spraying with slightly-warm water every morning.

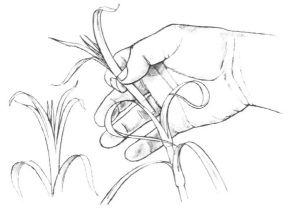

Rooted cuttings of perpetual carnations will be ready for stopping. This is done by breaking off the top of each young plant with a sideways movement

VEGETABLES AND FRUIT

Prick off seedlings During the month many seedlings, such as cauliflowers, lettuces and tomatoes, raised in the warm greenhouse or frame last month, will be ready for pricking out. Usually the ideal time is when the seedlings have made two true leaves each in addition to the first seed leaves (these are quite different from the true leaves and can be distinguished quite easily). Onions and leeks make only one seed leaf and are pricked off as soon as they can be handled conveniently. However, if you followed my advice and spaced the seeds singly, no pricking off will be necessary.

For general pricking off use John Innes or a peat-based seed sowing compost. Lift the seedlings with as little root injury as possible and dibble them in 2 in apart each way, making the soil firm around their roots. Water freely and shade for a few days while the tiny plants are recovering from the check of the move. You can either prick off into boxes or directly into the frame.

Make successional sowings Several vegetables that you have already sown will need to be resown during the month to provide a succession. You will need two or three more sowings of radishes (see page 17). For the first three weeks of the month these should be made in a frame unless you are in an exceptionally favourable district, for radishes must grow rapidly to be of any use. At the end of the month you can make a sowing outdoors in a warm sheltered border. Mustard and cress may be sown quite frequently in a warm frame or greenhouse. Sow lettuces in the greenhouse early in the month (see page 27). At the end of the month it will be safe to sow outdoors.

Treat peaches according to growth Peaches, nectarines and apricots in an unheated greenhouse will come into bloom early in the month and will require hand-fertilization followed by disbudding as described on pages 24 and 25.

Peaches and nectarines which were started in January should now have set fruit and you can begin to thin these; but as there is often a heavy natural fall during the stoning period at this early stage you should reduce the number of fruits per cluster just enough for them to have room to go on swelling without pressing against each other. More drastic thinning can wait until later.

In the Garden

FLOWERS AND SHRUBS

Sow sweet peas If you were unable to sow sweet peas in the autumn or in January under glass you should certainly make an outdoor sowing at the earliest possible moment now. Some growers are successful with sowings made in the open as early as the second week in February, but little is gained in this way as the soil is much more likely to be in the right condition during March. Sow the seeds 1 in deep and 2 to 3 in apart in rows 10 in apart, with a gap at least 4 ft wide between each pair of rows.

This is also the time to pinch out the tips of sweet peas sown in January, a task which must be done even if the peas are to be grown on the single stem (cordon) system. Side growths produce better flowers than the main stems.

Bed out spring-bedding plants If it was not possible to complete the planting of wallflowers, forget-me-nots, Canterbury bells, polyanthuses and double daisies in October, now is the time to get the plants into their flowering quarters. Do not delay this operation if weather and soil conditions are right (see page 164 for details).

Sow roses, trees and shrubs This is also a good time to sow seed of any shrubs and trees that may be available. It is not worth sowing just any rose seed but if you or any of your friends have made some special crosses, it is quite possible that they may yield good results. However, do not expect too much as one really worthwhile rose out of a hundred seedlings is quite good going. All these seeds should be sown outdoors in a sheltered border of finely prepared soil without any manure, or at most a sprinkling of bonemeal. If the seed has been stratified (see page 180), rub the mass of sand, pulp and seed through the hands to roughly separate out the seeds. Then everything can be scattered in the seed drills as evenly as possible. Sow in drills about $\frac{1}{2}$ in deep and press the soil down fairly firmly on top of the seeds but not so hard as to make it puddle. Many of the seeds may not germinate the first year, so be certain to sow in a place where you can leave them undisturbed.

VEGETABLES AND FRUIT

Sow spinach A small first sowing of summer spinach can be made in a sheltered border; preferably one with a southern aspect. Sow thinly in drills nearly 1 in deep and 1 ft apart. Other successional sowings will be made later.

Sow onions A most important sowing for early in March, if the weather is reasonably kind, is that of maincrop onions. Sow in drills $\frac{1}{2}$ in deep. The drills themselves should be 9 in to 1 ft apart, the latter if you are growing big bulbs for exhibition. As I have already remarked, it is almost impossible to make the surface of the onion bed too fine and light, but there should be plenty of richness in the way of animal manure below. With the top 4 in, mix only wood ashes and any similar soil-lightening materials so that the bulbs can swell without restriction.

Plant mint Now is the time to set about making a new mint bed. Lift some old plants or purchase the necessary roots; divide them up and spread them out thinly over the selected site, which should be in a reasonably open place, and cover with about $1\frac{1}{2}$ in of finely broken soil.

Plant rhubarb, horseradish and seakale You can make a new rhubarb bed if you wish now, or transplant old roots from one part of the garden to another. Be certain to dig out a hole big enough to take all the roots and allow the crowns to be just level with the surface of the ground. It is a spade job and not one that can be done with a trowel. The ground should have been well manured first and the position should be open or, alternatively, slightly shaded.

A few roots of horseradish are always useful, but you should be certain to plant them in an out-of-the-way part of the garden because once established this is an extremely difficult plant to get rid of. The roots are planted with a dibber 1 ft apart each way, and are dropped, right way up, well into the soil so that the crowns are 4 in beneath the surface. The only further cultivation that is necessary is an occasional hoeing to keep down weeds.

The seakale thongs that were removed earlier from the planting crowns and tied up in bundles (see page 194) can also be planted outdoors to form new beds. Cut the roots into pieces about 6 in long and make a nick or sloping cut at the bottom end of each cutting so that you may be certain to plant them the right way up. Plant with a dibber, making holes 6 in deep so that the cuttings are just level with the soil. Plant them 1 ft apart in rows 18 in apart.

New stocks can be obtained by sowing seeds outdoors now. Sow in drills 1 ft apart and ½ in deep.

Spray apple trees If apple blossom weevil has been troublesome (this is the pest which produces small white maggots which feed inside the opening flower buds, causing them to turn brown and refuse to open) spray with a suitable insecticide such as HCH, carbaryl or fenitrothion. If for any reason it was not possible to carry out tar oil spraying in winter, DNOC winter wash can be used now. This will kill aphids, capsid bugs, and many other pests, but not the apple blossom weevil. It is not as effective as tar oil in cleaning green scum, lichen and moss from the bark of old trees.

Under Glass

FLOWERS AND SHRUBS
Repot foliage plants and ferns Early March is a good time for potting summer and autumn-flowering plants and also all plants that are grown principally for their foliage. Winter-flowering plants are a different matter and are generally best repotted as soon as they have finished blooming. Now is the time to deal with palms, aspidistras, ferns of all kinds, including the so-called asparagus fern and *Asparagus sprengeri*, smilax,

coleus, crotons, cacti and succulents generally, dracaenas, marguerites, fuchsias, pelargoniums (this genus includes the familiar bedding geranium) and heliotropes.

It is usually advisable to give plants that are to be repotted a shift into a pot one size larger than that which they occupied before. If for any reason the plants are to be kept in the same size pot you must first reduce the size of the ball of soil around the roots. The way to do this is to tap the plant out of its old pot by rapping the rim of this upside down on the edge of the potting bench and holding one hand close up to the ball of soil to support it as it comes away. Then get a pointed stick and carefully loosen the soil around the edge of the ball without injuring the roots. If the compost is neither too wet nor too dry this can be done fairly readily. Do not remove all soil, but just sufficient

to get a reasonable quantity of new compost into the new pot. Even when potting for a size larger receptacle it is advisable to loosen roots a little in this way. After potting always give the plants a thorough soaking with water of room temperature and then transfer them to a slightly warmer temperature than that in which they were growing previously. Syringe every morning with tepid water, and shade from direct sunshine. These special precautions need only be maintained for a week or ten days, after which normal conditions should be resumed. The idea is to prevent the leaves from flagging during such time as new roots are being formed and to encourage rooting as much as possible.

A good general compost to use is John Innes potting compost No. 1. For some strong-growing plants John Innes potting compost No. 2 will give better results

Left: As soon as foliage plants have filled their pots with roots they can be transferred to pots one size larger. First ease some soil from the outer roots
Above: Then work in new compost with the fingers

Repotting spiny cacti is made less hazardous by using a folded paper collar to lift them out of their pots. Always use a gritty compost as good drainage is most important. It is also wise to place some gravel on top of the compost

and ferns will grow better in a peat-based mix or a mixture of two parts, by bulk, peat or leaf-mould, one part loam and one part coarse sand or charcoal.

Sow annuals for the greenhouse
A great many of the familiar hardy annuals that are grown for flowering in summer beds also make good greenhouse pot plants. Included under this heading are annual anchusa, browallia, calendula, annual chrysanthemums, clarkia, impatiens, larkspur, limonium, *Mesembryanthemum criniflorum*, mignonette, nasturtium, nemesia, nemophila, phacelia, salpiglossis, sweet scabious, ten week stocks, annual statice, ursinia and viscaria. Sow seed now in well-drained seed trays and germinate in the greenhouse in a temperature of 13 to 16°C (55 to 60°F). You will then have good strong plants starting to flower at the

end of May, just when your greenhouse has been cleared of most of the winter and spring plants. Prick off the seedlings 2 in apart each way into similar soil and trays as soon as they have made two true leaves each.

Pot rooted cuttings Another kind of potting which you should do at the earliest opportunity is that of late-summer and early-autumn rooted cuttings of tender bedding plants, including marguerites, pelargoniums, heliotropes, and fuchsias. These will be just starting into growth, and if you transfer them singly to 3- or 3½-in pots in the compost just mentioned they will soon grow into sturdy specimens. After potting, shade the plants for a few days, but stand them on the greenhouse staging in a light place as soon as growth recommences.

VEGETABLES AND FRUIT
Sow broad beans and celery
Make another sowing of broad beans in boxes for planting out (see page 27). If you were unable to make the first sowing through lack of heat it is now possible to

germinate the seeds in a practically unheated house or in a frame with soil-warming cables.

This is the time to make the main sowing of celery for a supply from October on through the winter. Treat the seeds exactly as described for the earlier sowing (see page 34).

Sow cucumbers These may be sown at almost any time of the year for successional cropping, but the average amateur gardener will find that a sowing made now will prove most useful for his general needs.

Sow brassicas in a frame If you were not able to sow cauliflowers in the greenhouse in early February, you should now sow seeds in a frame. It is even worth making this sowing as an addition to the greenhouse one if you choose a rather later variety than that sown before, because you will then prevent any chance of a break in the supply of curds in late summer and autumn. Sow thinly, as advised for cabbages. Summer broccoli (calabrese) can be sown in the same way. Brussels sprouts must have a long and steady season of growth if they are to be really successful. Sow now in boxes and germinate in a heated frame or in a slightly-heated greenhouse. If you also want a supply of cabbages in midsummer, sow an early variety now under exactly the same conditions as the sprouts.

Sow herbs Thyme, sage, marjoram and other herbs can be raised from seed sown in a frame or unheated greenhouse.

Mid March

In the Garden

FLOWERS AND SHRUBS

Sow hardy annuals This is a good time to make first sowings of all really hardy annuals provided the soil is in reasonably good condition. Thinly broadcast the seeds and cover with fine soil to about twice their own depth. The seeds should be sown where the plants are to flower. If the seedlings are too thick some of them may be transplanted later on, but the best flowers will be obtained from the unmoved plants.

Among the best annuals for sowing now are sweet alyssum, bartonia, calendula, annual candytuft, annual chrysanthemum, clarkia, collinsia, *Convolvulus tricolor*, annual coreopsis, cornflower, echium, eschscholzia, godetia, annual gypsophila, larkspur, *Lavatera rosea*, limnanthes, *Linaria macroccana*, linum (scarlet flax), annual lupins, malope, mignonette, nemophila, nigella, phacelia, carnation-flowered and Shirley poppies, annual rudbeckia, *Salvia horminum*, annual saponaria, annual sunflower, sweet peas, Virginian stock and annual viscaria.

VEGETABLES AND FRUIT

Sow carrots and leeks If the soil is in good working condition, make a small sowing of stump-rooted carrot outdoors, but choose a sheltered place. Sow very thinly, either broadcast or in rows 9 in apart, and cover with $\frac{1}{4}$ in of soil. The main sowings will be made in Mid April.

As already explained, the best leeks are raised under glass (see page 21) but if you do not possess a greenhouse, or even a frame in which you can install soil-warming cables, you can still have quite good leeks of your own raising by sowing outdoors now. Sow thinly in rows 1 ft apart and cover with $\frac{1}{4}$ in of fine soil.

Plant out cauliflowers Cauliflowers raised from a September sowing in a frame may now be planted outdoors if properly hardened off (see page 24). Lift the plants with as much soil and root as possible, and plant with a trowel on really good, well-dug soil. Allow 2 ft between the plants each way.

Sow peas Make a first sowing of an early culinary pea outdoors where the plants are to grow. I find the best method is to scoop out a trench with a spade. It should be just the width of a spade blade and not more than 3 in deep. Place the peas singly in this trench in two rows, one along each side, the peas should be spaced about 3 in apart in the lines and staggered on opposite sides of the trench. Then cover with 1 in of soil. The depression left will provide the tiny seedlings with some protection and will make watering a simple matter. Space the rows either 18 in apart for dwarf varieties or 3 ft apart for the taller varieties. Do not sow all your early peas at once or they will mature at the same time. Practise successional sowing every fortnight or so.

Plant early potatoes Even if you are not favoured with a particularly sheltered border you may now make a first planting of early potatoes. I have already given full particulars of the method to be followed in the notes on page 32.

Plant strawberries The best time for planting is at the end of August or early September, but if for some reason it was not possible to complete planting then, the work may be finished in March. Do not allow these plants to bear any fruit in the first year. If plants are available in pots some more may now be brought into the greenhouse for succession to those brought inside in Early February.

Protect early fruit blossom Outdoor peaches and nectarines should now be coming into flower and it is an excellent plan to protect these by hanging fine mesh netting in front of the trees. It might seem that this would afford no protection at all, but actually it makes quite a difference, causing eddies and preventing the slow, unbroken flow of air which always accompanies the worst frosts.

Under Glass

FLOWERS AND SHRUBS

Sow herbaceous perennials and alpines A great many herbaceous perennials and rock plants can be raised easily from seeds sown at this time of the year in either a

Opposite: Narcissus March Sunshine

frame or an unheated greenhouse. These include delphiniums, lupins, perennial gypsophilas, perennial statices, thalictrums, coloured primroses and polyanthuses, violas and pansies, campanulas, hypericums, meconopses, aquilegias and dianthuses. I make no attempt to give a full list because it is really worthwhile trying anything of which you can obtain seed. The method is to sow thinly in well-drained trays filled with John Innes or peat-based seed compost. Cover the seeds to twice their own depth with very fine soil and then place them in the frame or greenhouse and shade from direct sunlight. Remove the shading as soon as the seedlings can be seen.

Auriculas may also be sown now, but are best in well-drained seed pans, as the seeds are slow and irregular in germination. Place the seed pans in a frame or greenhouse and water as necessary by partial immersion rather than from a watering can. Sow very thinly so that seedlings can be pricked off as they appear.

Sow half-hardy annuals If you have no heated greenhouse and were therefore unable to sow half-hardy annuals in Late February you can do so now in a frame. This should be in a sheltered place and it is all the better if soil-warming cables are installed. The seeds may either be sown directly in the frame or in trays as with greenhouse germinated seeds. The latter method does make handling easier later on. Dahlias usually germinate very well in a frame now to make good flowering plants by August.

I find this is a good time to make a first sowing of asters. Seed will germinate easily enough earlier in the year, but the plants

Stopping chrysanthemums involves pinching out the growing tip of each plant. This encourages the production of side shoots

tend to get too big by planting time and are much more liable to damp off.

Sow cacti, fuchsias and pelargoniums This is a good time to sow seeds of cacti and succulents, fuchsias and also pelargoniums (if the latter are not required to flower much the first year). Sow the seeds very thinly in well-drained pots, using a light, sandy compost. Germinate in a greenhouse in a temperature of about 16°C (60°F). The pots containing the fuchsia and pelargonium seeds can be covered with glass and a sheet of paper but the cactus and succulent seeds should only be covered with glass as they germinate better in the light.

Stop chrysanthemums Many exhibition chrysanthemums should be stopped now (chrysanthemum specialists' catalogues will list suitable varieties). Stopping simply means pinching the growing tip out of each plant with the object of making it produce side shoots. If you aim to have very large blooms for

exhibition each plant must be kept to one stem and this must not be allowed to carry more than one flower. In this case you must only keep the uppermost of the side shoots that form after stopping. Rub the others out at the earliest opportunity. If you would rather have several smaller flowers per plant, you may retain about three of the best side shoots after this first stopping.

Start cannas and dahlias Start these into growth in a slightly heated greenhouse, a frame with soil-warming cables or even in an unheated well-constructed frame standing in a sheltered place. But beware of unheated frames if the sides are thin or have gaps between the wood through which draughts can penetrate. The method of starting dahlias is exactly as in the greenhouse (see page 29), except that there is no need to use boxes. The roots can simply be placed in the frames side by side and nearly covered with dry soil. Old canna roots may be in pots already. There is no need to repot them as this is better done after growth has restarted. If, however, you are purchasing new roots or are dealing with old bedding roots that have been overwintered in boxes, pot them singly in 6-in pots, in John Innes potting compost No. 1 or an equivalent peat-based mix.

Start begonia and gloxinia tubers If you have only a small greenhouse or one that is not too well heated, now is the time to start gloxinias and tuberous-rooted begonias into growth. I have already given full particulars regarding this (see page 16) and there is nothing further to add except that you will find it a good deal easier to maintain the required temperature of 13 to 16°C

(55 to 60°F) now than in January. Make the most of the sun's heat by closing the ventilators early in the afternoon. An excellent plan with houses that are not too well heated is to have heavy blinds which can be rolled down right over the glass as soon as the sun sets.

Pot greenhouse annuals If you were able to pot some annuals for the greenhouse in Early February the finest should now be ready for a further shift into 7- to 8-in pots, still using John Innes potting compost No. 1 or a peat-based equivalent.

Pot begonia and gloxinia tubers Tubers that were started in January and potted for the first time in Late February will almost certainly need a move into their flowering pots, 4 to 6 in in diameter, according to the size of the plants. Use the same compost and treat as before. Tubers set in fibre in Late February to start growth will probably be ready for a first potting.

Take dahlia cuttings Dahlias introduced to the greenhouse last month will now be making growth, and you can obtain a first batch of cuttings. Sever the firm young shoots when they are about 2 in in length. Some gardeners recommend taking each cutting with a small piece of tuber, but I regard this as wasteful. If the cuttings are severed just above the tuber, leaving a tiny stump still attached to it, this stump will soon send out two or three more shoots which can be taken as cuttings. If the shoot is severed with some of the tuber, no more cuttings will be obtained from there. The cuttings are prepared by trimming the base cleanly just below a joint, removing the lower leaves (if any) and inserting $\frac{3}{4}$ in deep in sandy soil. I find the simplest and quickest method in the long run is to put the soil into $2\frac{1}{2}$-in pots and place one cutting in each. Then there need be no further root disturbance. The cuttings should be rooted in a propagating case with a temperature of 16 to 21°C (60 to 70°F). Any sufficiently deep box with a piece of glass on the top will serve.

Select firm young growths about 2 in long for dahlia cuttings. Sever these above the tuber and just below a joint

Water rather freely. If desired, dahlia cuttings can be treated with a hormone rooting powder prior to insertion.

VEGETABLES AND FRUIT
Harden off vegetable seedlings Onions and leeks sown in the greenhouse in January, also cauliflowers, peas, lettuces and broad beans sown in Early February will now be better in a frame, where they can be hardened off for planting outdoors in April. Ventilate cautiously at first and be ready with sacks for cold nights, but gradually accustom the plants to full exposure.

Germinating period of vegetable seeds

The following table of germination times is only approximate. Actual times will vary greatly according to soil, warmth and weather. Given a sufficiently low temperature or dry soil, seeds will remain dormant indefinitely. The times below are for normal conditions at the usual sowing times.

Name	Time (days)	Name	Time (days)	Name	Time (days)
Beans, broad	8–12	Cress	5–8	Parsnip	21–28
Beans, French	10–14	Cucumber	5–15	Pea	7–12
Beans, runner	10–14	Endive	14–21	Radish	6–10
Beet	18–24	Kale	7–12	Savoy	7–12
Beet, seakale	18–24	Kohl Rabi	7–12	Spinach, summer	10–15
Broccoli	7–12	Leek	21–24	Spinach, winter	10–15
Brussels sprouts	7–12	Lettuce	10–15	Spinach, beet	18–24
Cabbage	7–12	Mustard	4–8	Swede	7–12
Carrot	17–24	Onion, spring-sown	21–25	Tomato	7–14
Cauliflower	7–12	Onion, August-sown	12–18	Turnip	7–12
Celery	18–28	Parsley	28–42	Vegetable Marrow	6–10

In the Garden

FLOWERS AND SHRUBS

Plant gladioli and montbretias
Make a first planting of gladioli, but do not plant all the corms at once. It is much better to make successional plantings over a period of about a month or six weeks, because this will lengthen the flowering period. Cover the corms with about 3 in of soil. The small 'primulinus' and miniature varieties may be 3 in apart in rows 8 in apart, but the large-flowered gladioli should be at least 6 in apart in rows 1 ft apart if you want the flowers for cutting. If they are merely to be used for bedding or in groups in the herbaceous border space them at least 6 in apart each way.

Ivy growing over walls can be clipped and then brushed over at this time of year

Montbretias are also planted now and these can all be planted out at once. If you are purchasing dried corms, I advise you to start them into growth first in trays filled with a very light compost mainly consisting of peat and sand. Just bury them in this, water moderately and place in a frame. Then, as soon as growth starts, transfer them to the beds in which they are to flower, planting carefully with a trowel and covering the corms with about 2 in of soil. A better method of culture is to obtain growing tufts (plants that have never been quite dried off) and plant these as advised for the started corms. Montbretias should be at least 4 in apart each way.

Plant tigridias Not everybody's flower, but they are very lovely and even though the individual blooms only last a day, they are followed by a succession of others. The bulbs are barely hardy and must be given a sheltered and sunny position. Plant now, placing the bulbs 3 in deep and about 6 in apart each way. Alternatively, tigridias can be grown in a sunny, unheated greenhouse, five bulbs in a 6-in pot in John Innes potting compost No. 1 or a peat-based potting compost.

Plant carnation layers Early autumn is usually considered the best time for planting rooted border carnation layers, but in very exposed places I prefer to pot the layers in the autumn and keep them in a cold frame during the winter. Then they are planted out doors at this time of the year, when conditions are getting steadily more favourable.

Plant autumn-sown sweet peas
Seize the first favourable opportu-

Young laterals of grapes must gradually be trained along the support wires. Each lateral should be stopped just after the second leaf beyond the flower cluster and any sub-laterals removed

nity to plant out sweet pea seedlings raised in pots in the autumn. Contrary to general practice when planting from pots, no attempt should be made to keep the ball of soil around the roots intact. Instead, very carefully shake the roots clear of soil and then plant equally carefully in deep holes prepared with a trowel. Spread the roots out and work fine soil around them, firming it thoroughly with the knuckles. For exhibition purposes the plants should be at least 9 in apart in the rows. Common practice is to grow double rows 1 ft apart with 5 ft alleyways between.

Clip ivy on walls This can be done very quickly with a pair of shears. Simply clip off the leaves, leaving the stems practically bare, and then brush them down with a stiff broom, getting out all dead leaves and dirt. The plants will look very bare at first, but will soon get new leaves and will be much better for the clean up.

VEGETABLES AND FRUIT
Sow broad beans and peas This is usually a good time to make

the first sowing of broad beans outdoors. The place chosen must be open, and really well cultivated. Sow the seeds 6 in apart in drills rather over 1 in deep and about 2 ft apart. The dwarf varieties can be grown as close as 15 in between the rows, but it is a mistake to crowd the bigger kinds.

Make a second sowing of early peas as described on page 46.

Sow lettuces Unless the weather is exceptionally bad or your garden is very cold, it should now be safe to make a first sowing of lettuces outdoors. You can choose a cabbage or a cos variety according to taste. Sow the seeds very thinly in drills $\frac{1}{2}$ in deep and about 1 ft apart for the large varieties or 9 in apart for the Tom Thumb or Little Gem types.

Sow spinach beet This is a very useful form of beetroot grown for its leaves, which are used like those of spinach. Sow now in drills 1 in deep and 18 in apart and thin out the seedlings to 9 in apart. This plant is sometimes known as perpetual spinach because it keeps on cropping all the summer and autumn and much of the winter as well.

Graft apples and pears Apple and pear stocks that are well

established and also old trees that were cut back for reworking (see page 12) may be grafted now.

Under Glass
FLOWERS AND SHRUBS
Harden autumn seedlings and cuttings Various seedlings and cuttings that have been in frames during the autumn and winter must now be hardened off. This simply means that more ventilation should be given, the lights being removed altogether during the day when the weather is mild and being tilted a little at night unless it is actually freezing or blowing very cold. The hardiest of these plants, and therefore the most able to stand exposure, will be pansies, violas, and violets. Antirrhinums (either from autumn seed or cuttings), penstemons, and calceolarias need a little more protection as yet.

VEGETABLES AND FRUIT
Sow French beans for succession You may now make a third sowing of beans in 8-in pots for cropping under glass to follow those sown in Late January and Late February. At this season it will be possible to maintain the necessary temperature in a well-made frame placed in a sheltered but sunny position and covered with sacks at night.

Prick off early celery Celery from the Late February sowing will be in need of pricking off into deeper seed boxes filled with John Innes potting compost No. 1 or a peat-based equivalent. Space the seedlings 2 in apart each way. Water freely and return to the greenhouse in an average temperature of about 13°C (55°F) for the time being, but gradually harden them off so that you can remove the boxes to a frame in April.

Sow celery and celeriac Celery may be sown in a frame in a very sheltered position, with soil-warming cables installed. Sow thinly either directly into the soil or in seed trays. Plants from this sowing will provide a succession for planting out after those raised earlier in the greenhouse.

Celeriac, which has the advantages that it will grow on soil that would be much too poor for celery, can also be sown now. The seeds are treated in exactly the same way as those of celery.

Pot early tomatoes and make further sowings Tomatoes sown in Late January should now be ready for their second potting into 4½- to 5-in pots of John Innes potting compost No. 1 or an equivalent soilless mixture. Pot the plants rather firmly this time and shade for a day or so.

A sowing of tomatoes made now will provide good sturdy plants for planting outdoors in June. Sow the seeds as before (see page 21) and germinate them in the greenhouse in a temperature of about 16°C (60°F).

Plant early cucumbers Cucumbers raised in Late February will now be ready for planting in growing bags or a specially prepared bed in a greenhouse maintained at a minimum temperature of 16°C (60°F). The growing bag or bed can be on the ground or on the staging, provided there is adequate light. Slates or sheets of corrugated iron make a good base. To make a special bed first spread some straw for drainage and then a 6-in layer of rough turfy loam or compost mixed with about one-third its own bulk of well-rotted stable manure and a good sprinkling of bonemeal and wood ashes. At intervals of 3 ft make low mounds, each consisting of about two bucketfuls of the same mixture and plant a cucumber on the summit of each.

Each plant should have its own supporting stake. As the plants grow, train the main stem up towards the apex of the house and tie the laterals to horizontal wires stretched 15 in apart 9 in below the glass. Water the plants freely and spray them twice daily with tepid water to keep the atmosphere moist. Little air will be needed at first, but open the top ventilators when the temperature reaches 24°C (75°F).

Sow cucumbers Good cucumbers can be grown in frames with soil-warming cables as well as in heated greenhouses. If sown now they will start to bear in June, just when the earliest hot-house cucumbers are getting past their first vigour. Spread compost prepared as for greenhouse cucumbers as described above, with a low mound in the centre of the space covered by each light. Sow two seeds on the centre of each mound. If both germinate, pull out the weaker seedling.

Sow aubergines and capsicums For cultivation under glass sow aubergines and capsicums (sweet peppers) in John Innes or a peat seed compost and germinate in a temperature of 16 to 18°C (60 to 65°F) in a propagating case.

Plant melons Melons raised in a warm greenhouse in Late February will be ready for planting. The method followed is exactly the same as for cucumbers (see above) and similar watering and spraying must be carried out.

Start vines in unheated houses It is now safe to encourage vines to start into growth even in unheated greenhouses. This is done by closing ventilators altogether at night and opening those at the top only a little by day. Spray every morning with water that is just slightly warm.

Pollinate and train early vines Vines started into growth last month will be coming into flower and will need hand pollination just like peaches. The young laterals must be pulled down little by little until they lie along the training wires. If more than one lateral forms at each spur, pinch out the growing point of the weaker at the earliest opportunity. The points of the flower-bearing laterals must also be pinched just beyond the second leaf formed after the truss. If any secondary laterals form, pinch these just beyond the first leaf. While the vines are in flower, raise the temperature to 18°C (65°F) at night, rising to about 24°C (75°F) by day. From this stage onwards you should soak the border occasionally with very weak liquid manure. Give sufficient to wet the soil to a depth of a couple of feet and repeat the application as soon as the soil looks at all dry an inch or two below the surface.

Crops in Season

In the garden Broccoli, cabbage, cauliflower, kale, leeks, spring onions, rhubarb, seakale, spinach beet.

Under glass Carrots, lettuce, mustard and cress, radish.

Mowers and mowing

Mowing grass not only converts it into a lawn but also has a profound effect on the composition of the turf. Some grasses and weeds die when kept cut very short and others thrive on close mowing. These effects are also influenced by the weather and it is when this is both hot and dry that the results of close mowing are revealed most starkly.

Broadly speaking, lawn grasses can be divided into two groups, the low-growing, narrow-leaved kinds such as the fescue and agrostis species and the taller, broader-leaved kinds such as perennial rye grass (*Lolium perenne*) and smooth-stalked meadow grass (*Poa pratensis*). Mixtures may be used of both fine and coarser grasses but for lawns that are to be close mown to give a very smooth, even surface it is the fine grasses that will predominate; whereas if the grass is left fairly long the coarse grasses will attain the ascendency. Fine grasses can be mown to $\frac{1}{2}$ in or less (as little as $\frac{3}{16}$ in for some purposes) whereas coarser grasses should be allowed to retain at least $\frac{3}{4}$ in of growth and maybe considerably more in some situations. So set the mower blades accordingly.

The method of mowing also has a bearing on the kind of turf produced. For the smoothest, shortest lawns the traditional cylinder type of mower is best and the more revolving blades it has the more even and less ribbed will be the cut. But multiple-bladed machines jam more readily if grass is long or wet and they require more energy to operate. For most gardens a hand-operated mower may have five blades, giving about forty cuts per yard of forward movement. However, the cutting rate can be more than doubled for power-driven machines to give a smoother finish.

Rotary machines cut like a scythe, relying on the sharpness and speed of movement of the blade and the inertia of the grass to give a good result. The revolving blade is always power driven but machines may be hand or power propelled. Some are supported on wheels which are adjustable to control the height of cut while others use the air cushion (hovercraft) principle and in these the blades are adjustable for height. Some models eject the cut grass at the back and others at the side. Side ejection leaves the cut grass lying in swathes which may have to be swept up. However, most rotary mowers can be fitted with boxes or bags to catch the mowings and so eliminate this extra work.

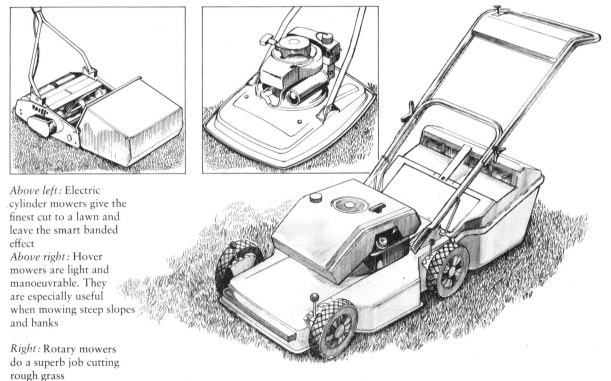

Above left: Electric cylinder mowers give the finest cut to a lawn and leave the smart banded effect

Above right: Hover mowers are light and manoeuvrable. They are especially useful when mowing steep slopes and banks

Right: Rotary mowers do a superb job cutting rough grass

Plants for March

There are some camellias that will bloom in autumn and winter but outdoors their flowers are then always at risk from the weather. By March they have a much better chance of survival and even if some flowers do get damaged by frost they will soon be replaced by new ones from buds that are more resistant then flowers to cold.

March is also the month when the forsythias first burst into bloom, filling gardens with such a blaze of golden flowers for a few weeks that there will be nothing to surpass it in the warmer months ahead. Only bullfinches can reduce it to insignificance and they are only likely to do this in secluded places where there is nothing to disturb them as they methodically peck off the flower buds. It is for the same reason that the early flowering almonds, peaches and ornamental plums so often give a far better display in town and suburban gardens than they do in the country where there may be less passing traffic to scare birds away.

In March primroses and polyanthuses will be becoming daily more numerous and beautiful as will some of the hardy exotic primulas, such as *Primula juliae*, with almost stemless, wine red flowers, and the numerous hybrids made between this Caucasian species and our native primrose which are collectively known as *P. juliana*.

In semi-shady places the dog's tooth violets and other species of erythronium will be opening their flowers, white, yellow or purplish pink according to variety. Some kinds have handsomely marbled leaves as an additional attraction.

Clematis armandii is the hardiest evergreen species and also one of the first to open its clusters of snowy white flowers. It enjoys growing on a west-facing wall where it gets plenty of shelter but not too much hot sunshine in summer. The Japanese quinces can also be trained on walls, even those facing north and in such places will be flowering in March if not earlier.

Herbaceous plants Adonis, bergenias, doronicum, hellebores, pulmonarias, primroses, polyanthus, *Ranunculus ficaria* vars., violets, winter-flowering pansies.

Below: Erythronium revolutum Pink Beauty
Top right: Primula juliae Wanda
Bottom right: Camellia japonica Bush Hill Beauty

Above: The early-flowering evergreen *Clematis armandii* looks well with varieties of flowering quince (chaenomeles)
Right: *Pulmonaria saccharata* is just as valuable for its handsome spotted leaves as it is for its flowers

Hardy bulbs, corms and tubers Anemone, chionodoxa, spring-flowering crocuses, *Cyclamen coum, C. libanoticum, C. repandum*, eranthis, erythronium, hyacinths, *Ipheion uniflorum, Iris aucheri, I. persica, I. sindpers, Leucojum vernum*, narcissus hybrids and species, *Romulea bulbocodium, R. clusiana*, scillas, tulips.

Evergreen shrubs *Azara integrifolia, A. microphylla, Berberis linearifolia*, camellias, daphnes, *Erica arborea, E. carnea, E. darleyensis, E. lusitanica, E. mediterranea*, mahonias, pieris, rhododendrons, *Ulex europaeus, Viburnum burkwoodii, V. tinus*.

Deciduous shrubs Chaenomeles, *Cornus mas, Corylopsis pauciflora, C. spicata*, daphne, forsythias, loniceras, *Magnolia stellata, Osmaronia cerasiformis*, prunus, *Spiraea thunbergii, Stachyurus praecox, Viburnum bodnantense, V. grandiflorum*.

Evergreen trees *Arbutus andrachne.*

Deciduous Trees *Acer rubrum, Alnus nitida, Magnolia campbellii, Parrotia persica*, prunus.

Hardy Climbers *Clematis armandii, C. calycina.*

Grafting and layering

Grafting is the process of joining one plant to another; usually the top growth of one (the scion) to the roots and possibly some portion of stem (the rootstock) of the other. It is a useful method of propagation for plants that cannot readily be made to grow from cuttings and which do not come true to type from seed. It also has value because the rootstock can exert influence on the scion, increasing or decreasing its normal vigour and possibly bringing it into flower or fruit earlier in life. There are many methods of grafting of which the following four are widely used.

Whip and tongue grafting is used when scion and rootstock

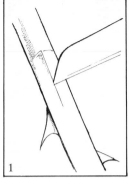

are of similar diameter. It is much used for fruit trees and is carried out in March or April when the sap is beginning to rise. The scions are prepared from the previous year's growth cut in winter and partly buried in a cool shady place so they are a little retarded but not withered. The scion is 4 to 6 in long and cut with several growth buds, one near the top. It is prepared by making a long sloping cut at the bottom. Half way up this first cut, make a second cut in the opposite direction to form a tongue. The rootstock is beheaded, usually 10 to 20 in above ground level but sometimes much more, and two similar cuts are

Budding
1 A T-shaped incision is made on the rootstock
2 The bud is usually cut with a shield-shaped piece of bark still attached, the sliver of wood inside being carefully removed
3 The bud is slipped into the cut and bound in place. No grafting wax is required

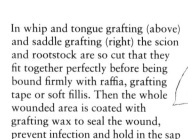

made at the top into which the scion can be fitted. The two interlocked tongues hold the scion in place while it is bound to the rootstock. Then the whole areas is coated with grafting wax. In a few weeks the two surfaces will join together around the cambium layer. This is the moist, greenish layer of actively-growing cells between the bark and the hard wood of the stem.

Saddle grafting is often used for rhododendrons but can be applied to many plants. Rootstock and scion should be about the same diameter. The rootstock is beheaded and then two upward cuts are made on opposite sides to form a pointed 'saddle'. The scion is split up the middle and trimmed so that it fits closely to the rootstock. The scion and rootstock are then bound together and grafting wax applied.

Rind grafting is useful when the rootstock is much stouter than the scion. The latter is prepared by making one long slanting cut. The rootstock is beheaded and a straight incision

In whip and tongue grafting (above) and saddle grafting (right) the scion and rootstock are so cut that they fit together perfectly before being bound firmly with raffia, grafting tape or soft fillis. Then the whole wounded area is coated with grafting wax to seal the wound, prevent infection and hold in the sap

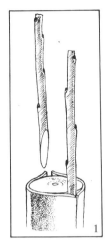
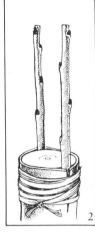
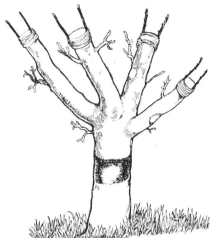

In budding the scion consists of a single growth bud. Any leaf is removed but the leaf stalk retained for ease of handling. The rootstock is prepared by making a T-shaped incision in the bark and lifting this on both sides of the down cut with the handle of the budding knife. The bud is slipped in so that its exposed cambium lies against that of the rootstock. The two are then bound together. Budding is

is made downwards through the bark for the extent of the cut in the scion. With the handle of the grafting knife raise the bark so the scion can be slipped under-neath, its cut surface lying snuggly against the exposed cambium of the rootstock. Several scions may be inserted around a large rootstock. Then all are bound in place and given a protective coating of grafting wax

Rind grafting (above)
1 Fit the scions in the slits in the bark of the rootstock
2 Bind the scions in place with raffia and then apply a liberal coat of grafting wax
3 If a large tree is being reworked, each branch may be cut back and grafted separately

Tip layering blackberry (right)

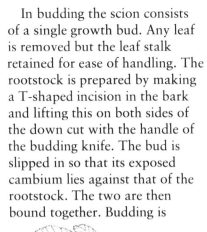

usually done in the summer months when the sap is flowing freely and the bark parts readily from the wood. The top growth of the rootstock is removed the following winter and thereafter growth should be permitted only from the scion bud.

Layering can be done at any time and some plants do it for themselves. Blackberry stems root and grow where their tips touch the ground and rhodo-dendron branches root where they lie on the soil. With many plants the process can be hastened by wounding the stem, preferably through or just below a joint that can be buried an inch or so deep in the soil and held firmly in place with a peg or stone.

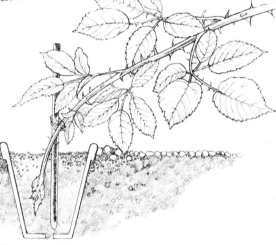

Layering a branch of a rhododendron

April

'A cold April. The barn will fill'

General Work

In the Garden

THIS IS a busy month for the gardener and many jobs delayed because of bad weather in March can still be undertaken. There is still time to plant hardy herbaceous perennials moved from the open ground, but the sooner the work is completed the better for these plants will now be making quite a lot of growth. Container-grown plants can be moved at any time provided they are sufficiently well established. However, be sure to keep roots and soil intact when removing the containers.

Plant gladioli for succession Throughout the month you should continue to plant gladioli in small batches for succession, as already explained in my notes for Late March.

Plant alpines Alpine plants are almost invariably grown by nurserymen in small pots and can be transplanted from these at any time of the year, provided sufficient care is taken. However, April is the ideal month when there is least risk and even plants grown in the open ground can be shifted now unless they happen to be in flower, for example, aubrietas, arabis and early saxifrages. These should be transplanted as soon as flowering is over. When planting from pots, simply tap the plants out, remove any crocks from the bottom of the root ball and loosen the mass a little with the fingers, but not so much as to damage any of the roots. Plant with a trowel and make firm. Only when planting in a scree is it advisable to shake all the soil from the roots and then these should be spread out carefully in the new compost.

Evergreen shrubs planted in an exposed position may need the protection of a hessian screen to keep off cold winds

Plant evergreen shrubs This is the best time for planting evergreen shrubs lifted from the open ground, but if continued spells of cold east wind should follow it may be necessary to erect some protection, either by making screens of sacking or fine mesh plastic netting, or by placing wattle hurdles or evergreen boughs in position, paying particular attention to the east and north sides. Later on, as the weather becomes warm, a nightly spray with tepid water will do good and mulching will help to keep the soil moist.

Propagate shrubs by layering This is a very simple method of propagating quite a number of shrubs and trees (see pages 56 and 57). It is worth trying practically any variety, with the exception of the big fruits, such as apples, pears, cherries and plums, and also very hard-wooded trees such as hawthorn and beech. Many evergreens grow freely from layers; rhododendrons, for example, and also laurels and aucubas. Rambler roses form roots without difficulty, and so do many of the more vigorous climbing varieties.

THE LAWN

Mow lawns more frequently From April onwards lawns will require mowing more frequently. Give a dressing of a good proprietary lawn fertilizer or of a mixture of two parts of sulphate of potash, one part of sulphate of ammonia, two parts of dried blood, to twenty parts of silver sand, blend well and apply at the rate of 6 oz per square yard. This is the time of year at which worm killers may be used most effectively. Choose a day when the soil is likely to be moist to a considerable depth and be sure it soaks well in. Later you should sweep up the dead worms.

VEGETABLES AND FRUIT

Make successional sowings You will need to make successional sowings during the month if you wish to maintain an unbroken supply of vegetables later on. In the main these are the same as for last month (see page 42). Radishes and mustard and cress may now be sown outdoors, but choose a warm, sheltered place. You should make two further sowings of lettuce at fortnightly intervals (see page 51). Similar instructions apply to spinach (see page 43). A further sowing of broad beans outdoors (see page 51) made towards the end of the month will ensure a crop in the early autumn. Further sowings of carrots will be necessary, but these I have dealt with separately (see page 68). Most important of all are at least two sowings of peas (see page 46). These are treated as before, but after mid April it is best to use a second early or maincrop variety rather than an early kind bred to grow and flower in the relatively cool days of spring.

Prepare celery trenches Some time during the month you should prepare the trenches for celery. They will not be wanted until June, but it is an advantage to prepare them well in advance so that manure and soil may become blended together. The trenches should be 15 in wide for single rows and 18 in wide for double rows, and they must be at least 3 ft apart. You can use the ground between the trenches for various salad crops. Remove the soil to a depth of 18 in and then break up the bottom as deeply as possible with a long fork, mixing in well-rotted manure or decayed vegetable refuse. Place a layer of manure and good top soil in about equal parts 9 in deep on top of the forked subsoil and a further layer of 6 in of good top soil over this. The celery will be planted later on in the 3-in deep depression. This shallow trench gives some protection to the young plants and makes it easy to flood them with water in dry periods.

Under Glass

General greenhouse management There will now be much less difficulty in maintaining a sufficient temperature in the greenhouse. It may even be necessary to have temporary shading for some plants during the hottest part of the day, especially in small houses which heat up very quickly. However, permanent shading will not be needed as yet. In general it is not wise to have the temperature running much above 21°C (70°F) in April, which means ample top ventilation on all sunny and fairly still days. Do not use the side ventilators yet, nor leave the door open, for fear of admitting damaging draughts.

Bedding plants and half-hardy annuals must be gradually hardened off. Later in the month you should remove them to frames if possible but prepare them gradually for this, by giving increased ventilation earlier in the month whenever the weather is favourable and keeping them as close to the glass as possible. In a mixed greenhouse it is sometimes difficult to reconcile the needs of all the plants at this stage, but much can be done by erecting shelves, a little below the top ventilators, where the plants that need cool conditions can be placed. Those varieties that require warmth can be kept on the staging and as near to the heating apparatus as possible.

From now onwards you will have to keep a sharp look-out for pests such as greenfly, thrips and red spider mites. Should any of these appear, fumigate at once using HCH smoke generators or pellets for greenfly and thrips and derris or diazinon spray for red spider mites. To obtain good results with fumigation, make sure that the greenhouse is as air-tight as possible. Close down all ventilators and doors, and leave the house closed for several hours. Plants which are to be fumigated should never be dry at the roots and treatment should not be carried out in bright

sunlight. Alternatively, spray with an appropriate insecticide.

The main batch of calceolarias, hippeastrums and autumn-sown schizanthuses will be approaching their flowering period and will benefit by fairly constant feeding with weak manure water or light applications of fertilizer. The former should only just colour the water, but where proprietary fertilizers are concerned you should consult manufacturers' instructions and certainly not exceed them. I find that it is better to halve the strengths they recommended but apply a little more frequently.

Prune and repot flowering shrubs in the greenhouse As soon as they have finished flowering remove the faded flower heads from Indian azaleas and cut back the flowering branches of deutzias and genistas quite close to the base. Both azaleas and camellias may be repotted, if necessary, as soon as they have finished flowering. Use a lime-free compost with a good sprinkling of bonemeal. At the most only use a pot one size larger than that occupied formerly but it is all the better if they can go back into the same size pots after teasing out some of the old soil with the point of a stick. After potting the plants must be returned to the greenhouse for a few weeks and should be sprayed every morning with tepid water.

General potting In addition to pricking off there will be a considerable amount of potting to do. Seedlings pricked off earlier may be getting overcrowded. Pot them singly into $2\frac{1}{2}$- to 3-in pots directly their leaves touch. The later chrysanthemum and carnation cuttings will be needing a move while dahlia cuttings can be potted into 3-in pots directly they are rooted, unless you inserted them singly in pots, in which case no move will be needed as yet. This also applies to rooted cuttings of abutilons, petunias and daturas taken in March. Begonias and gloxinias started as tubers in January and February and already potted once, will be in various stages of growth, as will many other young greenhouse plants and tomatoes. The safe plan is to tap a plant out of its pot occasionally and examine the roots. If the soil is just nicely moist right through you can do this quite easily without disturbing the plant at all. Simply turn the pot upside down, place one hand over the soil, and give the rim of the pot a sharp rap on the edge of the potting bench or greenhouse staging. As soon as you see white rootlets forming freely all round the side of the ball, transfer the plants to larger pots. The usual practice is to shift from 3-in pots into 4- or 5-in pots, and from these into 6- or 7-in pots. It is important to remember that too big a shift at one time is not desirable. By this stage most plants will appreciate a richer soil mixture such as John Innes potting compost No. 2 or even No. 3 for the really strong-growing plants such as chrysanthemums. Most plants should be returned to the greenhouse immediately after potting, but chrysanthemums are better in an unheated frame, where they may be hardened off gradually.

Stop early-flowering chrysanthemums From time to time during the month you should pinch out the growing tips of the rooted cuttings of early-flowering chrysanthemums required for spray flowering. The ideal moment to do this is when the cuttings are well rooted, growing freely and about 6 in tall. Most February- and March-rooted cuttings will reach this stage before the end of April. Note that this stopping applies only to plants that are to be grown for garden decoration or to produce a lot of flowers. The object is to produce a number of branches on each plant and with this end in view the plants will be stopped again in June. With plants grown for large individual flowers, either for exhibition or for cutting, a different method is followed (see page 86), so they must not be stopped now.

Much the same applies to the later varieties that are to flower under glass in the autumn but if some of these are required for exhibition on a particular date in October or November the time of stopping may need to be varied according to variety and locality. Commercial suppliers of chrysanthemums usually give detailed stopping instructions in their catalogues and these are useful as a guide but may need to be modified to suit local conditions. If plants are required solely for decoration or as cut flowers and the precise date at which they attain their peak of perfection is not important the later-flowering varieties can be treated in the same way as the earlies, that is, stopped when they are well rooted and growing freely.

Take cuttings It is still possible to take cuttings of bedding and greenhouse plants as I described on page 41, although the bedding plants will be comparatively late to flower. Some late-struck fuchsias, pelargoniums and salvias make admirable pot plants for the greenhouse in autumn. Continue to take cuttings of dahlias as they become available (see page 49). It should be possible to take further cuttings of winter-flowering begonias during the month (see page 41). Semi-tuberous-rooted begonias of the Optima type will now be starting into growth again and you can encourage them by giving them rather more water. As soon as the basal growths are a couple of inches in length you may remove some as cuttings, treating them as you would the other winter-flowering types.

VEGETABLES AND FRUIT

Prick off seedlings Throughout the month you will be kept busy pricking off many seedlings from sowings made in March.

Harden off plants in frames Onion, leek, cauliflower, pea, broad bean and lettuce seedlings moved to frames in Mid March will require full ventilation whenever the thermometer rises above freezing point and the wind is not very cold. They must be hardened off fully for planting out in Mid April. Similar remarks apply to violets, violas, pansies, penstemons, autumn-sown antirrhinums and other nearly hardy plants, but more tender kinds must still be ventilated with some caution.

Train and topdress early cucumbers Side shoots formed on the main stems of cucumbers planted in Late March must be stopped from extending too far or there will soon be such a mass of foliage in the house that the plants will get unhealthy. Pinch out

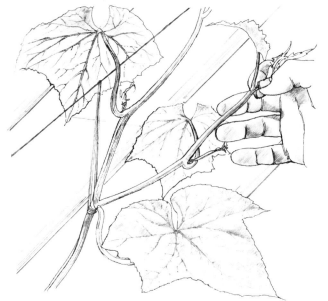

Stop greenhouse cucumbers by pinching out the soft tip of each side shoot. Remove the tips of secondary side shoots after two leaves have formed

Cucumbers in frames should be stopped after four true leaves
have formed. The resulting laterals are trained towards the
sides and eventually stopped

the soft tip of each side shoot as soon as it carries
two tiny fruits or when it is 2 ft in length, whichever
occurs first. If secondary side shoots appear, pinch
them out when they have made a couple of leaves.
The tip of the main stem must be pinched out as soon
as it reaches the apex of the house.

Keep a sharp watch and as soon as white rootlets
appear on the surface of the bed give a topdressing, a
couple of inches thick, of a mixture of equal parts of
good fibrous loam and well-rotted manure. Repeat
this later if necessary. The plants will want plenty of
water now that they are growing freely. You should
also spray them twice daily with tepid water and
damp down the paths to maintain plenty of moisture
in the atmosphere. Open the top ventilators a little
when the thermometer reaches 24°C (75°F). A light
permanent shading on the glass with one of the
proprietary shading compounds will be advisable
from now onwards. Spray the glass quite lightly,
heavy shading is not yet desirable.

Cucumbers sown in Late March and growing in
frames are trained in a slightly different manner from
those growing in greenhouses. The tip of each plant
is pinched out when it has made four leaves. Then
the resulting laterals are trained evenly over the bed,
being held in position with wooden or wire pegs.
These are stopped as soon as they reach the edge of
the frame or interfere with neighbouring plants.
Sublaterals, bearing flowers and subsequently fruits
are pinched out from time to time one or two leaves
beyond the flowers to prevent gross overcrowding
with foliage. Later on the old growths that have
finished bearing may be cut out to make room for
new growths.

Water the frame plants freely and ventilate very
sparingly on mild days only. Spray overhead in
sunny, warm weather.

Management of the vinery Whether heated or
unheated, the vinery will require fairly constant
attention throughout the month. In unheated houses
growth can be encouraged now by giving less
ventilation and rolling down blinds an hour before
sunset, so as to trap sun heat for the night. In a
heated vinery, growth will be in various stages
according to the time at which the house was closed.
Some vines will be in flower and will need a slightly
higher temperature and a drier atmosphere; more
ventilation should be given and spraying with water
discontinued for the time being. Training and stopping will be required (see page 52). Other vines a little
more advanced may be in need of fruit thinning
towards the end of the month (described on page 84).

Early April

In the Garden

FLOWERS AND SHRUBS

Prune flowering shrubs It is now time to prune the hardy fuchsias, such as *F. magellanica*, *F. gracilis* and *F. riccartonii*, *Buddleia variabilis* and its varieties, *Caryopteris clandonensis*, *Hydrangea paniculata*, *Leycesteria formosa*, *Perovskia atriplicifolia*, *Romneya coulteri* and *R. trichocalyx*, also all varieties of cornus (dogwood) and salix (willow) grown for bark effects. In each case pruning should be hard so last year's growth is cut back quite close to the older wood. However, with the buddleia and hydrangea you can allow a few branches to remain at three-quarter length to build up a main framework of growth if a large bush is required (for method see page 26).

Feed roses Give all your roses a dressing of a compound fertiliser. Use either a special proprietary rose fertiliser, in which case follow the manufacturer's instructions regarding rate of application, or a good general fertiliser, such as National Growmore at 4 oz per square yard.

THE LAWN

Sow grass seed This is usually a good time for sowing grass seed (see page 147), but wait a little if the ground is sticky. If grass seed is obtained pre-treated with a good bird repellent no further protection against birds will be necessary, but otherwise bird scarers or black thread stranded between small sticks should be used.

VEGETABLES AND FRUIT

Lift celery and leeks If any of these are still in the ground from last year, lift and heel them in behind a north wall or in any other cool place. This simply means digging a shallow trench, laying the leeks and celery in this and covering them with a little soil leaving their tops exposed.

Sow and plant asparagus Asparagus can be raised from seed sown now in a sheltered border outdoors. It is a slow process, as three or four years must elapse before the roots are large enough for cutting to start.

The best method of making a new asparagus bed is by planting sturdy roots. There are many different ways of growing asparagus but one of the best is by planting the crowns in single

---

Lift any leeks still occupying the vegetable plot and heel them in in a cool but protected spot

rows about 3 ft apart, with 1 ft between each plant. Lay the crowns in a shallow trench, spread the roots out as widely as possible and then cover them with fine soil until they are 4 in below the surface. Two-year-old crowns can be used, although commercial growers often prefer to use one-year-old plants. This method of growing in flat beds is suitable where drainage is good, but on heavy or poorly-drained soils it is better to make a raised bed about 6 in above the level of the surrounding ground.

Protect early potatoes Keep a close watch on the earliest potato bed now for shoots may appear. If they do, they will certainly need protecting by pulling some soil over them with a draw hoe. Alternatively you can scatter some dry straw or bracken on top.

Plant second-early and maincrop potatoes If the weather is good and the soil easy to work there is no point in delaying the planting

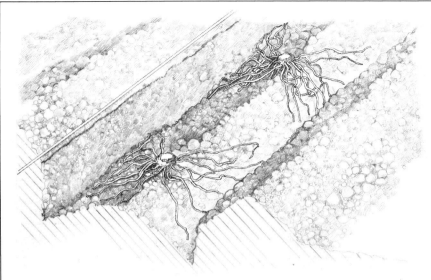

New asparagus beds can be made at this time by planting sturdy roots 1 ft apart in trenches 4 in deep. Get everything ready before planting as asparagus crowns should not be allowed to dry out

of second-early and maincrop potatoes. These crop more heavily than the earlies and therefore require more room. Allow at least 3 ft between the rows and 12 in between the tubers in the rows. I find that it is simplest and most satisfactory to plant with a spade, making the holes deep enough to allow the tops of the tubers to be covered with 3 in of soil. If the soil is inclined to be harsh and stony, surround each tuber with a few handfuls of peat or leafmould. Maincrop potatoes take longer to mature than second earlies, and will give a good succession in spite of the fact that they are planted at the same time.

Sow and plant globe artichokes These can be raised from seed, though a better method is to propagate selected varieties by suckers as the best forms do not come true from seed. However, if you would like to try seed, now is the time. Sow in drills 8 in apart, either in a frame or

sheltered border, and cover very lightly.

The best globe artichokes are propagated by suckers or offsets. Choose a really good piece of ground, well worked and thoroughly manured, and plant them firmly 3 ft apart each way. This will seem a lot of space, but it is necessary because the globe artichoke grows into a very large plant and will not give good results if overcrowded.

Sow kohl rabi This crop is a useful substitute for turnips in seasons or places where the soil is too dry for the latter. Sow the seeds in shallow drills 15 in apart.

Plant onion sets These are small onion bulbs especially prepared for spring planting. Space them 4 to 6 in apart in rows 1 ft apart, barely covering the little bulbs with soil. The bed should be prepared as for seed-raised onions.

Feed spring cabbages Give the spring cabbages now nearing maturity a topdressing of nitrate of soda, at the rate of $\frac{1}{2}$ oz per square yard, and hoe it in. A further dressing can be given in about three weeks' time.

Sow salsify This is by no means everybody's vegetable, but gourmets think highly of it. Sow the seed in shallow drills 1 ft apart. Choose an open part of the garden where the ground has been well dug and manured, preferably a year previously. The roots may be forked and useless if grown on freshly-manured ground so for this reason many gardeners plant salsify where the celery trenches were the previous year. No further manuring is carried out except a dusting of bonemeal in the autumn and an occasional sprinkling of a compound fertilizer while the plants are in growth.

Spray gooseberries and black currants If your gooseberries have suffered in the past from attacks of mildew, spray them a few days before the flowers expand with either benomyl or dinocap at the strength recommended by the manufacturer.

Black currants sometimes get very badly attacked by a mite which breeds within the buds causing them to swell up to a great size. This condition is known as big bud, and if any of your bushes are suffering from this you should spray them at once with lime sulphur wash at twice the normal winter strength recommended by the manufacturer. The effect will be to scorch the tiny leaves that are just appearing. The bushes will later recover but the mites will have been killed.

However, some varieties are sulphur shy including blackcurrant Wellington XXX and gooseberry Leveller. These susceptible varieties should never be given a sulphur wash.

Finish grafting fruit trees This is still a good time for grafting fruit

This attractive old stone trough is planted with sempervivums, sedums, thyme, and two tiny conifers which are growing between some well-placed rocks

trees in the open, although the earlier the better. I have already given instructions for this on pages 56 and 57.

Under Glass

FLOWERS AND SHRUBS

Pot seedlings of greenhouse plants Begonias, gloxinias and streptocarpus raised from seed in Late January and pricked off in Late February or Early March will probably be in need of a first potting into 3-in pots. Use John Innes potting compost No. 1 or an equivalent soilless mixture and stand in a light, well-ventilated place at a temperature between 13 and 16°C (55 and 60°F). If you were able to raise cyclamen

from seed last summer (see page 136), the seedlings will now be ready for transferring singly to 3-in pots filled with John Innes potting compost No. 1 or an equivalent mixture. The tubers should be kept on the surface of the soil, not buried. Firm moderately, water freely and then stand the plants on a shelf or staging in a light, airy part of the house. The temperature should not fall below 10°C (50°F); an average of just over 16°C (60°F) is ideal at this stage.

Rest winter-flowering plants Freesias that have been flowering during the winter must now be allowed to go to rest gradually. Place them on a shelf quite near the glass and gradually reduce the water supply. Treat arum lilies that have been used for winter flowering in a similar way. These should not be stood near the glass but kept in a cooler atmosphere. Old cyclamen that

have finished flowering should be given a decreasing amount of water though they should never be allowed to become quite dry. The young seedlings must be kept growing and must remain nicely moist all summer.

Sow zinnias in a frame If you make a sowing of zinnias in a warm, sheltered frame and keep the seedlings growing strongly without check, the plants will flower by July. The secret of success with zinnias is to maintain steady growth. Any kind of check is fatal. This is sometimes almost impossible to avoid with seedlings sown any earlier. Sow thinly in boxes or directly in the frame and cover with $\frac{1}{4}$ in of fine soil.

VEGETABLES AND FRUIT

Plant cucumbers Cucumbers from the Late March sowing will now be ready for planting in a heated greenhouse.

Mid April

In the Garden

FLOWERS AND SHRUBS

Sow hardy annuals Seed of the various hardy annuals will usually germinate more readily in Mid-April than in March, particularly if the soil tends to be heavy and cold. I have given details for an early sowing in the notes on page 46. These still apply and in addition a number of others can also be sown – notably nasturtiums of all types, calandrinia, sweet sultan, layia, leptosiphon, canary creeper, *Tagetes signata pumila*, *Mesembryanthemum criniflorum*, acroclinium, ursinia, venidium, dimorphotheca, salpiglossis and jacobaea. In sheltered gardens it is even possible to sow a number of half-hardy annuals outdoors with success, but if your garden is at all exposed I advise you to leave this until early in May. Given cloche protection, however, immediate sowing is possible.

Plant violas and pansies Plant out seedlings and rooted cuttings if they have been properly hardened off. A rather cool, semi-shaded position is best, though both will grow in full sun; the drawback is that they tend to finish flowering sooner. Well-worked, rather liberally manured ground will ensure fine blooms. Plant with a trowel and water in freely.

Prune evergreens Hardy evergreen shrubs grown as hedges or topiary specimens can be pruned with safety. If there is any really hard cutting back to be done, this is certainly the time to do it. Light trimming can be practised during the summer, but severe pruning is out of place then. Old, worn-out laurel hedges can often be renovated by cutting them back to within a foot of the ground at this time of the year. Of course, the stumps look terrible for a while, but given a little luck and some warm, showery weather, they will soon be a forest of vigorous new shoots, with fine, healthy leaves.

VEGETABLES AND FRUIT

Plant out vegetable seedlings Peas, onions, leeks, cauliflowers, broad beans and lettuces raised in the greenhouse and transferred to a frame in Mid March for hardening off may now be planted out where they are to mature, provided the weather is fairly mild. If it is frosty or winds are cold, wait a further week. All the ground should have been well dug and manured. The position chosen for the cauliflowers should be sheltered from the north and east if possible. Exhibition leeks are usually grown in trenches prepared as for celery (see page 60). However, quite good leeks can also be grown in ordinary beds if the plants are dropped into 9-in deep holes made with a dibber. With this exception, all other seedlings mentioned are planted with a trowel. Planting distances are given in the chart.

Sow winter greens All kinds of winter greens should now be sown. Brussels sprouts, cauliflower, broccoli and cabbages, either to follow the early sowing made under glass in Early March or as a first sowing, and kale, savoy and late-sprouting broccoli for the first time.

The simplest and most economical method is to broadcast as thinly as possible on a finely-prepared seed bed and cover with fine soil, which can be sifted over the seeds, to a depth of about $\frac{1}{4}$ in. Of course, you must take care to keep each patch quite separate and to label it clearly, because seedlings of winter greens are very much alike and you may find difficulty in identifying them later on if you get the seeds mixed. Remember that there are early, mid-season and late varieties of most of these brassica crops and that, by including some of each, the season of use can be greatly extended.

Vegetable	Space between plants	Space between rows
Broad beans	6 in	2 ft
Cauliflowers	2 ft	2 ft
Celery	1 ft	3 ft
Leeks	9 in	18 in
Leeks for exhibition	1 ft	18 in
Lettuces	6 to 9 in	1 ft
Onions	9 in	1 ft
Peas	4 in	18 in to 3 ft

Ring culture

Ring culture is mainly used for tomatoes and is capable of producing heavy crops. Young tomato plants are planted in good soil, such as John Innes No. 3 potting compost, in bottomless rings about 10 in wide and 9 in deep. These rings are usually made of tough, specially treated paper but could be of plastic or earthenware. They are placed about 18 in apart on a bed of some porous but otherwise inert substance such as pea gravel, well weathered boiler ashes or fairly small particles of heat-expanded clay (leca). This bed should be 6 in deep and insulated from soil below by a sheet of polythene.

The tomatoes should be well watered into the rings but thereafter all water, except for special feeds, must be applied to the bed of aggregate. It rises from this bed by capillary attraction into the soil in the rings and so to the roots. All feeding, whether with dry or liquid fertilisers, is applied directly to the soil in the rings.

Tomatoes grown in this way form two very different root systems; fine, fibrous, feeding roots in the rings and much coarser, water-searching roots in the aggregate. At the end of the season the soil in the rings can be discarded and the aggregate flushed out with water containing a little disinfectant.

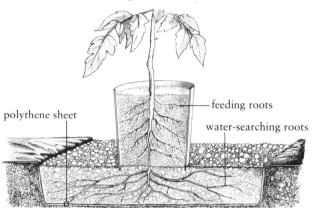

polythene sheet — feeding roots — water-searching roots

Winter-hearting cauliflowers succeed best in the milder parts of the British Isles; elsewhere it is probably best to settle for summer and autumn varieties, perhaps freezing any surplus for winter and spring use. Broccoli varieties divide into relatively quick maturing calabrese types for use in summer or early autumn, to slow-growing sprouting broccoli which takes the best part of a year to mature and is, therefore, valuable for spring use. Cabbages for spring cutting are also available but should not be sown until Mid July.

Sow maincrop carrots Now is the time to make the maincrop sowing of carrots. For this you will need an intermediate or long variety instead of the stump-rooted type. Sow thinly in drills about $\frac{1}{2}$ in deep and 1 ft apart. It is quite a good plan to make a small successional sowing of a stump-rooted variety as well and repeat a fortnight or three weeks later. From these sowings you will have tender young roots after midsummer but before the main crop is ready. These small varieties need only be sown in drills 9 in apart.

Sow parsley Make a small sowing outdoors to provide a successional crop to follow the one sown in Late February. Details of sowing are the same as before, except that there is no need now to choose a specially sheltered or warm position.

Spray apples and pears If apples were attacked last year by scab disease, spray now with benomyl, dispersible sulphur or captan, as recommended by the manufacturers. Pear trees should be treated with captan rather than lime sulphur, as the latter is inclined to cause scorching.

Under Glass

FLOWERS AND SHRUBS

Start achimenes and hippeastrums A second batch of achimenes (see pages 26 and 27) started now will ensure a succession of flowers in late summer and early autumn. Start any remaining hippeastrum bulbs into growth as well to provide late flowers (see page 21).

Start dahlias in frames If you were unable to start dahlias early, as recommended in Mid February or Mid March you can do so now. Simply arrange the roots close together in an unheated frame and cover the tubers with light soil. Water moderately, but give increasing supplies as growth commences. Cover the frame with plenty of sacks every night but remove these in the morning, unless it is very frosty.

Transfer bedding plants to frames You may now transfer most of the bedding plants and half-hardy annuals out of the greenhouse into frames for the next stage of hardening off. For the first few days after this move you should keep the frames closed and cover them well with sacks at night. Then admit a little air by day if it is fine, steadily increasing the gap until by the end of the month the lights are removed altogether for several hours on each mild day. Be particularly wary of days when the sky clears and the wind drops towards evening. At this time of year these signs often precede frost and lights should be temporarily closed. Your object should be to accustom the plants to full exposure, day and night, by the end of May.

If no frame is available, place the young plants in the coolest part of the greenhouse, possibly near the door, and a little later stand them in a sheltered, preferably sunny, place outside and cover them at night, whenever the weather is cold, with polythene supported on some kind of temporary framework to lift it clear of the plants.

VEGETABLES AND FRUIT

Sow and pot aubergines and capsicums Make a further sowing of aubergines and capsicums (see page 52) to give an outdoor planting. The seedlings from the Late-March sowing should be potted singly, in 3-in pots in John Innes potting compost No. 1.

Plant early tomatoes Tomatoes from a Late-January sowing should now be ready for their final position. You can grow them in boxes or plant them out directly into growing bags or a border of compost prepared on the staging or floor if the house is light with low walls or glass down to the ground. Nevertheless, I think 9- or 10-in pots are best for the first crop as the plants seem to come to maturity more rapidly. John Innes potting compost No. 2 is suitable.

Sow celery in frame To supplement earlier sowings of celery made in a warm greenhouse, or as an alternative to these if they could not be made, celery may now be sown in an unheated frame. The method is just the same as before (see page 34), the seed being sown thinly in well-drained trays filled with John Innes seed compost.

Prick off brassicas Cabbage, cauliflowers, broccoli and Brussels sprouts raised in frame or greenhouse in Early March will be in need of pricking off. Space them 3 in apart each way in a frame or, provided the weather is mild and they have been properly hardened off, in a sheltered border outdoors.

Sow French beans If you want a supply of French beans in July make a sowing now in seed boxes or pots; the latter method has the advantage that it avoids any

---

As soon as stoning is complete peaches and nectarines can be thinned to leave an average of one fruit per square foot

root disturbance later. Place one seed in each 2½-in pot, or in boxes plant the seeds 2 in apart each way. Cover with ¾ in of soil and germinate in the greenhouse or a frame fitted with soil-warming cables. A temperature of about 13°C (55°F) is necessary for germination, but no harm will be done if it happens to fall a little below this occasionally. Frost, however, will kill beans. The seedlings will be hardened off later on for planting out in Late May. Alternatively French beans can be sown under tunnel cloches outdoors where they are to crop. Sow seeds singly 2 in deep in a pair of drills 9 in apart to be covered by a single tunnel.

Thin peaches and nectarines In the warm greenhouse or conservatory, peaches and nectarines will have completed stoning by this time and it will be all the better if you can increase the temperature by 5°C (10°F) by day and night. Thinning can be completed as soon as the stones are formed. You can easily ascertain how far things have gone by removing and cutting open a fruit. If the stone is hard and almost full size, with a well-developed kernel, the stoning period is over. Leave an average of one fruit per 1 sq ft of tree area. Peaches in unheated houses should be set and you can start thinning as advised on page 42.

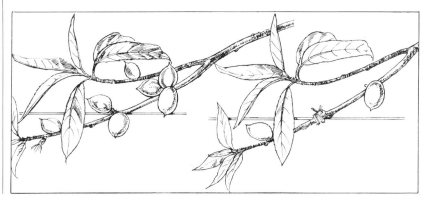

Plants for April

This is the month when the Japanese cherries really begin to assert themselves, filling gardens and lining many suburban streets with their opulent displays of bloom. They will have for company the equally magnificent magnolias and, as the month wears on, a steadily increasing number of ornamental crab apples (malus) some with rich red or crimson flowers, others with the usual white or pale pink.

April is also the peak month for daffodils and crocuses, though some have flowered earlier and there will still be a few late narcissi left over for May.

Tulips will be arriving in ever increasing numbers as the weeks slip by, the greatest colour in April coming from the early *Tulipa fosteriana*, *T. kaufmanniana* and *T. greigii* hybrids.

There will also be fritillarias to enjoy, the large upstanding crown imperials (*Fritillaria imperialis*) with dangling clusters of yellow or orange-red flowers, each cluster surmounted by a green top-knot of short leaves, and the much smaller more soberly coloured snake's head fritillaries, (*F. meleagris*) chequered in maroon and white, or sometimes white all over.

Doronicums will be among the first brightly coloured herbaceous perennials to flower and sunny banks, unmortared walls and rock gardens will be beginning to glow with the blues, purples, pinks and crimsons of aubrieta and the yellow of *Alyssum saxatile*, a plant well named Gold Dust and a true herald of the sun.

Aubrieta and *Alyssum saxatile* look especially attractive growing over a drystone wall

Herbaceous plants *Adonis vernalis, Bellis perennis flore-pleno,* bergenias, *Brunnera macrophylla,* doronicums, *Helleborus corsicus, H. orientalis, Iris chamaeiris, I. innominata, I. japonica,* myosotis, polygonatums, primroses and polyanthus, pulmonarias, wallflowers.

Hardy bulbs, corms and tubers *Allium neapolitanum,* anemones, chionodoxas, crocuses (large flowered), cyclamen, *Endymion hispanicus, E. non-scriptus* (bluebell), *Erythronium revolutum, E. tuolumnense, Fritillaria acmopetala, F. assyriaca, F. imperialis, F. meleagris, F. persica, F. pontica, Ipheion uniflorum, Iris bucharica, Leucojum vernum,* lily-of-the-valley, muscaris, narcissi, *Puschkinia scilloides,* romulea, scillas, trilliums, tulips.

Evergreen shrubs *Berberis darwinii, B. hookeri, B. linearifolia, B. lologensis, B. stenophylla,* camellias, *Ceanothus arboreus, C. rigidus, Daphne burkwoodii,* *D. cneorum, D. tangutica,* ericas (as March, see page 55), mahonias, *Osmanthus delavayi, O. burkwoodii,* pieris, *Prunus laurocerasus,* rhododendrons, *Rosmarinus officinalis, Skimmia japonica, Viburnum burkwoodii, V. tinus, Vinca major, V. minor.*

Deciduous shrubs Chaenomeles, *Colletia infausta, Cytisus ardoinii, C. monspessulanus, C. praecox,* forsythias, *Magnolia soulangiana, M. stellata, Prunus glandulosa, P. tenella, P. triloba,* rhododendrons, ribes, *Rubus spectabilis, Spiraea arguta, S. prunifolia, S. thunbergii, Viburnum carlesii, V. juddii.*

Deciduous trees *Acer platanoides, A. rubrum,* ornamental cherries and peaches (prunus), amelanchiers, *Magnolia denudata, M. kobus, M. liliiflora, M. salicifolia, M. soulangiana, M. veitchii,* malus (crab apples).

Hardy climbers Akebias, *Clematis alpina, C. armandii, Ercilla volubilis, Stauntonia hexaphylla.*

In addition many rock plants are at their best this month.

Below: Magnolia soulangiana
Bottom: Doronicum plantagineum (leopard's bane)
Below right: Fritillaria meleagris and *F.m.* Aphrodite

In the Garden

FLOWERS AND SHRUBS

Plant antirrhinums and penstemons Antirrhinums raised in the autumn from seeds or cuttings and also penstemons from autumn cuttings may be planted in their flowering quarters if they have been thoroughly hardened off.

Thin hardy annuals Hardy annuals sown outdoors in Mid March where they are to bloom will be in need of a first thinning. Simply pull out the feeblest seedlings until the remainder are left a clear 2 to 3 in apart each way to give them room to develop. A further thinning will be necessary in May. You can transplant some of the seedlings elsewhere if you wish but as a rule those with long, unbranched tap roots do not recover well from the shift. These include annual lupins, eschscholzias, poppies, clarkias,

Sweet peas can be trained in a number of ways. They look most attractive clambering up tripods in the herbaceous border or can be grown more formally up bamboo canes in rows

godetias, gypsophilas, Virginian stocks and mignonette. Be sure to firm the soil around the seedlings you leave.

Plant sweet peas Sweet peas raised in the greenhouse during January will be ready for planting out, provided they have been hardened off properly. The method to follow is exactly the same as that for planting out September-sown sweet peas (see pages 50 and 51).

Those planted in Late March should be well established, and it will be time to provide each plant with a bamboo cane at least 7 ft long. This must be pushed really firmly into the soil, and it is a good plan to link all the canes together at the top with string or wire, securing this at each end to a stronger post. You should reduce the number of shoots to one per plant, choosing the sturdiest, and lead this towards its cane with raffia or string.

If the Early March-sown plants have 2 to 3 in of growth, as they should by this time, pinch out the tip of each plant. These late-sown peas are usually grown naturally over bushy pea sticks and are not trained as a single stem up

bamboos, so there will be no need to reduce the number of shoots that form as a result of the stopping. They look well in small groups or climbing up tripods among herbaceous plants. They may also be trained on screens, pergolas and arches with other climbers, including roses.

Prune forsythias This is the time to prune forsythias if you want to keep them moderately small, or to train them against a wall. Cut back as many as possible of the flowering branches to younger stems that have not yet flowered or to new shoots just starting. With wall specimens any small laterals that have not flowered and cannot conveniently be tied in can be cut back severely.

VEGETABLES AND FRUIT

Sow endive Make a small sowing of endive; it makes a welcome change from lettuce in summer salads. Sow the seeds thinly in drills $\frac{1}{2}$ in deep and 1 ft apart.

Sow globe beetroot You can now make a sowing of globe beetroot in a fairly sheltered border. This earliest sowing need not be a very large one, as it will be followed by another in May. Sow the seeds 2 in deep in rows 1 ft apart. I find the most economical method is to place three seeds every 6 in along the rows and then reduce the seedlings to one at each station later.

Spray gooseberries If you considered it necessary to spray your gooseberries, with benomyl or dinocap before flowering in Early April, you should certainly

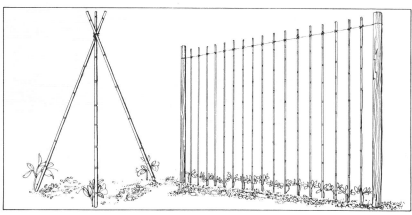

Sow three globe beetroot seeds at stations 6 in apart

repeat the treatment as soon as the petals have fallen and you can just see the tiny, fertilized fruits.

Remove greasebands from trees You should now remove and burn greasebands that have been round the main trunks or branches of apples, pears, and other fruit trees since September.

Under Glass

FLOWERS AND SHRUBS

Sow annuals for the greenhouse You can now make a second sowing of hardy and half-hardy annuals for flowering in pots in the greenhouse (see pages 33 and 45). Plants from this late sowing will provide a succession of flowers after the first batch is over.

Sow greenhouse primulas Make a first sowing of primulas that flower in the greenhouse during winter such as *Primula sinensis* and its variety *P.s. stellata*, *P. obconica*, and *P. kewensis*. Do not sow all your seeds of the first three now, but keep some for a second batch in Late June. Sow the seeds thinly in John Innes or a soilless seed compost. I think they are better sown in well-

drained pots or pans rather than boxes. Cover the seeds very lightly with fine soil and germinate in the greenhouse in a temperature of about 16°C (60°F). Cover each seed vessel with a pane of glass until germination takes place. If they begin to dry out hold the pots nearly to their rims in a bucket of water until droplets appear on the surface of the compost; do not water from overhead.

Take chrysanthemum cuttings This is the time to start taking cuttings of chrysanthemums that are to make dwarf specimens in pots. You can root them in boxes or beds of soil exactly as the earlier chrysanthemum cuttings, though I think a better method is to insert them singly in 2½-in pots or three round the edge of a 3-in pot. Allow them to root either in a cool greenhouse or a frame. By no means all varieties are suitable for this method of culture but lists of those that are suitable are given in the catalogues of most chrysanthemum nurseries.

VEGETABLES AND FRUIT

Sow runner beans Make a small sowing of runner beans in exactly the same way as the early sowing of French beans (see page 69). If you germinate them in the greenhouse you will have some nice forward plants for putting out early in June and these will give

---

Crops in Season

In the garden Broccoli, cabbage, cauliflower, kale, leeks, lettuce, spring onions, rhubarb, seakale, spinach beet.

Under glass French beans, carrots, lettuce, mustard and cress, radish.

---

you a crop of beans several weeks before the earliest outdoor sowing. Alternatively the sowing can be made under tunnel cloches where the plants are to mature as described for French beans.

Sow marrows, ridge cucumbers and melons Later on you are sure to want marrows, and you may be glad of a few ridge cucumbers as well. Sow some seeds singly in 2½- to 3-in pots and germinate them in the greenhouse or in a frame with soil-warming cables in a temperature of 16°C (60°F) or thereabouts. They will germinate more quickly if you cover the pots with thick paper but this must be removed as soon as the seed leaves appear. Melons that are to be grown in a frame should also be sown now and germinated in the same way.

Train and pollinate melons The training of melons is not unlike that of cucumbers (see page 63). It is, however, necessary to restrict each plant to about four fruits. These should be spaced as evenly as possible over the plant. There are two kinds of flowers, male and female, but only the latter will produce fruits. You can recognize the females because each will have a tiny fruit on its stalk just beneath the petals. These flowers must be pollinated by hand, and all on any one plant at the same time. You can arrange to get four suitable blooms open at once by judicious pinching. Backward blooms can be hastened by stopping the shoots on which they are growing one leaf beyond the flower, while forward blooms can be retarded by allowing the shoot to grow unstopped. Scatter pollen transferred from the male blooms to the females with a paintbrush, doing this when the sun is out.

May

'Button to chin 'till May be in;
Cast not a clout 'till May be out'

General Work

In the Garden

ACTIVITY OUTSIDE in May is not just confined to gardeners for greenfly are likely to make their first appearance during this month. Keep a sharp look out especially on the young growths of roses and fruit trees. At the outset it is easy enough to kill all the insects by spraying once or twice with a reliable aphicide such as dimethoate, formothion, pirimicarb or bioresmethrin. The first two are systemic, which means that they enter the sap of the plant where they gradually decompose but cannot be washed off by rain. If systemics are used on food crops, care must be taken not to eat the crop until the prescribed safety period, printed on the label, has elapsed. For further information on pest and disease control and the use of chemicals in general, see the section covering this subject on page 210.

Feed plants in full growth It is a very good plan to feed plants that are growing fast. At this time of the year most herbacous plants are making a big effort and many of them are forming their flower stems. Spring-sown vegetables are also growing freely and need plenty of nourishment. Therefore it is a good policy to give all such plants a small topdressing of a compound, quick-acting fertilizer early in the month and hoe this in.

Kill slugs Slugs are also likely to be much in evidence now and may do a lot of damage to tender seedlings, especially lettuces and delphiniums, unless you take measures against them. There are numerous proprietary pellets which may be sprinkled round plants to protect them.

FLOWERS AND SHRUBS

Thin and stake herbaceous perennials It is usually a mistake to allow herbaceous perennials to retain all the growth they produce. Much better results can be obtained by thinning out the shoots a little at this time of the year. Delphiniums and Michaelmas daisies in particular repay rather drastic thinning. Retain some of the sturdiest shoots and nip off the rest. Before the stems get too long and begin to flop about, place stakes in position and loop the stems to these with garden twine. Usually it is best to allow several stakes to each plant, thrust in close to the clump but leaning outwards towards the top, so that as growth extends and is tied in it will be spread out and get its full ration of light and air. As an alternative, twiggy branches may be pushed into the soil around the plants; as the plants grow they will hide the branches and be supported by them.

Plant aquatics May is the best month of the year for planting water lilies and other aquatic plants (see pages 78 and 79).

Thin out rose growth Examine rose bushes and standards occasionally during the month and pinch out any badly-placed or overcrowded shoots. Those growing inwards and tending to crowd the centre of the plant are the ones most likely to cause trouble later.

VEGETABLES AND FRUIT

Make successional sowings Once again there will be a number of sowings to be made during the month to provide a succession of vegetables after those raised from earlier sowings. Lettuces, spinach, turnips, radishes and mustard and cress should be sown exactly as explained in the General Work for April (page 60), with the exception that it is now more than ever advisable to sow the first three in a partially shaded position. They will not stand a great amount of summer heat as this makes them run to seed. You should make a couple of sowings of maincrop peas to give you a chance of continuing the crop well on into the autumn. Make a further sowing of endive (see page 72) towards the end of the month, and another sowing of kohl rabi about the middle of the month (see page 65).

Protect brassica seedlings Lightly dust all seedlings of cabbage, broccoli, cauliflower, Brussels sprouts, kale, turnip, swede and other brassicas with HCH, carbaryl or derris to kill flea beetles before they have a chance to do any harm. The treatment can be repeated occasionally if any flea beetles are seen or if small holes appear on the leaves.

Stake peas Successional batches of peas will be growing freely during the month and these must be staked as soon as they are a couple of inches in

This is the time to stake herbaceous perennials. Twiggy branches can be pushed in around the plants and will, in time, become almost hidden by the foliage

An alternative method is to push in several stakes round a clump, each leaning slightly outwards. As the stems grow, they are tied into the canes

height. Even the dwarf peas should have small bushy twigs or some other type of support to keep them erect. At the same time draw a little soil into a ridge on each side of the row. This will serve to protect the young plants and will also make a trough into which you can pour water and liquid manure later.

Thin onions and root crops Various crops sown in drills out of doors will be in need of thinning during the month. The sooner this can be started, once the seedlings can be clearly seen, the better but I do not advise you to complete the thinning all in one operation as there may be some casualties yet.

Recommended thinning distances are as follows.

Vegetable	Distance between plants
Globe artichoke	6 in (for planting Early April)
Asparagus	1 ft
Carrots (stump-rooted)	3 in
Carrots (long or intermediate)	4 in
Kohl rabi	9 in
Leeks	4 in (transplant in July)
Lettuces	6 in–1 ft (depending on variety)
Onions	6–9 in
Turnips	4 in

It is always advisable to increase these distances if you wish to have large vegetables for exhibition. Seedlings of lettuce may be transplanted elsewhere if you water them in well. The seedlings of root crops are of no value for transplanting. Pull out the weakest and least promising seedlings first, and be careful not to disturb those you leave more than you can help. Firm the loosened soil with the knuckles. This is

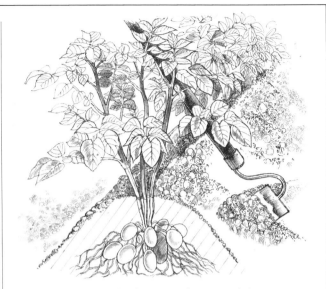

Protect early potatoes by drawing soil up around the stems as they grow

particularly important with onions, as the dreaded onion fly frequently lays its eggs in the loose soil caused by careless thinning. As a further precaution against this pest sprinkle 4% calomel dust along the rows of onions, keeping it in a narrow band on each side of the plants.

Earth up early potatoes As the earlier crops of potatoes push their shoots through the ground draw more soil around them for protection. A few degrees of frost will injure these shoots and there can be no certainty about the weather until May is well advanced. The very earliest outdoor crops planted in Late February in sheltered borders will be well advanced in growth and it will not be possible to protect them with soil alone. Keep some dry straw, bracken, or evergreen boughs at hand and strew these thickly over the bed when frost threatens.

Potatoes in frames must be ventilated as freely as possible on mild days but be sure to close them again early in the afternoon if frost threatens. Incidentally, it is wasteful to lift whole roots of frame potatoes when the tubers form. Scrape away the soil from them as they grow, remove the biggest tubers and then return the soil once more. The smaller tubers will continue to swell and you can collect them later on. You may well be able to harvest the first tubers this month.

Thin peaches and nectarines The young fruits on outdoor peaches and nectarines should now be about the size of marbles and you must start to thin them out. The work is done in exactly the same way as with indoor peaches (see page 42) and so I need not go into it again in detail here. Do not forget that there may be a natural fall during the stoning period with outdoor peaches and nectarines just as with glasshouse-grown varieties and that it is not wise to complete thinning until this is over. Disbudding, that is removal of unwanted young shoots, should also be carried out.

Apricot trees may be allowed to carry more fruits, about thirty per square metre (three or four per square foot) and disbudding is nothing like as drastic, well-placed laterals being merely stopped and not rubbed right out.

Treatment of vines Outdoor vines will be growing freely now and you must regulate their growth in much the same manner as that of indoor varieties. Reduce the number of laterals to one per spur, retaining those that are showing flower trusses. Stop them

beyond the truss but before they have grown so far as to interfere with neighbouring vines or the laterals from other rods.

Indoor vines will be in various stages of growth according to the time at which you started them, and I refer you to my notes for Late February, Late March and General Work for April (pages 35, 52 and 63) for information on pollination, stopping and thinning. The early vines started in Late February will need increased ventilation, using side ventilators as well as those at the ridge, now that the weather is getting warmer. A heated, stagnant atmosphere is a certain cause of cracking. There is no need to keep the evaporating trays filled with water any longer for early vines as a rather dry atmosphere is an advantage. Keep the top ventilators a little open throughout the night, even though this necessitates the use of a little more artificial heat when the weather is cold.

Aquatics

Aquatics can be planted in beds or mounds of soil made in an empty pool which is then gradually filled with water but a simpler method is to plant in baskets and sink these where required. Special plastic baskets can be obtained for this purpose. Ordinary garden soil can be used, preferably fairly heavy soil and with a sprinkling of bonemeal, about 2 oz to each 2 gal bucketful of soil.

Baskets containing marginal plants, which like to grow in shallow water, can be stood on bricks or pieces of rock to bring them to the correct level. Most water lilies will thrive in 1 ft depth of water and only the very strongest kinds will survive in lakes 3 ft in depth. Every two or three years the baskets should be drawn out of the pool and the contents tipped out. The plants can then be divided if necessary

and replanted in fresh soil.

Pools are often constructed with a shelf around the edge so allowing for two depths of water, probably 18 to 24 in at the lower level and 9 in or thereabouts at the shelf. Such pools may be pre-formed of a light rigid material such as fibre glass, or can be shaped by excavating the soil and covering it with a flexible

plastic or butyl liner or they can be made of concrete. The first is the easiest, the last the most permanent but also probably the most expensive, in labour and materials. Fresh concrete will allow lime and other chemicals to escape into the water, with possible harm to plants and fish, so concrete pools must either be sealed with some inactive com-

Aquatic plants are planted in baskets in garden soil which is then covered with small stones to keep it in place

Under Glass

General greenhouse management As sun heat gains still more in power you will have to be increasingly careful in shading plants. Foliage plants, particularly many ferns, suffer a lot if exposed too long to intense light and heat. Tuberous-rooted begonias and gloxinias also need some shade.

Another consequence of the increased heat is that plants will require considerably more watering, in particular cucumbers and tomatoes. The earlier-raised plants should be growing freely and will loose a lot of water on warm days. You must examine all the plants in your greenhouse daily, although it does not follow that all the plants will require water every day. Where plants in clay pots are concerned, rap these with a hard piece of wood, such as a cotton reel pushed on to the end of a thin bamboo cane. If the pot gives a ringing note the soil within it is dry but if it has a dull heavy sound, the soil is probably moist enough. I say 'probably' because the test is valueless if the pot happens to be cracked. Broken pots always give a dull note, so see that you are not misled. Plastic pots cannot be tested in this way.

More ventilation can be given by day and usually it is safe to give a little ventilation at night. I prefer to rely exclusively on the top ventilators except with plants that have been grown under cool conditions from the outset. Side ventilators are valuable in the summer, but in the spring they are liable to cause damaging draughts. One thing that you must guard against from now onwards is a sudden rise of temperature early in the morning. As soon as direct sunlight first strikes the greenhouse a quick rise in temperature will take place. A vast amount of damage in amateurs' greenhouses must be done every year during the spring and summer on bright mornings between about 5 and 8 a.m. This can be prevented by fitting automatic ventilator openers.

pound or be filled with water and emptied several times before they are finally stocked.

Fountains playing into pools do no harm to plants or fish and may actually do some good by helping to aerate the water. A very slow flow of natural un-heated water is also helpful, though seldom practicable unless the pool is fed by a stream, but fast-moving water makes it difficult to grow anything except tough marginal plants.

Suitable plants for the deeper water are water lilies (nymphaea), water hawthorn (aponogeton), and floating heart (nymphoides). Good marginal plants are bog arum (calla), marsh marigold (caltha), water irises, skunk cabbage (lysichitum), arrowhead (sagittaria), zebra rush (*Scirpus zebrinus*), reed mace (typha) and pickerel weed (pontederia).

The variegated foliage of *Iris pseudacorus* provides a strong foil to the candelabra primulas in this waterside planting

FLOWERS AND SHRUBS

Pot and stop perpetual-flowering carnations Carnations grown from cuttings taken during the winter and early spring are all likely to be ready for their final move into pots 6- to 7-in in diameter some time during the month. Do the work as soon as the 3-in pots are comfortably filled with roots but before they show the slightest tendency to become pot bound. Use John Innes potting compost No. 2. Pot firmly and then arrange the plants in a frame, keeping the lights on if it freezes or the wind is very cold, but removing them altogether when it is mild.

From time to time break out the ends of the first side shoots resulting from the March stopping. The ideal time to do this is when the shoot has made about eight joints. Two complete joints should be broken out. Do not deal with more than one shoot per plant at a time but spread the work over a period so that the plant does not suffer any severe check to growth.

Thin out chrysanthemum growths During the month chrysanthemums that were stopped during March and April will be making new growths known as 'breaks'. You will have to decide just how many of these you require to each plant and then rub the rest out as soon as possible. The actual number retained will depend upon the type of chrysanthemum and the purpose for which you are growing it. With exhibition Japanese chrysanthemums that are being grown for the biggest flowers possible, only one shoot must be retained on each plant. Three stems per plant is usually the ideal number to leave on incurved varieties that are being grown for exhibition. The reason for leaving more with these is that great size is not desirable, quality and form are the imperative points and these are best obtained by having several blooms per plant. Decoratives that are being grown for cutting may also have three stems from the present stopping. They will be allowed to carry still more when they break again in June.

Pot on greenhouse plants If you struck cuttings of fuchsias and pelargoniums in March and you wish to grow on some of the plants in pots for autumn and winter flowering, they will need potting now into 5-in pots. Use John Innes potting compost No. 1 or a soilless equivalent. Pinch the points out of fuchsias to encourage bushy growth. Return the plants to the greenhouse for a week or so after potting. At the end of the month they may go to a sunny frame for the summer. Similar remarks apply to rooted cuttings of coleus and other greenhouse plants. Some of the later cuttings of all these plants will be in need of a first potting into 3-in pots.

Cuttings of winter-flowering begonias rooted last month must be potted as soon as they are well rooted. Pot them singly in 3-in pots, using the same compost as that used for the pelargoniums and fuchsias. Place them on the staging in the greenhouse with an average day temperature of 18°C (65°F), not falling below 13°C (55°F) at night, and shade from direct sunshine.

VEGETABLES AND FRUIT

Train and feed cucumbers Cucumbers in heated greenhouses and frames will be in various stages of growth. All will require regular training and stopping as already described (see pages 62 and 63) and all must be watered freely and ventilated very sparingly. A damp, warm atmosphere is what cucumbers like and only on really mild days should a little air be admitted. From this time onwards a permanent shading should be applied to the glass to prevent sun scorch.

The earliest plants in full bearing will need regular feeding with liquid fertilizer used according to makers' instructions. Choose one with approximately equal proportions of nitrogen, phosphoric acid and potash. If you note white rootlets on the surface of any of the beds, top-dress at once with an inch-thick layer of old manure or compost, well broken up.

Fruit under glass Peaches and nectarines that were started into growth in January will begin to ripen their fruits during May and you must no longer spray them with water. Ventilate as freely as possible without letting the temperature fall below 16°C (60°F) by day or 10°C (50°F) by night. Later trees will be in various stages of growth and will require thinning and disbudding as described in my notes for General Work during March and April (pages 42 and 66). Apricots should be thinned moderately if overcrowded and laterals must be pinched out from time to time to prevent unnecessary formation of wood.

Caring for pools

Water in the garden can be used for its gleaming surface and mirror-like reflections, for its movement and sounds and as a medium in which to grow aquatic plants. It is not, as a rule, possible to combine all these uses without one or more suffering. Absolutely clear water can seldom be maintained for long if plants are grown in it, since weeds and algae will almost certainly invade the water at periods and cause it to cloud. Only by changing water repeatedly or treating it with chemicals such as copper sulphate or chlorine can clarity be maintained and neither is good for plants.

The condition of the water can be improved by growing submerged plants such as elodea and myriophyllum which release oxygen into the water. These plants also provide valuable cover for fish but since their growth is dense they cloud the water and, in excess, can fill it completely. They may need to be thinned out from time to time.

Pools in which plants are to be grown are best sited in open, sunny places since most aquatics

Clear any leaves and twigs off the surface of the pond, especially in autumn, with a net

A submersible pump is necessary to recirculate the water down a fall or cascade. The constant recirculation of water has the added advantage of keeping up the level of oxygen for fish and plant life

prefer this and water lilies require bright light to open their flowers. But sunshine and warmth also encourage growth of weeds and algae so again there can be a conflict of interests.

Fountains and cascades are usually operated by pumps which recirculate the water. This is both economical and satis-factory for plants and fish since it avoids the necessity for constant changing of the water which can cause harm to life if the water comes from a purified and possibly chemically-treated mains supply. Natural stream water does not suffer from this handicap.

Inevitably debris of various kinds, such as leaves and twigs, will collect in pools, even in those that are completely unstocked with plants or fish. It will need to be removed occasionally, more frequently, probably, from unstocked rather than from stocked pools since in the former it is more noticeable and unsightly.

Early May

In the Garden

FLOWERS AND SHRUBS

Plant dahlia tubers If you have not been able to start dahlia tubers into growth in either a greenhouse or frame you can plant them outdoors now. Cover the tubers with 3 in of soil and then they will be quite secure against frost. It will be some weeks before shoots appear above ground.

Sow annuals If you want flowers of hardy and half-hardy annuals outdoors in early autumn, now is the time to sow them. The seeds should be broadcast where the plants are to flower and covered lightly with soil as described earlier (see page 46).

Harden off bedding plants During Early May bedding plants in frames must receive as much ventilation as possible, though it is still unwise to expose any of them to frost. Take the lights right off by day if the weather is fine, but replace them in the afternoon should there be a threat of frost. A clearing sky in the afternoon is to be regarded with suspicion at this time of the year as, more often than not, it is an indication that there will be a sharp frost at night but radio and television weather forecasts are the most reliable indicators of frost. Pelargoniums, fuchsias and marguerites, also almost all half-hardy annuals sown in Late February should be fully hardened off and ready for the open ground by the last week in May; but it is advisable to give dahlias, heliotropes, scarlet salvias and cannas a further week of protection as they are more susceptible to cold.

Spray roses Give roses an early spraying with benomyl to prevent black spot disease establishing itself on the young leaves. A systemic insecticide such as dimethoate or formothion can be used at the same time to kill early aphids.

THE LAWN

Treating weedy lawns May is a good month for using lawn sand or finely powdered sulphate of ammonia to kill small, broad-leaved weeds on the lawn. What actually happens is that the chemical lodges on broad leaves and scorches them but slips harmlessly off the upright narrow blades of grass. It is most effective in dry weather. If you use sulphate of ammonia, be certain to distribute it as evenly as possible and not to use more than $\frac{1}{2}$ oz per square yard. You can give a second application a few weeks after the first provided there has been some rain meanwhile to wash the former dose away. Commercial lawn sand should always be used strictly according to the manufacturers' instructions given on the packet.

An alternative and even more effective method is to use one of the selective hormone weed killers such as MCPA, or 2,4-D. These are sold under various trade-names and are generally offered in liquid form for lawn use, though they can also be obtained in combination with a granular lawn fertilizer.

VEGETABLES AND FRUIT

Start to cut asparagus From now onwards, for something like six weeks, you should be able to cut good asparagus from established beds. It is, however, a great mistake to cut any shoots at all until the roots are well established. I certainly do not advise you to cut a single shoot until the second year after planting and it may even be worth waiting until the third year.

Sow main crop beetroot This is the time to sow the main crop of beetroot. For the heaviest crop you should choose a long-rooted or intermediate beet rather than a globe variety but many home gardeners prefer the relatively small roots of the globe type. Sow the seeds in drills 1 in deep and 1 ft apart. If you space the seeds, which are quite large, at about 2 in apart it will be a very simple matter to thin the seedlings to about 6 in later.

Sow dwarf French beans It should be safe to make a sowing

Asparagus should only be harvested from established beds. Cut the spears when they are about 4 in high

of dwarf French beans in the open if you were not able to raise any plants under glass last month. Sow the seeds singly about 6 in apart in drills 2 in deep. An economical method is to have two drills about 9 in to 1 ft apart, then an alleyway about 2½ ft wide, then another couple of rows, and so on.

Plant out winter greens Cauliflowers and Brussels sprouts sown in Early March should be planted outdoors in their permanent quarters at the first opportunity. Of course, they must be properly hardened off first, but it should be easy to have accomplished this by now.

It is better to plant with a trowel rather than with a dibber, even though the job will be slower. Usually it is sufficient to plant 2 ft apart in rows 2½ ft apart, but these distances may need to be varied a little according to the size of the varieties you are growing. Seed packets usually give adequate information on these points.

Cover strawberry beds Place clean straw around and between strawberry plants. The object of this is twofold: mainly to protect the fruits later on from mud splashings, but also to provide a mulch and so conserve soil moisture, a most important point in the cultivation of good strawberries. Alternatively, black polythene film can be used and this has the added bonus of preventing weeds growing as well as conserving soil moisture.

Mulch fruit trees Spread a fairly thick layer of well-rotted farmyard or stable manure, or failing this spent hops (not hop manure, which contains chemicals), around fruit trees and bushes of

An informal ground cover of *Helleborus corsicus* and white and purple honesty (*Lunaria annua*) in a woodland garden

all types, also raspberries. This is known technically as a mulch, and it is very valuable for three reasons: it provides the trees with much-needed nourishment while they are in growth; it helps to retain moisture in the soil by preventing surface evaporation, and it also keeps down weed growth.

Spray apple trees against scab It is at just about this time that the expanding blossom buds on apple trees reach the point of development described by growers as 'pink bud stage'; that is, the first trace of pink petal

colouring can be seen. This is the ideal moment for applying a second application of dispersible sulphur, benomyl or captan as a preventive of scab disease. You must not delay beyond this stage or the disease may spread rapidly, particularly in warm, humid weather. The actual details of application are exactly the same as for the Mid April spraying (see page 68).

Under Glass

FLOWERS AND SHRUBS

Sow cinerarias Sow a few seeds of cinerarias if you want to have plants in flower by December. The seeds will want a little warmth to encourage germination so early, but the ordinary greenhouse temperature of 13 to 16°C (55 to 60°F) will be ample. Sow very thinly in well-drained pans filled with John Innes or a soilless seed compost. Cover lightly with some compost and shade until germination begins.

Allow nerines, arums, freesias and lachenalias to go to rest Gradually reduce the amount of water given to nerines and place the plants in the sunniest part of the greenhouse. The object is to ripen the bulbs and allow them to go to rest. The foliage will gradually turn yellow and die down. Freesias and lachenalias (not treated in Early April) will benefit from a similar thorough baking in some sunny place. Once their foliage dies down no water need be given until July or August. Later batches of arum lilies that have flowered in a cool house and those earlier forced roots must also be allowed to go to rest. Do not attempt to bake them in the sun after the fashion of nerine bulbs but gradually reduce the water supply. When the foliage dies down, lay the pots on their sides and give no more water until August.

Feed, disbud and pollinate tomatoes Tomatoes will be in various stages of growth. The earliest will have set some fruits

Pinch out the side shoots of tomatoes as soon as they are large enough to handle

by this time, later batches may be just coming into flower, while those from March sowings will be ready for potting on into 5-in pots early in the month. With all these you must remove side shoots regularly.

Aid pollination by tapping the flowers. This is most effective if done about midday when the sun is shining.

The earliest plants will benefit from a topdressing of old, well-rotted manure or compost thoroughly broken up and spread evenly over the existing compost to a depth of about 1 in. You can give an additional liquid feed once a week. Use a good proprietary fertilizer but be sure to use a weak solution. I prefer to dilute with twice as much water

as the manufacturer recommends and then feed rather more frequently.

Keep the main stems tied up regularly and pinch out the growing points of the plants as soon as they reach the ridge.

Train and feed melons You will now be able to see the result of your pollination last month. If sufficient fruits have set on each plant, well and good; but if only one or two have set, remove them and start all over again, fertilizing the requisite number of female flowers all on the same day. As soon as white rootlets appear on the surface of the bed, top-dress with 1 in of well-rotted manure or compost thoroughly broken up. Water very freely. Continue to pinch out the points of side shoots so that the house does not get overcrowded with foliage. Maintain a rather moist atmosphere and a day temperature averaging 21°C (70°F).

Start to thin the early grapes Bunches of grapes in a fairly warm glasshouse will be ready for their first thinning. The ideal time to start is about a fortnight after the grapes first set. Use a pair of scissors with pointed blades and start thinning at the bottom of the bunch. Leave the extreme point of the bunch but remove all the berries that are within $\frac{3}{4}$ in above it. Berries at the top of the bunch can be left almost twice as thick as this, those between being given an intermediate amount of room. Do not touch the berries by hand but use a small forked stick to turn the bunches if necessary.

Vines started into growth in Late March will be in need of pollination, training and stopping (see page 52).

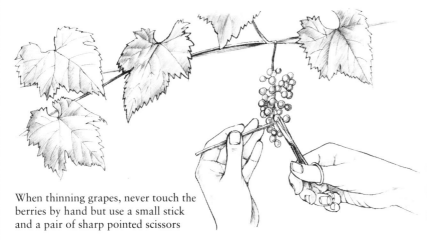
When thinning grapes, never touch the berries by hand but use a small stick and a pair of sharp pointed scissors

Mid May

In the Garden

FLOWERS AND SHRUBS

Clear ground for summer bedding Late May will be the time to make a start at planting the summer bedding subjects and so you must clear the ground of spring bulbs. Lift daffodils, hyacinths and tulips as carefully as possible with all the roots that you can get and heel them in temporarily in any out-of-the-way, but preferably sunny, place. Heeling in simply means making a trench about 6 in deep, laying the bulbs in this with their leaves exposed to sun and air and covering the roots and bulbs with soil which should be made moderately firm. It is useless to take the bulbs up and dry them straight away, for they have not yet finished their growth and would be too weak to do any good another year, but if heeled in as described you will get some flowers next season.

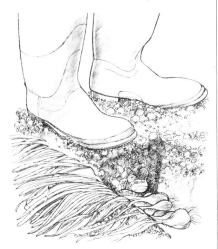

Bulbs which have been growing in land needed for summer bedding plants can be lifted, with as much root as possible, and replanted in an out-of-the-way corner of the garden to finish ripening

Plant early-flowering chrysanthemums By this time early-flowering chrysanthemums raised from cuttings taken in February and March should be sufficiently hardened off to be planted outdoors in the beds in which they are to flower. Choose a good open place and well-manured, deeply-cultivated ground if you want blooms of the highest quality. For cutting it is best to have the plants in beds by themselves, 15 in apart in rows 2 to $2\frac{1}{2}$ ft apart; but they can also be used to fill up spaces in the herbaceous border, in which case they should be spaced 15 in apart each way. Plant with a trowel, taking care to make holes large enough to accommodate all roots without doubling them up. Gently firm and water freely if the soil is dry.

Plant out hardy perennial seedlings If you were able to sow hardy perennials and alpines in a greenhouse or frame in Mid March you may now plant the seedlings outdoors in a nursery bed where they can grow on undisturbed throughout the summer. The soil should be good but not heavily manured. Alpines prefer no manure at all. Set the plants in rows about 1 ft apart leaving from 3 in to 1 ft between the plants according to their spread. Violas, primroses and polyanthuses succeed best in a partially shaded place, but the other plants mentioned in Mid March (see page 46) prefer a sunny position. Similar remarks apply to herbs raised from seed and to hardy perennials raised from root cuttings in January.

VEGETABLES AND FRUIT

Plant out celeriac Celeriac raised from seed in Late March may now be planted outdoors. Choose an open position and reasonably rich soil and plant 1 ft apart in rows 18 in apart.

Sow Chinese cabbage This is more like a cos lettuce than a cabbage and can be used raw as a salad or cooked like cabbage. Sow thinly in rows 1 ft apart where plants are to mature.

Sow chicory This crop is often neglected by gardeners but it is a most useful vegetable and a welcome change from seakale and endive in the winter and spring. It is blanched and eaten raw or cooked. Sow seeds now in a sunny place and on rich, deeply dug ground. Sow sparingly in drills $\frac{1}{2}$ in deep and 1 ft apart.

Sow runner beans It is now time to make a good sowing of runner beans in the open. Sow the seeds individually or in pairs about 8 in apart in two lines 10 in apart. If you require more than one double row, leave at least 6 ft wide between each set. Cover the seeds with 2 in of soil. If you sow the seeds in pairs and they all germinate you will need to single the seedlings out later on.

Sow sweet corn Sweet corn may be sown out of doors where the plants are to grow. Sow the seeds in pairs 1 ft apart in the row and allow 2 ft between the rows. Thin out later to one plant at each station. Alternatively sow in $2\frac{1}{2}$-in pots, two seeds in each.

Paeonia lutea Souvenir (tree paeony) needs a well-drained soil and a sunny but sheltered position

Germinate in a frame or greenhouse. Remove the weakest seedling from each pot and plant outside during the first week in June.

Prick out winter greens It is a mistake to let winter greens get overcrowded in the seed beds. Prick out all the seedlings from the Mid April sowing into a nursery bed in the open. This should be well broken down on the surface and fairly rich. Plant the seedlings 3 in apart in lines 8 in apart. Do the same to any seedlings left over from the March sowings, but give these rather more room.

Dust strawberries If you have had any trouble with mildew on strawberries, now is the time to take preventive measures by dusting the leaves thoroughly with benomyl, flowers of sulphur or dinocap. Alternatively, spray with benomyl, captan or thiram. Benomyl also gives good control of botrytis, a disease that causes the fruits to rot.

Spray pear trees By this time most of the blossom will probably have fallen from pear trees, and it will be necessary to spray again, this time with captan or benomyl, if there is much danger of scab attacking the trees during the summer. The ideal period is between a week and ten days after blossom can first be shaken from the topmost branches. The details of application are exactly the same as before flowering (see page 68). If caterpillars have been troublesome in previous years, it is also an excellent plan to spray with a good insecticide, such as derris or carbaryl, or to mix such an approved insecticide with the fungicide according to manufacturers' instructions.

Under Glass

FLOWERS AND SHRUBS

Stop chrysanthemums If early-flowering chrysanthemums required for specimen blooms and planted out early in the month are not showing a break bud (flower bud) at the extremity of the central growth, stop them now by pinching out the tip and first pair of leaves. Note well that this instruction applies only to plants that are being grown for large specimen blooms. If your object is to have a large number of comparatively small flowers, two stoppings are necessary, one in April and the other in June.

Pot late-flowering chrysanthemums It should now be possible to get most of the late-flowering chrysanthemums, including Japanese exhibition varieties, incurves, decoratives, and singles, into their final flowering pots. Exception, of course, must be made for late cuttings, some of which may as yet be barely rooted. Flowering pots for the early-rooted cuttings should be 8 to 9 in in diameter according to the strength of the plants, while for Late March cuttings, 6-in pots should prove adequate. John Innes potting compost No. 3 is the best for all these different kinds.

Remove greenhouse plants to a frame You can further clear the

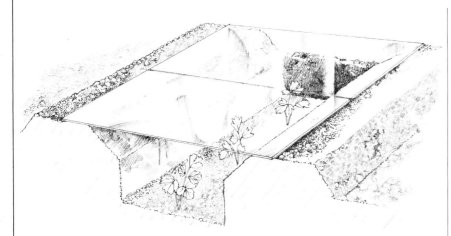

Plant early celery in a trench and protect with sheets of glass or plastic

greenhouse by removing a good many of the winter and spring-flowering plants to a frame; but keep plenty of sacks at hand for use at night during the first week or so, as we often have treacherous weather about the middle of May. In addition to forced bulbs, shrubs, and bedding plants, about which I have already given advice (see pages 61 and 69), you can now clear out arum lilies, freesias, vallotas and any perpetual-flowering carnations that have for the time being finished flowering. It is not worth keeping the various greenhouse primulas, cinerarias and calceolarias for another year after they have finished flowering. All should be raised annually from seed.

If no frame is available it will be wise to leave plants where they are for a further fortnight, except in the mildest parts of the country where they can be stood outdoors now.

Greenhouse cyclamens, both seedlings raised last August and old flowering plants, will also be better in a shady frame during the summer. The old corms must be kept almost, but not quite, dry from now onwards until the middle of August, but the seedling plants should be maintained in growth all the time, and that means giving them an ample water supply.

VEGETABLES AND FRUIT

Pot and harden off aubergines and capsicums Plants from the first sowings in Late March should now be moved into 6- to 7-in pots in John Innes potting compost No. 2. Seedlings from the second sowing in Mid April should be potted singly in 3-in pots in John Innes potting compost No. 1, and should be gradually hardened off in readiness for planting outdoors in early June. Pinch out the tips of all aubergine plants when 6 to 8 in high.

Prick off and plant celery Celery sown in Mid April will require pricking off into a frame. Give the seedlings plenty of space for they will be growing fast now. Planting 4 in apart in rows 6 in apart will not be overdoing it. Ventilate carefully at first but freely after a week or so.

It will not be possible to keep the earliest celery, sown in Late February in boxes or frame beds, any longer without risk of checking them severely in transplanting, so plant them now out into the trenches dug in April. There is still danger of frost sufficient to kill the plants, so you must keep some protection at hand. The simplest and best method is to draw up some soil to form a ridge on each side of the shallow trench and then to lay some ordinary frame lights or sheets of clear polythene over this, so converting the whole trench into a contemporary frame. Set the plants 1 ft apart in a single line down the middle of the trench if it is a narrow one, or in two lines, one at each side of the trench, if it is a wide one. Water in well as celery loves moisture and will fail if allowed to get dry.

Plant tomatoes in unheated greenhouses When you have cleared the greenhouse sufficiently you can plant it with tomatoes for a late-summer crop. Little or no artificial heat will be needed for these from now onwards if you are careful with ventilation. If your greenhouse is fitted with blinds it is a good idea to lower them on frosty nights. The tomatoes can be grown in pots as advised for the early crops (in Late March), or you can have them in growing bags, either on the staging or on the ground, or in the greenhouse border. In any case the plants should be at least 1 ft apart in rows which should be 2½ ft apart. An alternative method, which certainly makes working easy, is to have two rows about 15 in apart and then an alleyway 3 ft wide. Make the soil very firm around the roots. The best compost is good fibrous loam, with a little well-rotted manure, or John Innes potting compost No. 3. Water the plants in freely after planting or potting and provide each with a cane for support.

Setting up a greenhouse

The utility of any greenhouse is considerably extended if it can be heated sufficiently to exclude frost at all times. The range of plants that can be grown will still further increase the higher the minimum winter temperature up to a useful maximum of about 18°C (65°F), but as every 3°C rise in minimum temperature can double the fuel bill clearly economics enter largely into what is desirable.

The most economical heating is usually that taken directly from a domestic system. Fan assisted electric heaters can be excellent for small greenhouses. Natural gas is economical and paraffin heaters are relatively cheap and easy to install. Wherever practicable heating should be thermostatically controlled both for the good of the plants and to economise on fuel.

Staging and shelves are almost essential if many pot plants are to be grown but crops such as tomatoes and cucumbers are usually grown on the floor of the house to make use of the maximum height available and this is also necessary for some tall plants such as chrysanthemums.

Automatic ventilation is a great convenience, especially for gardeners who have to be away from home at lot. The simplest type operates by the expansion and contraction of a heat-sensitive compound contained in a cylinder which moves a piston which itself opens and closes the ventilator by hinged levers. A separate apparatus is required for each ventilator but in small houses it may be adequate to have only one ventilator automatically controlled any others being hand operated.

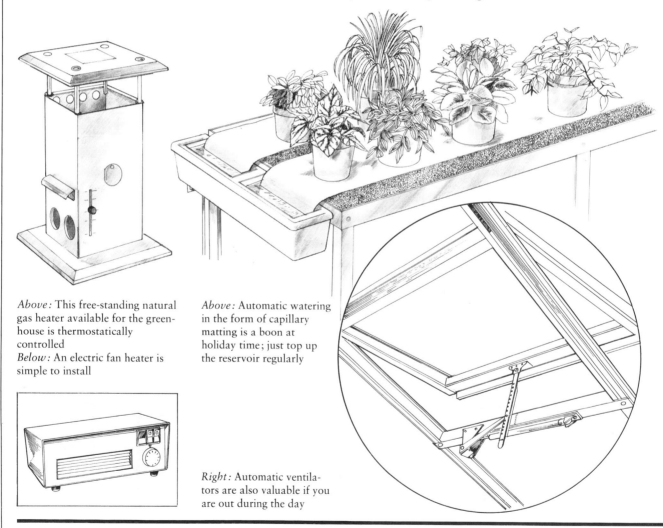

Above: This free-standing natural gas heater available for the greenhouse is thermostatically controlled
Below: An electric fan heater is simple to install

Above: Automatic watering in the form of capillary matting is a boon at holiday time; just top up the reservoir regularly

Right: Automatic ventilators are also valuable if you are out during the day

Firm shelves and staging are most important in a greenhouse as is a hard central path of concrete or paving slabs. Blinds to protect plants from the burning rays of the sun can also be used to conserve heat at night during the winter. Louvre windows can be fitted in the sides of the greenhouse in increase ventilation and air circulation

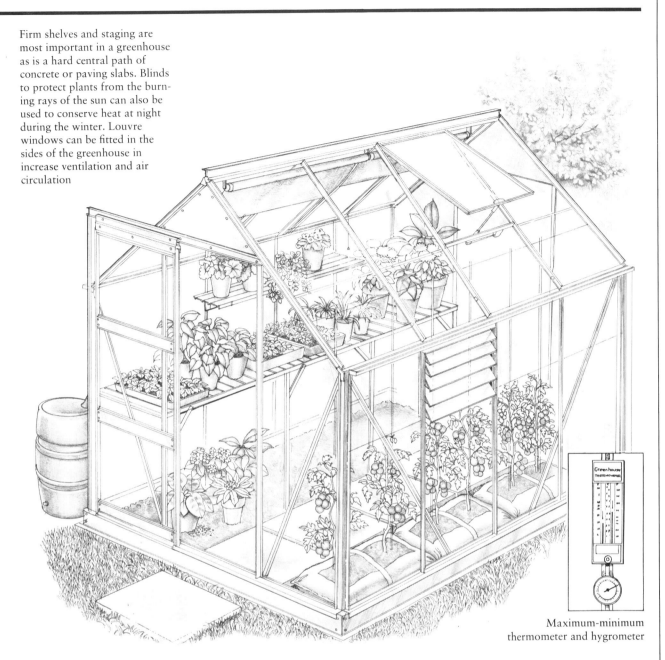

Maximum-minimum
thermometer and hygrometer

Automatic watering can also be convenient, though it is seldom a complete alternative to hand watering. The simplest method is the capillary bench, a solid staging or shallow plastic tray covered with a 1- to 2-in layer of coarse sand or a plastic capillary mat. The sand or mat are kept constantly wet by various devices and pot plants standing on them draw up moisture as they require it by capillary attraction. In warm weather capillary benches perform the additional task of keeping the air moist.

Shading is essential for many plants in summer and is also useful in preventing temperatures from rising too high in sunny weather. Blinds fitted inside the house and easily raised or lowered as necessary are ideal. They need only be on the sunny (southerly) side of the house.

A maximum-minimum registering thermometer is almost essential as without it it will be impossible to keep a check on temperature fluctuations. A hygrometer to register humidity is useful but not essential. Probes can also be obtained which, when pushed into the soil, indicate the moisture level. Some are combined with a light meter to register light intensity.

Plants for May

In gardens with lime-free soil, and particularly where there is light overhead cover from widely spaced trees, this is the month when rhododendrons and azaleas become dominant in many gardens. No shrubs are capable of making a more solid and varied colour display and there is also immense variety in size, habit and leaf character. Yet there are many other shrubs, both evergreen and deciduous, which are not so limited in their soil requirements, are at their best in May and can be grown in almost every garden that has reasonably fertile soil.

This is the month when the laburnum and the hawthorn, both lime lovers, come into flower and when *Clematis montana* and the numerous varieties of wisteria can cover buildings with bloom or clamber to the top of high trees to tumble out in a spectacular floral display.

The snowball trees are easy to grow and their ball-shaped clusters of white bloom are beginning to open in May. There are two species, *Viburnum opulus* Sterile, a British plant, and *V. plicatum* which comes from Japan. Viburnums also have 'lace-caps' forms in which the globular flower heads are replaced by flat clusters, each with a centre of little beady flowers surrounded by an encircling halo of white. Ceanothus will provide a haze of soft blue over a long period if given a sunny, well-drained spot. Several species will bloom again in September.

Rock plants are still abundant and tulips reach their peak of glory in May, the late-flowering varieties carrying on into June. Wallflowers fill the air with their spicy perfume, forget-me-nots and bluebells make wide carpets of blue in the woods and it sometimes seems that so much is happening all at once that there can be little to follow later on. Of course, it is not true and already in May there are early roses, such as Canary Bird and *Rosa cantabrigiensis*, to remind one of the splendour which this genus alone will unfold throughout the summer. The first of the peonies and bearded irises are also forerunners of many more to come in June and there will even be slender spikes of blue on *Veronica gentianoides* as reminders of a herbaceous genus that will continue to give pleasure until the autumn.

Laburnum and *Viburnum opulus* Sterile with the lacy tiers of *V. plicatum* in the foreground

Above: Deciduous azaleas, rhododendrons and polyanthus provide a blaze of colour through the spring months
Below right: Rosa omeiensis pteracantha

Herbaceous plants *Adonis autumnalis*, aquilegias, bellis, brunnera, centaurea, dicentras, doronicums, eremurus, euphorbias, forget-me-not, geraniums, irises (many species and hybrids), *Lychnis viscaria*, mertensias, peonies, polygonatums, pyrethrum, *Ranunculus aconiti-folius flore pleno*, *Saxifraga umbrosa*, *Smilacina race-mosa*, trollius, *Veronica gentianoides*, violas and pansies, wallflowers.

Hardy bulbs, corms and tubers Alliums, anemones, endymions, erythroniums, fritillarias, hyacinths, *Ixio-lirion montanum*, *Leucojum aestivum*, lily-of-the valley, muscari, narcissus, ornithoglaums, trilliums, late-flowering tulips.

Evergreen shrubs As April (see page 71) also hybrid azaleas, *Buddleia globosa*, ceanothus, *Choisya ternata*, *Crinodendron hookeranum*, *Daphne collina*, ericas, *Leucothoe cateshaei*, *Olearia phlogopappa*, sophoras, *Yucca whipplei*.

Deciduous shrubs Deciduous azaleas, cytisus, *Deutzia gracilis*, *Enkianthus campanulatus*, exochordas, genista, kerria, kolkwitzia, leptospermum, magnolias, tree peo-nies, piptanthus, *Poncirus trifoliata*, roses, *Rubus delicio-sus*, spiraeas, staphyleas, syringas (lilacs), *Tamarix tetrandra*, *Viburnum opulus*, *V. plicatum*.

Deciduous trees *Aesculus hippocastanum*, *Cercis sili-quastrum*, crataegus, davidias, halesias, laburnums, malus, paulownias, *Prunus padus*, *Robinia pseudoacacia*, sorbus species and hybrids, *Viburnum lantana*.

Hardy climbers As April (see page 71) also *Clematis macropetala*, *C. montana*, wisterias.

Late May

In the Garden

FLOWERS AND SHRUBS

Plant out summer bedding If the weather appears reasonably settled and you have followed out instructions regarding hardening off, now is the best time to plant out the majority of bedding plants and half-hardy annuals. Plant with a trowel, giving roots plenty of room and firming the soil thoroughly round them. Water in liberally if the soil is dry. The exceptions are dahlias, heliotropes, scarlet salvias and cannas which are all very susceptible to the cold and are better kept where they can be protected easily until the first week in June.

Plant out chrysanthemums It is possible to grow many of the late decorative chrysanthemums without keeping them in big pots all the summer. Plants from 4- to 5-in pots are planted outdoors now exactly like the early border varieties (see page 85) and are allowed to grow on in the open ground until September or Early October, when they are lifted, carried into the greenhouse and either placed in big boxes or planted in beds of soil. One great advantage of this method is that the plants do not need constant watering during the summer. An alternative method is to plant in wire or plastic baskets and sink these in the soil. Some roots will probably grow out into the surrounding soil but it is still easier to lift plants grown in this way than those planted out straight into the soil.

Remove side shoots from sweet peas Early sweet peas that are being grown on the single stem (cordon) system will need regular attention from now on in the way of removal of all side shoots and tendrils. Be careful not to pinch out flowering stems by mistake; it is quite easy to tell these, as the flower buds are evident even at an early stage.

The later sweet peas will need staking and tying in (see page 72).

Plant up containers This is the time to fill window boxes, hanging baskets and ornamental vases with their summer occupants. To hang over the edge you can have ivy-leaved pelargoniums, trailing lobelia, *Campanula isophylla*, *Lysimachia nummularia aurea*, and *Asparagus sprengeri*, while good plants with a more erect habit are zonal pelargoniums, marguerites, fuchsias, petunias and bedding calceolarias. Give the plants a thorough watering after planting. The hanging baskets must be well lined with sphagnum moss or punctured black polythene before filling with compost to prevent this from being washed through.

To plant up a hanging basket, first line it with a generous layer of sphagnum moss or perforated black polythene before filling with compost

Introduce trailing plants such as *Campanula isophylla* through the sides as you fill with compost, firming as you go

Finally plant the top of the basket. Plant with upright subjects in the centre and trailers round the edge. Soak well before hanging in position

VEGETABLES AND FRUIT

Plant out French beans If you were able to raise some French beans in boxes in Mid April, and have hardened the plants carefully in a frame, you may now plant them out with safety. Choose a reasonably sheltered place and be ready to cover the plants at night with some sheets of newspaper should the weather turn suddenly frosty. Plant the beans 6 in apart in rows 18 in apart.

Sow marrows and ridge cucumbers Marrows and ridge cucumbers can now be sown outdoors where the plants are to grow. Sow the seeds singly or in pairs about 3 ft apart, cover them with 1 in soil, and then invert flower pots over them as an additional protection. It is common practice to prepare marrow beds by building up a mound of turves, but in view of the fact that the plants can do with any amount of moisture, it is really much better to dig out a large hole and fill this with chopped turves, good compost or, better still, a mixture of turfy loam and well-rotted manure. It is then a comparatively simple matter to flood the bed with water from time to time. Ridge cucumbers are better on low mounds of turf, compost and well-rotted manure, for they need all the sun they can get to make them grow rapidly. Still, do not build up the mounds too steeply or watering will be a problem.

Spray cane fruit Raspberries and loganberries and also to a lesser extent blackberries, sometimes suffer severely from a disease known as cane spot. Purplish patches of decayed tissue appear on the canes, gradually encircling

Keep a lookout for any weak spindly raspberry canes and remove them to avoid overcrowding. Leave about six good canes on each plant

them and cutting off the supply of sap. If you have had any of this trouble in former years, spray now with benomyl or thiram.

Thin out raspberry canes Look over the raspberry plants and reduce the number of new canes if these are very numerous. There is no point in having more than six canes per plant, and these should be quite close to the clump for preference. Raspberries have a habit of sending up suckers all over the bed, and unless you remove them from the alleyways it will be almost impossible to get between the canes to pick fruit later on.

Spray apples By this time the blossom will probably be falling from all but the latest-flowering apples. About ten days after it can first be shaken from the topmost branches is the ideal time to give yet one more spraying with benomyl, dispersible sulphur, or captan as a protection against scab disease (see page 68).

If in former years maggots have been found in the young apple fruits during June causing many of these fruits to fall, the trees should be sprayed with HCH, dimethoate or fenitrothion now. The pest involved is the apple sawfly.

The small caterpillars of the codling moth also eat their way into apples but the attack comes a little later. Codling moth caterpillars usually bore right into the core of the apple. Sawfly larvae often leave a ribbon-like scar on the skin of the apple and the sticky frass they produce has an unpleasant smell.

Under Glass

FLOWERS AND SHRUBS

Start achimenes A final batch of achimenes (see page 26) started now, will carry the display of flowers well on into the autumn.

Pot begonias and gloxinias Begonias, gloxinias and streptocarpuses from an early sowing in Late January should be ready for removal to their flowering pots. Do not be in a hurry, however, if roots are not showing freely around the sides of the present

These well-planted baskets containing pendulous begonias, petunias, pelargoniums and lobelia should provide flowers all summer long if watered frequently

soil balls. Over-potting does no good, but then neither does over-crowding. The flowering pots should be 5 to 6 in in diameter. Use John Innes potting compost No. 1 or an equivalent soilless mixture as before (see page 61). Water freely, place in the green-house, and shade from direct sunshine.

Prick off primulas Greenhouse primulas sown in Late April will need to be pricked off into other trays. Use the same compost as for seed sowing and space the seedlings about $1\frac{1}{2}$ in apart each way. Water them in well and then place them in a sheltered

frame. The plants will be better in frames for the rest of the summer. Ventilate rather sparingly at first, but freely once the seedlings take hold of their new soil.

VEGETABLES AND FRUIT
Plant melons and cucumbers Melons raised in the greenhouse in Mid April, may be planted in

Crops in Season

In the garden Asparagus, broccoli, cabbage, lettuce, spring onions, mustard and cress, radish, rhubarb, seakale, spinach.

Under glass French beans, carrots, cucumbers, lettuce, mustard and cress, potatoes, radish.

frames. Prepare a compost as described for cucumbers (see page 52) and allow one plant for each full-sized garden light 6 ft by 4 ft. Plant on a small mound of compost in the centre of the space covered by the light. Pinch out the point of each plant when it has made about five leaves.

Cucumbers raised from seed in Mid April for cultivation in unheated frames may also be planted in exactly the same way as melons. Subsequent training is the same as for cucumbers in frames (see page 62).

Opposite: Wisteria floribunda is most suitable for training up walls and over pergolas as it is less vigorous than other species

Patios

Patios, terraces and courtyards can provide clean and dry areas to be used in comfort at all seasons of the year. They permit an enormous degree of ingenuity and originality in design and construction but there are some basic considerations which it is wise to take into account.

First, since they are likely to be largely paved, they will catch and hold a lot of water when it rains heavily so they must be given a slope (or slopes) which will direct the water to where it can most conveniently be disposed of. This may involve making a land drain or gravel-filled channel at the lowest point directing the water to a natural outlet or into a rubble-filled soakaway sufficiently large and deep to cope with quite a lot of water.

Secondly, paving slabs are much less likely to get out of true if they are set in mortar but there is no need for this to cover the whole site. It will actually be better to have three or four large blobs of mortar under each slab, sufficient to hold them securely yet leave gravel or sand infilling to drain away surface water.

Gravel is an alternative surfacing material and can often be used effectively; the gritty surface of loose gravel providing a pleasant contrast to the smooth surface of paving slabs. Panels of cobblestones are also effective and, since they are uncomfortable to walk on, they can be used to deter people from moving where they are not wanted; for example, close to valuable plants and around those growing in panels of soil left in the paving.

Concrete is a cheaper and more flexible material than paving slabs and can be given many interesting finishes by varying the aggregate used and also by raking or brushing the surface when it is nearly dry.

Bricks, especially if old and pleasantly coloured, make delightful paths and panels and can be

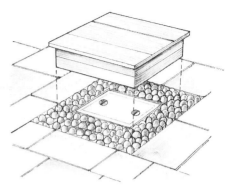

A manhole cover can be concealed by a simple removable wooden podium

laid in patterns, herringbone, ringed, on edge and so on. However, bricks can become dangerously slippery when wet, especially if green scum (algae) has been allowed to grow on them. It needs to be removed by scrubbing from time to time.

Manholes sometimes present a problem but can be concealed in potentially decorative ways by incorporating them in the paving pattern and covering them with loose slabs or even with a low wooden podium as a display place for a plant container or an ornament.

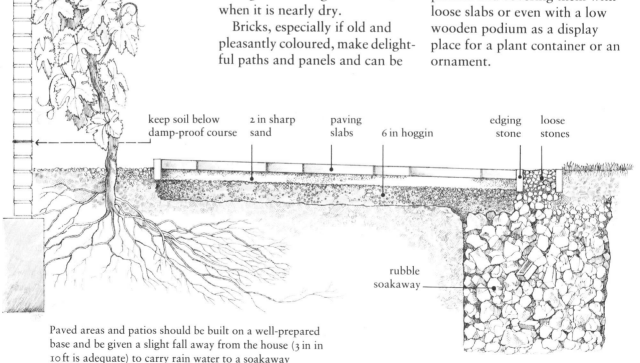

keep soil below damp-proof course   2 in sharp sand   paving slabs   6 in hoggin   edging stone   loose stones

rubble soakaway

Paved areas and patios should be built on a well-prepared base and be given a slight fall away from the house (3 in in 10 ft is adequate) to carry rain water to a soakaway

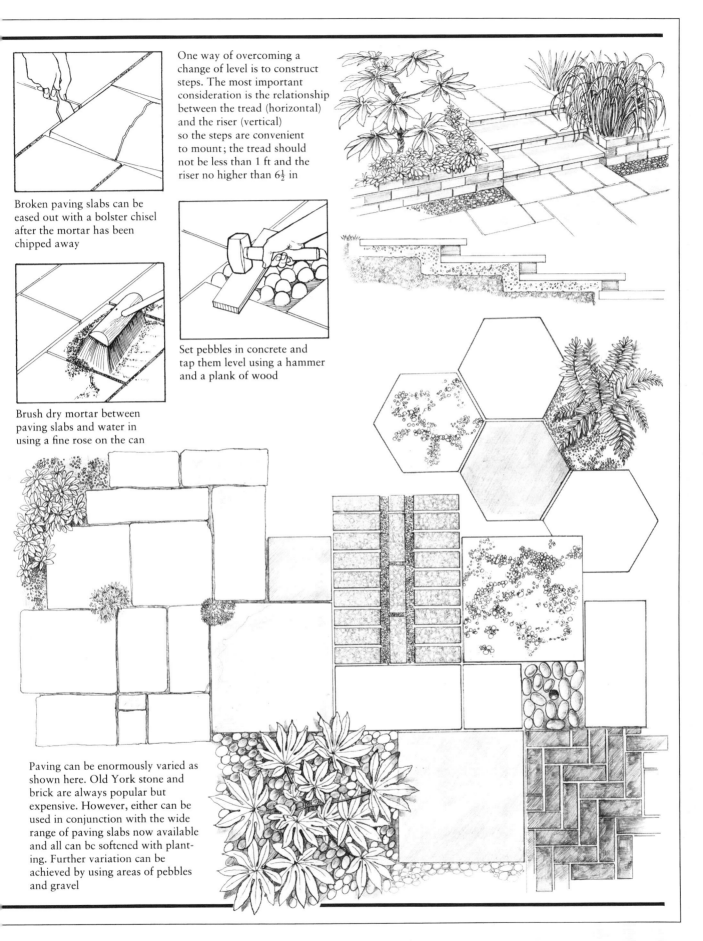

Broken paving slabs can be eased out with a bolster chisel after the mortar has been chipped away

Brush dry mortar between paving slabs and water in using a fine rose on the can

One way of overcoming a change of level is to construct steps. The most important consideration is the relationship between the tread (horizontal) and the riser (vertical) so the steps are convenient to mount; the tread should not be less than 1 ft and the riser no higher than $6\frac{1}{2}$ in

Set pebbles in concrete and tap them level using a hammer and a plank of wood

Paving can be enormously varied as shown here. Old York stone and brick are always popular but expensive. However, either can be used in conjunction with the wide range of paving slabs now available and all can be softened with planting. Further variation can be achieved by using areas of pebbles and gravel

June

'Calm weather in June sets corn in tune'

General Work

In the Garden

SUMMER HAS almost arrived and the roses are coming into bloom. Bees and butterflies abound, but not all the insects in the garden are so useful or appear as beautiful. Aphids (greenfly, blackfly etc.) will be about and are likely to become more of a nuisance this month unless you take appropriate measures to destroy them at the first sign of attack (see page 74). Caterpillars may also put in an appearance. Usually they can be poisoned before they have done much damage by spraying with one of the numerous insecticides available such as derris, HCH, carbaryl or malathion. Continue to use a proprietary slug bait.

Red spider mite can become a nuisance on fruit trees at this time of year, infecting the undersides of the leaves and causing them to turn a mottled greyish-gold colour. If this occurs spray at once with derris, dimethoate or malathion and repeat after ten days or a fortnight.

FLOWERS AND SHRUBS
Stake and disbud border carnations Border carnations will be forming their flower stems and these must be staked as necessary. Beginners often do this incorrectly. The natural habit of the border carnation is to arch its flower slightly and not hold it stiffly erect, so any ties you make must be sufficiently low down the stem not to interfere with this natural arching habit. If you make ties all the way up to the bud, rain will collect in the expanding flower and spoil the petals and hot sun will complete the damage.

Another important task if you want to have really

If large-flowered roses are being grown for exhibition, suitable stems should be disbudded. This involves the removal of all the side buds, leaving just the terminal bud to develop. The latter should then grow into a much larger bloom

fine blooms is to remove the side shoots that form on the flower stems and to remove all flower buds except the terminal one on each stem as advised below for roses.

Disbud roses for exhibition Roses will be forming their flower buds freely throughout the month, and if you want some big blooms for exhibition or cutting you must disbud hybrid tea (large flowered) varieties from time to time. This simply means that all the side buds on each stem should be nipped out at as early a stage as possible, retaining only the big terminal one.

Trim hedges You can trim evergreen hedges lightly at any time during the month. If you grow *Berberis darwinii* as a hedge, the best time to trim it is immediately the flowers fade. Cut the flowering shoots back sufficiently to give the hedge a neat appearance.

VEGETABLES AND FRUIT
Continue to feed plants in full growth Vegetables that are growing freely will be all the better for one or two applications of a quick-acting fertilizer or some soakings with weak liquid manure.

Make successional sowings Successional sowings are almost the same as those given for last month (see page 76). Lettuces, endive, radishes, mustard and cress, and turnips should still be sown at intervals. It is too late for sowing maincrop peas, but it is not a bad plan to make a sowing at the beginning of the month of a second early variety which will mature more rapidly. Choose an open place for this last crop, for late-sown peas in the shade are certain to be ruined by mildew. All the salad vegetables and turnips will be better in a rather shady place.

Blanch leeks If you planted leeks in trenches during Mid April you must start to blanch them as soon as they are well established and growing freely. The best method is to make tubes out of stiff brown paper, slip one of these over each plant, fastening it to a cane and drawing a little soil up around its base. The tubes should be about 6 in in length and about 3 in in diameter to ensure adequate blanching.

Lift autumn-sown onions as required During June the bulbs of autumn-sown onions will have attained sufficient size to be used. Do not lift the whole crop yet, however, for the bulbs will not be properly ripened. Simply dig up a few onions at a time as you require them.

Stake peas Peas sown last month must be staked in the same way as the earlier batches (see page 76).

Earth up potatoes The earthing up of all March- and April-planted potatoes must be completed during this month. This is not a task to be finished at one operation. Better results are obtained by drawing the soil up round the potato stems a little at a time. Go over them about three times in all, eventually leaving the bed in a series of broad, flat-topped ridges.

Plant winter greens Throughout June you should miss no opportunity of planting out winter greens, including Brussels sprouts, broccoli, kale and savoy. Usually these should be planted about 2 ft apart in rows 2½ ft apart but, as different varieties grow to varying sizes, you should consult the seedsman's notes on the packet. Make the soil really firm around the roots; none of the cabbage family does well in loose soil, and for this reason the beds should be well trodden before planting. Then after planting, run a hoe through the surface to leave a dust mulch which will lessen soil moisture loss.

Remove runners from strawberries If left to their own devices, strawberries will make innumerable runners during the summer and early autumn. You should remove these, cutting them off close to the main clump unless you require some for propagation (see Early July).

Spray raspberries against fruit maggots If you have had trouble in previous years with maggots in the ripe fruits of raspberries spray twice during June with derris, fenitrothion or malathion; the first time when the raspberry flowers are beginning to fall and the second when the earliest fruits turn pink. Do not eat fruits for one week after using fenitrothion.

Finish thinning peaches You will be able to complete the thinning of peaches, nectarines and apricots on walls as soon as the stones are formed (see page 77). Continue to disbud peaches and nectarines and pinch out the laterals of apricots to encourage fruit spurs to form.

Treatment of vines Continue to train outdoor vines and pinch out the tips of secondary laterals when they have made one leaf. This will prevent the vines from getting overcrowded with foliage. The early varieties will need thinning (see page 84).

Up till this month outside borders usually need little or no watering, but from now on they should be watched closely and watered freely if they show

This is the time to plant out winter greens. All brassicas need to be firmed in really well

signs of getting really dry. In order to conserve moisture it is a good plan to spread a 3-in mulch of well-rotted strawy manure over the border after watering.

Under Glass

General greenhouse management As the weather gets warmer ventilation must become even more free. Keep a sharp watch on the thermometer at the beginning of the month, however, and be ready to close the ventilators quite early if it shows a tendency to drop rapidly, for early June nights can be very treacherous. The average night temperature at this time of the year for the majority of popular greenhouse plants should be 16°C (60°F). Keep the top ventilators open a little at night when the weather is mild and ventilate really freely by day as soon as the thermometer registers 18°C (65°F). Side ventilators and doors can be opened wide on hot, sunny days.

Plants that are still making growth or are producing flowers must be watered with increasing freedom as the days become hotter. It is advisable to examine pot plants daily during the summer. Watering is best done in the morning. However, remember some greenhouse plants will be going to rest and will not need water.

Steps should now be taken to blanch leeks which have been planted in trenches. First, a thick paper collar is fastened round each plant and then earth is drawn up round the bases with a hoe

The dainty hybrid musk rose Ballerina twines round the column of this graceful statue

FLOWERS AND SHRUBS

Pot on perpetual-flowering carnations and chrysanthemums If you did not pot on all the young stock of perpetual-flowering carnations last month you should certainly complete the work before the end of June. Deal with the most forward plants first and gradually work through the whole batch. Continue to stop first laterals a few at a time as they make their eighth joint.

Backward or late-struck chrysanthemums should also be dealt with at the earliest opportunity. Very late cuttings of special varieties grown for forming dwarf specimens in 5- to 6-in pots (taken in Late April), must be placed in their flowering pots as soon as they have filled their first 3-in pots with roots.

Stop early-flowering and decorative chrysanthemums If you are growing some early-flowering chrysanthemums with the object of getting a large number of comparatively small flowers (see pages 62 and 86), the plants will require a second stopping some time during this month. The ideal time is when the most forward side shoots caused by the first stopping are 1 ft in length; but stopping must be completed by the end of the month. Similar remarks apply to the late-flowering decoratives and singles, except that these are almost always better for two stoppings, whether the object in view is to get several medium-size blooms or only a few big ones. If the latter is your aim, then you must reduce the number of side shoots that grow after the stopping, keeping only from six to a dozen per plant according to its strength.

VEGETABLES AND FRUIT

Train, feed and renovate cucumbers Cucumbers in greenhouses and frames will be in various stages of growth, and I refer you to my previous notes for details of treatment (see pages 62 and 80). Some of the earliest plants in the warm greenhouse will be getting past their prime, but they can be renovated and induced to go on bearing for another month or so by cutting out old laterals that have borne fruit and training young laterals in their place. See that shading material does not get washed off the glass. Strong sunshine may cause much damage. Keep the atmosphere really moist by frequent spraying with water and by wetting the paths.

Management of fruit trees There is little to add to my remarks on this subject in May (see page 80). Ventilation can be very free whenever the weather is mild, and you may open side ventilators by day as well as those at the ridge. Ripening can be assisted by removing a leaf here and there to expose fruits to the sun, or propping them forward with the aid of ordinary wooden plant labels.

As soon as you have cleared the earliest trees of their fruits, recommence spraying at least twice a day with clean water. There is no better preventive of red spider mite and thrips, two pests that always prove troublesome in a hot dry atmosphere.

Indoor vines These will be in various stages of growth and I refer you to my previous notes (see pages 63 and 78) for particulars regarding stopping, thinning and other operations. These tasks are the same both for late and early vines. You must be very careful about ventilation whatever the state of growth. Excessive heat should be avoided. Late vines in unheated houses will require much more moisture in the atmosphere, which means that you must keep evaporating trays filled with water, or thoroughly wet the paths two or three times a day. If red spider mite should appear, spray the foliage with clear water once or twice daily.

Early June

In the Garden

FLOWERS AND SHRUBS

Sow St Brigid anemones Anemones of the St Brigid and de Caen types can also be raised from seed sown outdoors now and will flower next summer. Choose a sunny, sheltered position and sow the seeds very thinly indeed in drills $\frac{1}{2}$ in deep and 9 in apart. The reason that I stress the importance of thin sowing is that then no transplanting will be necessary and the plants can grow on unchecked in the seed bed until they have flowered next year.

Sow perennials and biennials Most perennials and biennials, if sown out of doors now, will make good sturdy plants for placing in flowering quarters in the autumn. The only exceptions are forget-me-nots and Brompton stocks, which I find are better

sown rather later. They get too big if sown now, tending to flower before the winter; this is always a bad point. The most useful biennials are Canterbury bells, various verbascums and *Coreopsis grandiflora*. Perennials which are almost invariably treated as biennials are wallflowers, *Cheiranthus allionii*, foxgloves, sweet Williams, double daisies, Iceland poppies and *Campanula pyramidalis*.

Among the easiest perennials to raise from seed are aquilegias, lupins, oriental poppies, hollyhocks and delphiniums, also easy rock plants such as aubrietas, *Alyssum saxatile* and *Campanula carpatica*; but there are many other things that you can try if you can obtain the seeds. Sow thinly in drills 6 to 8 in apart and cover with from $\frac{1}{4}$ to 1 in of soil, according to the size of the seeds. Violas, pansies, primroses and polyanthuses may also be sown now outdoors, but it is preferable to choose a rather shady place for these.

Plant tender bedding plants The few tender bedding plants that I

advised you to omit from the May planting may now go outdoors into their flowering quarters. These plants include dahlias, begonias, scarlet and other bedding salvias, heliotropes and cannas, also a few choice foliage plants, such as abutilons, cordylines, ricinus, *Zea mays* and *Calocephalus* (*Leucophyta*) *brownii*. Details for planting are exactly as for those plants put out in May (see page 92).

Place chrysanthemums outside Exhibition and decorative chrysanthemums grown in pots will be better out in the open from now onwards. If you have many of these plants I advise you to make a special standing ground for them in an out-of-the-way place. The soil should be well covered with ashes or gravel to give good drainage. The plants are then arranged in straight rows at least $2\frac{1}{2}$ ft apart, so that you can move between them easily for watering, tying and bud taking. Drive a good strong stake into the ground at either end of each row, stretch a couple of wires between the pairs of stakes and then attach each cane to the wires. This is the ideal method with exhibition chrysanthemums grown with a single stem. With big decorative plants the horizontal wires get in the way.

Plunge shrubs in pots outdoors From now until the end of September, any shrubs and roses that have been grown in pots for early flowering, and are either still in the greenhouse or have been removed to shelters or

Chrysanthemums grown in pots can be stood out on gravel or ash beds during the summer months. It is important to provide each plant with a strong stake

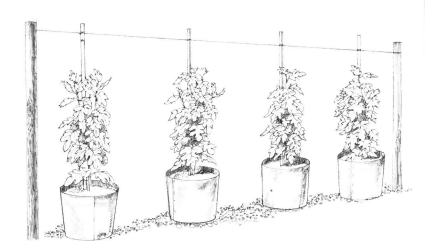

Many indoor plants benefit from being outside in a plunge bed during summer. This consists of a deep bed filled with free-draining material

frames, will be much better in a sunny but not scorchingly-hot position outdoors. This also applies to greenhouse heaths, Indian azaleas, camellias and acacias. The ideal method is to prepare a deep bed of sifted ashes or coarse sand and to plunge the pots up to their rims in this. Watering will be considerably reduced by this means and the soil in the pots will be maintained at a more even temperature. Never choose a position that is exposed to cutting draughts, as, for example, near an alleyway between buildings. Spray daily with clear water throughout the summer to ward off attacks by red spider mite. This is particularly necessary with Indian azaleas.

VEGETABLES AND FRUIT

Thin out seedlings Various vegetable seedlings from April and May sowings will be in need of thinning (see page 77).

Pinch broad beans The earliest broad beans should now have set about three clusters of pods each and it is wise to stop them growing any taller by pinching out the tip of each plant. This may prevent an attack by black-fly, because this pest invariably goes for the young growing tips and if there is no soft growth it will seek food elsewhere. Incidentally the stopping will hasten the development of the pods.

Plant celery You can plant out celery with safety and without the necessity for any protection. Details of work are the same as for the earliest crop (see page 87). Set out all plants that are 3 in high or more. Backward seedlings and those from late sowings may wait for a few weeks yet. Water in freely.

Plant runner beans Runner beans which were raised in boxes under glass in April will be ready for planting out in double rows 10 in apart, allowing 8 in from plant to plant in the rows. If you have more than one row of beans they should be at least 6 ft apart, because when they grow up they cast a considerable amount of shade. For this same reason it is an advantage if all the rows can run north-south, as then each row does stand a chance of getting some direct sunshine.

You must either provide a stout stake for each plant or grow them up bean netting. These stakes should be at least 8 ft long and must be thrust as firmly as possible into the ground. There are many ways of finishing the task, but none that is simpler than to cross the sticks at the top and then place other sticks horizontally in the forks so made. Bind all the sticks together where they meet and you will have a support for your beans that will stand any amount of wind. Netting will need to be suspended from some secure support such as a pole laid across sturdy uprights. A well developed row of runner beans presents a large surface to the wind, like a large sail, and so requires substantial support.

An alternative is to grow some as bush plants by the simple process of pinching out the growing points of the shoots from time to time. Quite a good crop of beans can be obtained in this manner, though, of course, it will not be so heavy, nor will the beans be quite so fine, as those from plants grown in the more usual way up stakes.

Plant out aubergines and capsicums Plants that have been properly hardened off can now go outdoors. Choose the sunniest and warmest place available and plant in fairly rich soil or in grow bags. Space plants 12 to 15 in apart and, if there is more than one row, leave 2 ft between rows. Place a good cane to support each plant.

Plant out sweet corn Any plants sown under glass in Mid May should be planted outside in a sheltered position. Space in blocks with 1 ft between plants and 2 ft between rows.

Plant marrows and ridge cucumbers Marrows and ridge cucumbers raised under glass and properly hardened off may be planted out on a prepared bed (see page 93). If the weather is cold and there is any likelihood of a frost, keep some big flower pots at hand and invert one over each plant every evening, removing it in good time the next morning. The plants should be at least 3 ft apart each way in beds. Pinch out the tip of each plant when it has made about six or seven leaves; then train the laterals that form evenly around the plant to fill the bed and pinch the tip out of each as soon as it reaches the edge of the bed.

Plant tomatoes Tomatoes that have been well hardened off in frames may be planted outdoors in a sunny, sheltered position. A border or growing bag positioned at the foot of a fence or wall with a southerly aspect is the best possible place for the plants, which should be 15 in apart. If you have more than one row,

space them 2½ ft apart. The soil should be in good condition, but not too richly manured, as it is wise to let tomatoes set a few fruits and then to feed regularly with any reliable tomato fertilizer.

Under Glass

FLOWERS AND SHRUBS

Prick off cinerarias Cinerarias sown early in May must be pricked off 2 in apart each way in seed boxes filled with the compost recommended for seed sowing. Stand in a frame and ventilate freely.

VEGETABLES AND FRUIT

Feed and fumigate tomatoes The earliest tomatoes will be ripening now, while even the latest batches planted in Mid May will be setting fruits during the month. All must be watered freely, every day when the weather is warm, and should be fed regularly as I described on page 84. Plants in flower should be pollinated, as explained on the

same page. Stop the plants when they reach the apex of the house and continue to remove side shoots as before. A topdressing of well-rotted manure will help the later plants.

Whitefly may become a nuisance now. If it does, fumigate at once with lindane smokes, putting the pellets or canister on the path in the evening, setting light to them and then keeping the house closely shut up until the morning. Repeat twice, at intervals of four or five days, to catch the adult flies as they emerge from the scales which are unaffected by the fumigant. Alternatively spray with malathion, bioresmethrin, permethrin or pirimiphos-methyl.

Ventilate freely, keeping the top ventilators partly open during mild nights, and opening doors as well as side ventilators on very warm days. Cut back some of the lower leaves on early plants to expose the fruits to the light and so hasten ripening.

Perennial weeds

All these weeds can prove a problem in the garden if allowed to spread. Ideally they should be dug out (see page 219 for further details).

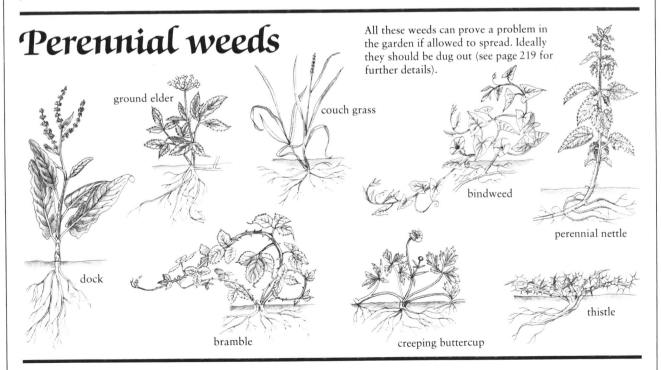

ground elder

couch grass

bindweed

perennial nettle

dock

bramble

creeping buttercup

thistle

Roses in the Garden

Contrary to popular belief roses thrive among other shrubs and herbaceous plants provided they are given adequate room, are not allowed to be overrun by other plants and have their fair share of sunlight, moisture and plant food. But the roses that look best in company are seldom the same varieties as those that are most popular for rose gardens. These bedding roses tend to carry all their flowers at the ends of erect stems, all about the same height so that they make solid sheets of colour. Roses in mixed borders need to have far more individuality of habit, height and flower character. Shrub roses are ideal for the purpose and also some of the old garden roses and fairly short-stemmed climbers. These latter can be grown with little or no support and allowed to spread out arching branches wreathed in flower for much of their length or can be trained on tripods or short pillars. They need to be pruned more lightly than those in rose beds, the operation being mainly confined to the removal of a few of the oldest stems and cutting out of weak, diseased or damaged stems, leaving the rest to go their own way and establish the individual characteristics of each variety. Selection can include some varieties chosen largely for the beauty of their foliage or heps and the flower shapes –

Bush roses add fullness to a mixed border where they provide a long season of colour

singles, semi-doubles, quartered, 'cabbage' as well as the currently popular high-centred hybrid teas. Some very vigorous climbing roses can be allowed to ascend trees that are not in themselves particularly ornamental. Varieties suitable for this kind of planting are Kiftsgate, Seagull, Wedding Day, *Rosa longicuspis* and some forms of *R. multiflora*. Some slender climbers can actually be encouraged to use the much stiffer rose stems as natural support. The less rampant varieties of clematis look delightful clambering into big rose bushes or climbers.

RECOMMENDED VARIETIES
Aloha – muted rose pink, big bush or short climber
Ballerina – pink and white single, small shrub
Blanc Double de Coubert – white, shrub
Buff Beauty – apricot yellow, wide shrub
Chinatown – yellow, shrub
Constance Spry – rose pink, single, wide shrub
Eye Paint – red and white, bush
Fantin-Latour – pink, shrub
Felicia – salmon-pink and yellow, shrub
Frau Dagmar Hastrup – pink, large heps, wide shrub
Fritz Nobis – salmon pink, shrub
Frühlingsgold – bright yellow, semi-double, large shrub
Frühlingsmorgen – deep pink and yellow single, wide shrub
Golden Showers – yellow, climber
Golden Wings – yellow, wide shrub
Handel – cream and pink, climber
Heidelburg – light crimson, large shrub or climber
Iceberg – white, bush
Joseph's Coat – yellow and red, large bush or climber
Königin von Dänemark – soft pink, shrub
Macrantha – light pink, shrub
Matangi – vermilion and white, bush
Nevada – creamy white, large shrub
Penelope – creamy pink, large shrub
Raubritter – pink, low wide shrub
Rosa gallica Officinalis – deep pink, bush
Rosa moyesii Geranium – red, large heps, large shrub
Rosa rubrifolia – purplish pink single flowers, mauve grey leaves, large shrub
Roseraie de l'Hay – magenta, large shrub
Swan Lake – white and pink, large shrub
Uncle Walter – bright crimson, bush
Zéphirine Drouhin – carmine pink, climber

Top: Roses Zéphirine Drouhin and Golden Showers with *Clematis* The President
Centre: *Rosa macrantha* and *Linum narbonense*
Bottom: Shrub rose Constance Spry with *Geranium* Johnson's Blue

Mid June

In the Garden

FLOWERS AND SHRUBS

Divide auriculas, polyanthuses and primroses Any of these which are growing in the open may be lifted and carefully divided if they are particularly good selected varieties. With ordinary mixed strains, however, it is better to raise a new stock each year from seed, as the old plants tend to get weakened by attacks from greenfly, red spider mite and other pests.

Divide mossy saxifrages Old clumps of mossy saxifrage may be divided, and this a good policy if they are tending to get brown in the centre. Discard the brown pieces altogether and replant the green clumps in a semi-shady place in soil that contains plenty of leafmould or moss peat. Water freely for a few weeks.

VEGETABLES AND FRUIT

Thin chicory Chicory sown in Mid May will require thinning. Leave the seedlings 9 in apart.

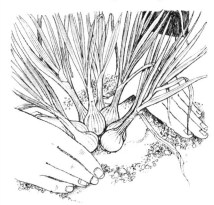

Expose shallot bulbs at this time of year by scraping away some of the surrounding soil to allow them to ripen off thoroughly

Sow stump-rooted carrots Make a last sowing of stump-rooted carrots outdoors. These will come in at about the same time as the main-crop carrots and will be more tender and delicately flavoured for immediate use. The main crop is principally of value for storing for winter use.

Sow and thin Chinese cabbage If this vegetable was sown in Mid May thin seedlings now to 8 in. Make a further sowing for succession.

Sow French beans Make one more sowing of French beans in a sheltered place outdoors in the same way as advised on pages 82 and 83. This will provide you with plants that will crop in September and continue until the first sharp frosts.

Sow parsley Make a third small sowing of parsley for succession (see pages 32 and 68).

Dig early potatoes The earliest potatoes planted at the end of February will probably be ready for digging. Lift one or two roots and see what kind of crop there is. There is no point in waiting for the tubers to mature. So long as they are big enough to be used, lift them, but only as you actually require them for use. It is a great mistake to dig too many early potatoes at once for they lose quality rapidly when taken out of the ground.

Expose shallot bulbs Shallots will now be approaching their ripening period and you should draw the soil away from the bulbs a little in order to allow them to swell freely and get the full benefit of sunlight.

Stop cutting asparagus It is most unwise to cut asparagus after the third week in June. Allow the plants to make foliage now so that new crowns may be formed for next year. Give the bed a small dressing of any good compound fertilizer. If you prefer to make your own mixture, use three parts of superphosphate of lime, two parts of sulphate of ammonia and one part of sulphate of potash at the rate of 2 oz per square yard.

Start to thin apples and pears You will now be able to see how many fruits have been formed on your apple and pear trees. It is no use leaving too many as they will only be misshapen, small and poor in quality. Usually one per spur is enough, and two should be regarded as the maximum. If there are more than this the weakest or least satisfactory will have to be removed, and you can begin to do this now, but do not complete the work yet for there is usually a fairly heavy natural fall later in the month. Be content at the moment to thin the fruits to about four per cluster, removing any that are noticeably poor, badly shaped or spotted. You will find a pair of pointed scissors most serviceable for this work.

Spray apples against codling moth If in former years grubs have been found feeding inside apples during July and August it is probable that the codling moth is responsible, and steps should be taken now to prevent further damage. Spray all apple trees at once with derris, carbaryl, fenitrothion or malathion, making sure that the fruitlets are covered. It would be advisable to spray again in about three weeks' time, to catch any later-hatching grubs. This pest is easily confused with apple sawfly (see page 93).

Under Glass

FLOWERS AND SHRUBS

Lift anemones in frames Anemones of the St Brigid and de Caen types, grown in frames for winter and spring flowering, will have completed their growth by this time and should be lifted. Shake the tubers clear of soil and place them in trays, surrounding them with a little dry peat moss. Then stand the trays in a cool dry place. The corms will keep safely under these conditions until you wish to plant them again.

Repot auriculas If you grow auriculas in pots now is the time to repot them. Shake the old soil from the roots and make certain that these have no woolly aphids upon them. This, by the way, is the same pest that causes the white woolly patches on apples, and is often known as American blight. If it should be present wash the roots in a solution of derris or HCH. Then repot either in 3½- or 4-in pots, reducing the size of the plants if necessary and using a rich loamy compost with some leafmould added and a little sand. Pot firmly, water freely and place in a frame or a sheltered place outdoors. You can remove offsets with roots if you wish and pot them separately.

Sow greenhouse calceolarias
Sow the large hybrid greenhouse calceolarias now in well-drained seed boxes filled with soil- or peat-based seed compost and give the lightest possible covering of fine sand, for the seed is very small. Cover the boxes with paper and place the seeds in a frame to germinate. This is better than a greenhouse as it can be ventilated more freely. There is nothing more likely to harm greenhouse calceolarias than excessive heat.

Pot cyclamen into flowering pots
About this time cyclamen seedlings that were potted individually in Early April will be ready for their final potting into 5-in pots. Use John Innes potting compost No. 1 again but add a little well-rotted manure to it if possible. As before, be careful not to bury the tuber. After potting, arrange the plants in an unheated frame and shade from sunshine for a few days. After this the plants may have more light, but should always be shaded from very hot sunshine and must be ventilated freely, indeed the lights may be removed

Cuttings of pinks are taken in the form of 'pipings'. These are 4- to 5-in lengths of stem pulled out from a joint and inserted in sandy soil in a frame

Pot on cyclamen into 5-in pots. Always be careful to leave the top of the tuber exposed

altogether most of the time and only replaced when the weather is stormy or cold.

Take pink pipings Now is the time to propagate pinks by means of cuttings. Select healthy-looking shoots 4 to 5 in in length and pull them out at a joint. This is known as taking a 'piping'. Insert these pipings firmly, 2 in deep and about 4 in apart each way, in sandy soil, preferably in a frame, but failing this in a shady border outdoors, and keep well watered. If in a frame shade from direct sunlight. They should be well rooted and ready for planting out by the end of September.

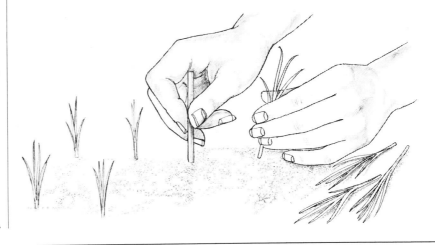

Plants for June

Now that summer has arrived herbaceous borders really come into their own. First to make a big splash are the Chinese peonies, the June-flowering irises, gaudy Oriental poppies, upstanding lupins and anchusas – the bluest of all the taller perennials. They will be followed very quickly by delphiniums, various campanulas, primulas of many kinds, violas and lychnis.

It is important with all this colour about to have plenty of good foliage to set it off and cool it down. Those kinds of pulmonaria that have heavily silvered leaves and have already played one role as spring-flowering plants, now take on a new usefulness for their foliage. *Scrophularia aquatica variegata* is an ugly name for a handsome plant, and the various species of dianthus, including the old-fashioned garden pinks, besides having beautiful and sweet smelling flowers, also have good grey leaves which are very attractive at the front of a border.

There are also excellent varieties of iris with variegated leaves and all the hostas have handsome foliage whether it be green, blue-grey or variegated. Some of these plants, including the scrophularia, will thrive best of all near water where the soil is moist and the foliage can develop to the full. This is also the place for most of the Asiatic primulas including *Primula florindae* with big heads of primrose-coloured flowers like giant cowslips.

June is the month when the rock roses and the sun roses (cistus and helianthemum) are at their best, especially if they are given a suitably sunny place. Unlike the primulas, these are plants that dislike too much water and appreciate good drainage. Sometimes they literally flower themselves to death after a few years so prodigal can they be with bloom and seed, but they are easy to grow from seed or summer cuttings and it is a wise precaution to raise a few young plants each year for use as replacements. In more shaded spots there will be plenty of interest in the rock garden where dainty alpine primulas, erinus and dryas, to name but three are still flowering.

As June days become longer and warmer, roses

Mixed borders are at their peak in June when the foliage is still fresh. The shrubs behind add depth to the planting.

Above: Cistus purpureus
Above right: Decorative summer foliage of *Pulmonaria saccharata* and *Scrophularia aquatica variegata*

become ever more numerous until by the end of the month they can be nearing their peak. Some rhododendrons also flower late, including most of the invaluable Hardy Hybrids and the many forms of *Rhododendron ponticum* the purple species which is the only one to have naturalised itself widely in Britain.

Herbaceous plants Achilleas, anchusas, *Anthemis cupaniana*, aquilegias, *Armeria plantaginea*, aruncus, astrantia, campanulas, centaureas, coreopsis, crambe, delphiniums, dianthus (pinks), dictamnus, digitalis (foxgloves),

Primula florindae

eremurus, erigerons, geraniums, geums, heucheras, incarvilleas, irises, *Kniphofia caulescens*, libertias, lupins, lychnis, meconopsis, nepetas, *Papaver orientale*, peonies, polemoniums, polygonatums, potentillas, pyrethrums, smilacina, thalictrums, *Trollius ledebouri*, verbascums, *Veronica gentianoides*, violas and pansies.

Hardy bulbs, corms and tubers Alliums, camassias, *Gladiolus byzantinus*, English, Spanish and Dutch irises, lilies, ornithogalums, turban ranunculus, *Scilla peruviana*.

Annuals For hardy annuals see page 46.

Bedding plants Ageratums, Canterbury bells (campanula), fuchsias, lobelias, marguerites, pelargoniums.

Evergreen shrubs *Abelia floribunda*, carpenteria, ceanothus, cistuses, cotoneasters, crinodendrons, daboecias, *Helichrysum rosmarinifolium*, *Jasminum humile*, kalmias, leptospermums, *Olearia macrodonta*, *Phlomis fruticosa*, pyracanthas, rhaphiolepis, *Rhododendron discolor*, *R. griersonianum*, hardy hybrid rhododendrons, stranvaesia, *Viburnum rhytidophyllum*, vincas.

Deciduous shrubs Abutilon, deciduous azaleas, *Buddleia alternifolia*, *B. globosa*, *Colutea arborescens*, *Cornus kousa*, *Cytisus scoparius*, deutzias, fremontias, genistas, hedysarums, indigoferas, kolkwitzias, magnolias, neillias, philadelphuses, potentillas, *Robinia hispida*, roses, *Rubus deliciosus*, *Spiraea cantoniensis*, *S. nipponica*, *S. vanhouttei*, *S. veitchii*, syringas (lilacs), *Viburnum opulus*, *V. plicatum*, weigelas.

Evergreen trees Embothriums, *Prunus lusitanica*.

Deciduous trees Aesculus, *Fraxinus ornus*, laburnums, *Magnolia acuminata*, *M. tripetala*, *Malus coronaria*, *M. hupehensis*, *M. ioensis*, *Robinia pseudoacacia*, sorbus, styrax.

Hardy climbers Clematis, *Hydrangea petiolaris*, loniceras (honeysuckles), roses, wisterias.

Late June

In the Garden

FLOWERS AND SHRUBS

Cut back aubrietas, arabis and perennial candytuft Aubrietas, arabis and perennial candytufts may be cut back quite considerably as soon as they have finished flowering if you wish to prevent the plants from spreading very far. In any case, it is a good plan to remove the faded flowers before seed pods form. The work can be done very quickly with a large pair of scissors, or, where large clumps are concerned, with garden shears.

Sow Brompton stocks and forget-me-nots This is a good time to sow Brompton stocks to stand the winter and flower outdoors next May and June. It is possible to germinate the seeds in the open, but I find it better to sow in boxes and place these in a frame. Here the seeds can be shaded from strong sunshine and protected from rain storms until they germinate. Cover the seeds very lightly with sandy soil and water moderately. Forget-me-nots may be sown at the same time, but these germinate freely enough in a shady place in the open. Sow in drills ½ in deep and 6 in apart.

Lift and divide June-flowering irises This is the ideal time for lifting and dividing all the May- and June-flowering flag irises, as most of the plants will be starting to make new roots. Of course, it is not wise to lift and divide the clumps every year, but after four or five years they tend to get overcrowded and to exhaust the soil. Then you should dig them up carefully with a fork, cut off the old central portions of bare rhizome, discarding them altogether, and replant the healthy outer growths with 3 to 4 in of rhizome attached to each. Plant in well-prepared soil which has been dusted with superphosphate of lime at the rate of 2 oz per square yard. If you use animal manure, work it in rather deeply, so that it does not come in contact with the rhizomes. These should only just be covered with soil.

Prune flowering shrubs Any shrubs that flowered during May or early June can be pruned now, but this is not to say that pruning is always necessary. Much depends upon the purpose for which the shrub is being grown and the amount of space that you can spare it. For example, evergreen ceanothuses must be pruned annually when grown against a wall, but there is no necessity to prune them at all if they are cultivated as bushes in the open. The method for wall-grown specimens is to cut back to within 1 in or so of the main branches all side shoots that are growing away from the wall.

Brooms may become very straggly if they are not pruned annually. You must never cut back into very hard, old wood, but it is quite safe to clip the bushes lightly now, shortening the young flowering shoots to within an inch or so of the older branches. Lilacs, rhododendrons and azaleas need no regular pruning of a severe nature, but it is a great advantage to cut off the faded flower trusses and so prevent the formation of seed. *Clematis montana* and other early-flowering kinds may be cut back sufficiently to keep them within bounds. The popular *Chaenomeles speciosa* (cydonia, japonica) must be pruned when grown against a wall. The best method is to shorten side shoots a few at a time, working over a period of several weeks.

Any crowded clumps of May- and June-flowering irises can be lifted and divided. Cut off the old bare rhizome and replant the outer portions

Examine grafted fruit trees to see if the scion is showing signs of growth. If it is, cut through the grafting wax and raffia tie. If this is not done there is a danger of strangling the scion

Start to bud roses It is usually possible to start budding rose stocks at about this time, though much depends on the weather. If June is very dry, one may have to wait until well on into July, whereas if the weather is wet it is sometimes possible to start budding even earlier than this. The test is to make an incision in the stock and then attempt to lift the bark away from the wood. If it comes easily and cleanly budding can proceed at once, but if it drags away unwillingly it is better to wait a while. The method is described on pages 56 to 57.

VEGETABLES AND FRUIT
Start to prune gooseberries and currants You can save yourself a great deal of winter work, and incidentally improve the yield of your gooseberry and red and white currant bushes by summer pruning. Start this now, but do not attempt to complete it all at once. Summer pruning does not apply to black currants. The

ideal is to spread the work over a period of about six weeks. Then the bushes will not suffer any check from sudden loss of foliage. Pruning consists in cutting off the ends of all side shoots when they are about 6 in long. Shorten them to about 3 in.

Examine grafted fruit trees It is a good plan to examine any fruit trees that you grafted in March or April to make quite sure that all is in order. If the stock appears to have swollen a good deal, remove the grafting wax and make sure that the tie is not strangling the scion.

Under Glass

FLOWERS AND SHRUBS
Pot cinerarias The first batch of cinerarias, sown in Early May, will do better singly in pots now. Use John Innes potting compost No. 1 or a soilless equivalent and return the plants to a frame after potting. Ventilate freely.

Sow cinerarias and primulas To provide a succession of flowers after those from the Early May sowing you should now make a second sowing of cinerarias. The

seeds are treated in exactly the same way as before, except that now no artificial heat will be needed to effect germination. You can even place the seed pans in a frame if you are short of space in the greenhouse.

It is also an excellent plan to make a second sowing of *Primula sinensis* and its variety *stellata* to flower after the earliest plants sown in Late April. *P. malacoides* may be sown now for the first time. It grows more rapidly than the others, and there is nothing to be gained by sowing earlier.

VEGETABLES AND FRUIT
Train and feed melons Melons in the heated greenhouse should be swelling well by now and you must sling the fruits up in special melon nets to take their weight off the stems. Gradually reduce the amount of atmospheric moisture and give increased ventilation, but without reducing the average day temperature of 21°C (70°F). This will assist ripening.

Melons in frames will be making side shoots as a result of having their growing tips pinched out. Retain four per plant and train them to the four corners of the bed, pegging them down to its surface. Pinch out their tips when they reach the limits of the bed. Flower-bearing sublaterals will soon be formed. Fertilize about half a dozen female flowers at the same time (see page 73). Keep the plants well watered and topdress the bed with 1-in layer of well-rotted manure as soon as white rootlets appear on the surface.

Crops in Season

In the garden Asparagus, broad beans, shorthorn carrots, cauliflower, lettuce, mustard and cress, spring onions, onions, peas, potatoes, radish, rhubarb, spinach, turnips.

Cherries, gooseberries, raspberries, strawberries.

Under glass French beans, cucumbers, tomatoes.

Grapes, peaches, nectarines.

July

*'If the First of July be rainy weather
It will rain, more or less, for four weeks together'*

General Work

In the Garden

THE GARDEN is now full of flowers. In order to ensure that the show continues throughout the summer months you should regularly remove any blooms or flower spikes that are so faded as to be no longer decorative. This applies to early-flowering herbaceous plants, bedding plants and annuals and also to roses. The object is to prevent seed formation, which weakens the plant unnecessarily. Exception may be made if one wants some seeds of any special thing, but then the best plan is to reserve one particular plant of this variety for seed bearing.

While dead heading, keep an eye open for any sign of caterpillars, red spider mites, thrips and greenfly which are still sources of danger. Take prompt measures to destroy these pests as soon as they put in an appearance (see pages 74 and 98). Fungal diseases, such as mildew, rust and black spot, are likely to be on the increase as the weather gets warmer. Occasional spraying with benomyl, thiram, captan or some other good fungicide is the only certain method of keeping them down. It is wise to spray roses every fortnight or so as a precautionary measure, for it is much easier to prevent diseases than to cure them. Other good remedies for black spot of roses and rose mildew are maneb and dinocap which should be sprayed on the leaves according to manufacturers' instructions.

Thin and disbud dahlias If you want some extra fine dahlias for exhibition, you must thin out the plants and only allow them to bear a restricted number of flowers. A good strong plant of one of the large-flowered varieties may carry three stems, but no

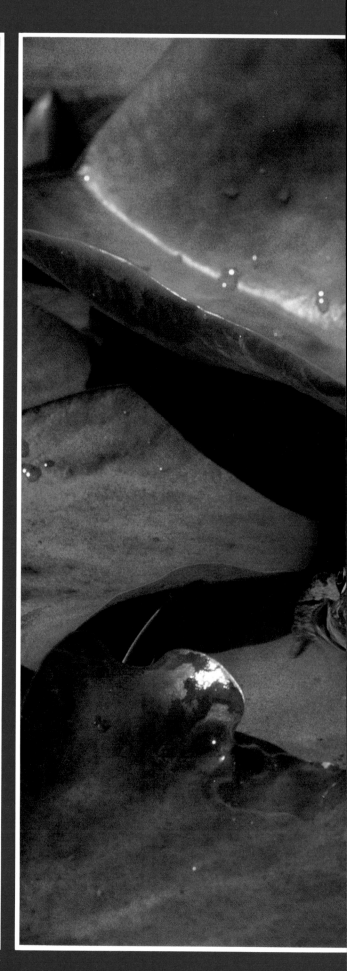

more. Remove others, keeping only the sturdiest. Then, when the flower buds appear, remove all except the central terminal one on each stem. Plants that are only grown for garden decoration do not need this drastic restriction and may be allowed to grow naturally. All will benefit from liberal soakings of weak liquid manure every few days.

Continue to trim hedges You can continue to trim evergreen hedges and topiary specimens as necessary to keep them neat and tidy.

Continue to bud rose stocks You can continue to bud throughout the month so long as the bark parts readily from the wood of the stock (see page 113). Sometimes, if the weather gets very hot and dry, the stocks refuse to work properly. You should then stop for the time being.

THE LAWN
Remove grass box from mower During this month and August, when the weather is likely to be hot, it is an excellent plan to remove the grass box from the lawn mower and let the tiny clippings fall on to the lawn. They will act as a mulch and will protect the roots from scorching.

VEGETABLES AND FRUIT
Continue to feed plants in growth You should keep feeding all plants that are making rapid growth as I advised in my notes for May and June (see pages 74 and 100). For winter greens planted during May and June, nitrate of soda may well be used in place of a compound fertilizer. Give two applications, each of $\frac{1}{2}$ oz per square yard, at an interval of about three weeks.

Continue to thin seedlings Various vegetables sown last month for succession must be thinned out before they become overcrowded (see page 100).

Make successional sowings These are in the main the same as for last month (see page 100). Sow turnips for the last time about the middle of the month. You can be rather more generous with the seed, as this crop will supply roots for storing. One more sowing each of lettuce, endive and summer spinach should meet all requirements. It is necessary to choose a shady place for all these crops, for heat

and drought will make them run to seed prematurely. Mustard, cress and radishes can be sown as before, also in a cool position.

Plant celery During the month you can make further plantings of celery as plants from late sowings become available. It is not wise to shift the plants to the trenches while they are very small. Wait until they are at least 3 in in height and can be lifted with a nice ball of roots (see pages 87 and 104).

Continue to plant winter greens Continue to plant out all winter greens as you clear ground of early crops, such as dwarf peas, early potatoes and the first sowings of turnips and salad vegetables. So far as possible, choose showery weather for this work, but do not delay long on this account. If July is persistently dry, push on with the planting and then water freely for a few days.

Plant March-sown leeks Leeks from the Mid-March sowing may also be planted, as opportunity occurs. Plant with a large dibber in holes 9 in deep, dropping the leeks right down into these. Do not refill the holes with soil, simply water in thoroughly. This deep planting will blanch the stems without the need for earthing up. The leeks should be 1 ft apart in rows 18 in apart.

Continue to blanch leeks The process of blanching leeks grown in trenches must be continued gradually, as explained on page 100.

Cut globe artichokes From now onwards you can cut the heads of globe artichokes as they become avail-

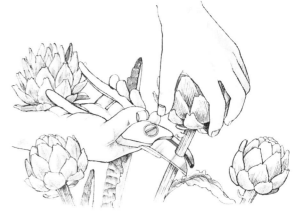

Globe artichokes should not be cut the first summer after planting. In subsequent years cut the heads when they are nice and plump but before the scales have opened and become hard and tough

Regular damping down of the greenhouse path helps maintain a humid atmosphere and deters red spider mite

able. On no account leave any on the plants so long that they begin to flower. The ideal time to cut them is when they are nice and plump, but before the scales begin to open out too much.

Feed and train tomatoes Outdoor tomatoes will be growing freely and forming their flower trusses. Keep each plant to a single stem and nip out all side shoots at the earliest opportunity. Water freely during dry weather and, as soon as the bottom truss is set and you can see the tiny fruits swelling, spread a layer of well-rotted manure or compost round the plants. From that time onwards feed every week with small doses of any good tomato fertilizer.

Thin grapes Thinning of the fruits will now become general with outdoor vines, and as the process is exactly the same as for indoor varieties I refer you to my earlier notes on page 84. A thick mulch of well-rotted manure or compost spread over the border will help the vines tremendously at this time.

Under Glass

General greenhouse management There is really little to add to my remarks in the General Work for June on this subject. Heating for all ordinary greenhouse plants will now be quite unnecessary. Indeed the problem usually will be to keep the house sufficiently cool by day. This is particularly so in very small houses, which must, in consequence, be ventilated freely and shaded carefully. Shading for a few hours each day may even be necessary for such a sun-loving crop as tomatoes. Occasional damping down of paths and walls will also help matters, but spraying of the plants must be done cautiously when the sun is shining brightly as drops of water lying on the leaves can act like burning glasses, concentrating the light and heat on a small area.

FLOWERS AND SHRUBS

Pot on greenhouse plants Spring-struck cuttings of zonal pelargoniums required for autumn flowering in the greenhouse are almost sure to need potting on into 6-in pots during July. Similar remarks apply to other greenhouse plants raised from spring cuttings taken in March, except that sometimes even bigger pots may be required. In this connection I refer you to my general remarks on potting in the notes on page 61, and would remind you that it is rarely wise to shift plants into pots more than two sizes larger than those in which they are already growing. Use the same compost as before but coarser in texture, and press it more firmly around the roots unless it is a peat compost.

VEGETABLES AND FRUIT

Tend tomatoes There is really nothing to add to my remarks on indoor tomatoes made last month (see page 105). Cut back more foliage as you clear the lower trusses of fruit. Free ventilation, steady feeding and ample watering are important points to watch.

Feed and train cucumbers Plants in frames will now be tending to take the place of those in greenhouses, although even the latter may be kept going for a surprising time by frequent removal of all side growths that have ceased to bear and their replacement by young growth. Spray and water constantly to keep up the necessary moisture in soil and air. Ventilate rather more freely, especially when the temperature shows signs of rising above 27°C (80°F), but do not allow the air to get dry on this account or you are sure to have trouble with red spider mites and thrips. Heavier shading will help to keep the temperature down. Continue to stop and train the plants in frames. Regulate growth in such a manner that the beds are never overcrowded but you are continually getting a new supply of laterals with

flowers. Be very careful to cut the cucumbers directly they are fit to use. If a few hang and ripen, the plants will soon stop bearing.

Management of fruit under glass Peaches, nectarines and apricots under glass must be treated according to their state of growth (see pages 80 and 102). As trees are cleared of ripened fruits spraying with water should begin again on a daily or twice daily basis. Ventilate freely by day, but do not let the temperature fall below 13°C (55°F) at night. Even July nights can be chilly occasionally.

Protect vines from mildew Mildew may become troublesome from now onwards, covering leaves and grapes with a white, mealy growth. If there is the slightest sign of this disease, give increased ventilation and dust foliage and fruits with flowers of sulphur or spray with dinocap. Make certain that the border is not short of water, for dry soil combined with a damp, unventilated atmosphere are sure causes of mildew.

Shanking sometimes occurs at this time of the year. This is a physiological disorder which causes the footstalks of the berries to die, with the result that the berries themselves suddenly collapse. It is caused by poor soil or a cold, wet subsoil. Remaking of the border the following autumn is the best remedy.

Herb gardens

It is possible to use herbs to make an independent and highly attractive feature of the garden, as can be seen in such well known gardens as Sissinghurst Castle and Wakehurst Place.

Several of the most popular and useful herbs, thyme, sage, fennel, mint and chives among them, are perennials which can be given semi-permanent positions where they can be left undisturbed for years. Others, such as parsley, summer savory, sweet marjoram, basil, borage, coriander and dill are annuals and yet others such as angelica and caraway, are biennials and these must be renewed annually from seed.

The perennials can also be raised from seed in the first place if desired but, as only a few plants are likely to be required, it is usually more convenient and economical to obtain them as young plants, preferably in spring, and plant where required. Bay leaves, which are sometimes used for flavouring, are obtained from *Laurus nobilis*, a slightly tender evergreen tree.

All herbs like open, preferably sunny places and reasonably fertile soil. From May to October many can be gathered as required, but for winter use they must be cut, dried and stored (see page 120).

Opposite: A particularly fine border dominated by angelica

Paving slabs make gathering herbs easier in wet weather

Hardy annual herbs such as borage, chervil, coriander, dill and summer savory are best sown outdoors in April where they are to grow. Half-hardy kinds such as sweet basil and sweet marjoram can be sown in a greenhouse or frame, or in a sunny window in March, the seedlings pricked out and potted singly and hardened off for planting out in late May. Biennials, such as angelica and caraway, are sown outdoors in May or June and transplanted in September. Perennial kinds are best planted in March or April but fennel is usually raised from seed like the biennials.

Early July

In the Garden

FLOWERS AND SHRUBS

Lift tulips and hyacinths Tulips and hyacinths will now have completed their growth and may be lifted and cleaned. Lay the bulbs in shallow trays and stand them in a dry, cool, airy place, but not in full sun. Dead tops can be removed and the bulbs sorted out into two sizes, the biggest for flowering again next year (though do not rely on them for the most important display) and the smaller ones to be planted in good soil in an out-of-the-way place to grow on. If your garden is only small it will be best to throw these small bulbs away, for they will scarcely be worth the space they take up. Anemones of the St Brigid and de Caen types and also turban ranunculuses, are treated in much the same way, the tubers being lifted as soon as foliage has died down. Store in a dry, cool place until planting time. Crocuses can also be lifted now, but only if they are over-crowded or you need the ground for something else. If you do have them out, get them replanted quite soon; they gain nothing from being out of the ground.

Stand out pelargoniums Show and regal pelargoniums will have practically finished flowering by this time and will be better out of the greenhouse. Stand them in the open in any sunny, fairly sheltered place and gradually decrease the water supply, practically withholding it for the last fortnight in July. If it rains a lot, lay the pots on their sides. The object is to check and ripen growth and give the plants a rest.

VEGETABLES AND FRUIT

Sow carrots A small sowing of stump-rooted or intermediate carrots made now is often amply justified, especially if the season happens to be a bad one for carrot fly. This fly does all its damage early in the summer so seedlings from a July sowing usually escape. In any case, young carrots in the autumn are very welcome.

Finish planting celery All remaining celery seedlings should now be planted out in the trenches as soon as possible (see pages 87 and 104). The last plants to be dealt with will be those from the Mid-April sowing in a frame.

Spray potatoes Do not wait until disease attacks your potatoes, but spray them now with a copper fungicide or zineb. The potato blight disease is common and some of your plants are likely to become infected unless you take this precaution. In any case spraying is repaid because it lengthens the season of growth and so indirectly increases the weight of the crop. When spraying, be very careful to cover the under, as well as the upper, sides of the leaves.

Gather herbs This is the time to gather most herbs for winter use. Do not delay until they have flowered or you will lose much of the flavour. Tie the stems into small bundles and suspend these head downwards from a beam or hook in a cool, dry and airy shed or room. When thoroughly dry the leaves can be stored in tightly-stoppered jars or tins in any reasonably cool dry place.

Peg down strawberry runners Strawberry plants tend to deteriorate after a few years, so it is advisable to raise a few new plants every year to take the place of old, worn-out ones. All that is necessary is to peg down some of the plantlets that form on the runners. Each runner will form a number of plantlets but, for propagation, the one nearest the parent plant is the best and the tip of the runner beyond this should be pinched out. It is not usually wise to peg down more than three or four plantlets round each old plant.

There are two methods of doing the work. One is simply to press the plantlet down on to the soil in the strawberry bed and hold it in position with a wooden or wire peg. The other is to fill a 3-in flower pot with a mixture of loam, leafmould and sand.

Hang herbs in bunches in a cool, airy place to dry.

120

Strawberry runners are most conveniently propagated by pegging them down into pots of compost sunk into the ground. In this way they are easily transplanted when they have rooted

Plunge this into the strawberry bed and peg the plantlet into it. The second method is the better of the two because, when the rooted runners are severed from their parent plant later on and are removed to a new bed, there need be no serious root disturbance. The pot, complete with roots, is simply lifted from the strawberry bed and the ball of soil tapped out intact. But rooting in pots does mean a little more watering is required. If you can get all the runners you require now, so much the better, for early rooting gives the best results, but if there are not enough runners at the moment you can continue to peg down throughout the month as the runners develop.

Cut off any runners you do not need, because they only weaken the plant. Continue to do this throughout the summer.

Burn straw on strawberry beds
If you have had any mildew or other disease on your plants or if they have been badly attacked by greenfly or other pests and the beds have been covered with

straw, set fire to the straw as soon as you have gathered all the fruits. This will burn off all the foliage and leave the bed looking very bare and sad for a week or so, but the crowns themselves will not be damaged and will soon produce healthy new growth. If the beds were not strawed the leaves can be cut off with shears or a sharp sickle, then gathered up and burned. Of course, you must not do these things to plants around which you intend to peg down runners.

Complete thinning of apples and pears It is now the time to complete the thinning of apples and pears (see page 108). Reduce the fruits to one or two per spur.

Remove plum branches attacked by silver leaf Silver leaf is a disease caused by a fungus that actually infects the wood of plums and occasionally apples and pears. It cannot be counteracted by spraying, and the only method of preventing its spread is to cut off and burn affected branches, afterwards painting wounds with Stockholm tar or a proprietary wound dressing. By law, wood killed by silver leaf must be removed before 15th July. The leaves of diseased branches have a distinctive silvery appearance. The only other disease which may be confused with this is mildew, but the latter produces a white, mealy outgrowth on the leaves. With silver leaf there is no outward fungal growth until a later date, and then it is on the dead wood. At this time of the year there is just the tell-tale silvery sheen to the foliage. The variety Victoria is particularly susceptible to attack, while Blaisdon Red, Yellow Pershore and Rivers' Early Prolific are resistant to it.

Start to summer-prune cherries and plums You can now begin to summer-prune cherries and plums growing on walls. It is not worthwhile trying to apply this method of pruning to large bushes and standards, for these are better allowed to grow rather freely. With the one exception of the Morello cherry, the method is the same for all varieties.

Side shoots which have been growing during May and June should be shortened by about one-third each, but leaders terminating main branches are left unpruned. Do not do all the work on any one tree at once, but spread it over a period of about six weeks. In this way trees will suffer less check to growth.

Morello cherries bear their best fruits on young wood, and so are disbudded just like peaches and nectarines. Side shoots growing on the fruiting laterals are gradually rubbed off or pinched back a few at a time with the exception of two on each lateral, one near its base and one at its tip. The former will replace it after the winter pruning, while the latter serves to maintain a good flow of sap to swell and ripen the fruits.

Under Glass

FLOWERS AND SHRUBS
Complete stopping of carnations
By this time you should complete all the second stopping of perpetual-flowering carnations (see page 80). If the plants are stopped later than this they will not begin to flower until well on in the new year, and carnations are much in demand at Christmas and even before. Roughly speaking, five months must elapse before a stopped growth can produce any flowers.

Plants for July

This is the month when many annuals and bedding plants really begin to make their presence felt. Some of them will already have been flowering in June but now their flowers will be becoming more abundant and the early kinds will be joined by later ones, including many annuals sown in spring in the open ground where they are to grow. Those sown in open ground have a fairly short season but this can almost always be lengthened if the fading flowers are regularly removed before they have a chance to set seed.

Early June should be the peak period for the first display of most bedding roses. Hasten the second flush by cutting off the fading flowers with a sufficient length of stem to encourage rapid growth from a shoot already formed or a growth bud that looks plump and ready for action.

By this time planted pools and streamsides should be making their full contribution to the pleasures of the garden. Water lilies will be flowering, though not until the sun has shone on them for a few hours, and many of the marginal plants will be at their best. One can expect irises in plenty, including the magnificent Japanese varieties, astilbes and the taller filipendulas which carry their flowers in fluffy clusters rather than in tapering plumes, and even some of the hostas which, though grown primarily for their leaves, can make a welcome contribution. Primulas, too, will continue to bloom, especially the candelabra varieties, so called because they carry their carmine, vermilion, pink or yellow flowers in a succession of

Mixed annuals including *Papaver somniferum*, *Layia elegans*, *Agrostemma milas*, *Malope trifida* and *Malcomia maritima*

Above: This well-stocked mixed border includes varieties of campanulas, violas, antirrhinums and delphiniums

Top: A secluded seat shaded by *Robinia pseudoacacia* Frisia
Above: A paved area softened by planting surrounds a pool

whorls of diminishing size, rather like a candelabra turned upside down. In favourable conditions many of these will spread by self-sown seed and if some of the seedlings appear in unwanted places they can be carefully lifted and replanted elsewhere.

Herbaceous plants Achilleas, aconitums, alstroemerias, anthemis, *Artemisia lactiflora*, aruncus, astilbes, astrantias, buphthalmum, campanulas, centaureas, centranthus, *Chrysanthemum maximum*, cimicifugas, *Clematis integrifolia*, *C. recta*, coreopsis, delphiniums, dianthus (border carnations, pinks, sweet Williams), dictamnus, digitalis, echinacea, echinops, erigerons, eryngiums, gaillardias, galegas, geraniums, geums, gypsophilas, heleniums, heleopsis, hemerocallis, heucheras, hostas, inulas, kniphofias, *Lavatera olbia*, liatris, *Linaria purpurea*, linums, lysimachias, lythrums, macleayas, meconopsis, mertensia, monardas, nepetas, oenotheras, penstemons, phlox, platycodons, polemoniums, polygonums, romneyas, *Scabiosa caucasica*, sidalceas, solidagos, thalictrums, *Tradescantia virginiana*, verbascums, *Verbena rigida*, veronicas.

Hardy bulbs, corms and tubers Alliums, cardiocrinums, crocosmias, *Cyclamen europaeum*, gladioli, lilies, tigridias.
Annuals See page 46 (hardy) and 33 (half hardy).
Bedding plants See page 111 also begonias dahlias.
Evergreen shrubs Abelia, calluna, carpenteria, cistuses, erica, escallonias, hebes, *Hypericum calycinum*, lavenders, myrtus, *Olearia haastii*, phlomis, senecios, teucrium, vincas, yuccas.
Deciduous shrubs *Ceanothus delilianus*, *Clethra alnifolia*, *Colutea arborescens*, *Cytisus battandieri*, fuchsias, genista, hoherias, hydrangeas, hypericums, philadelphus, potentillas, roses, sorbarias, *Spartium junceum*, spiraeas, *Tamarix ramosissima (pentandra)*.
Evergreen trees *Eucryphia cordifolia*.
Deciduous trees *Aesculus indica*, *Castanea sativa*, catalpa, eucryphias, liriodendron, tilias.
Hardy climbers Berberidopsis, clematis, eccremocarpus, *Jasminum officinale*, *Lathyrus latifolius*, lonicera (honeysuckles), *Passiflora caerulea*, roses, schizophragmas, *Solanum crispum*, *S. jasminoides*, trachelospermums.

In the Garden

FLOWERS AND SHRUBS

Prick out perennials and biennials Perennials and biennials sown in Early June will be in need of pricking out into a nursery bed. This should be in an open position except in the case of violas, pansies, primroses and polyanthuses, which grow more quickly in partial shade.

The ground must be well forked and reasonably rich, but not recently manured with dung. If the soil needs feeding, give a very light dressing of hop manure and fork this in. Lift the seedlings up as carefully as possible and if the ground is dry it is a good plan to give it a thorough watering the day before you intend to move the seedlings. Replant them with a trowel in rows about 9 in apart. The bigger plants, such as hollyhocks, delphiniums and lupins, should be 9 in apart in the rows, 6 in will be sufficient for plants such as wallflowers, double daisies, *Cheiranthus allionii* and primroses, while violas and pansies may be as close as 4 in. Pinch out the tips of wallflowers and cheiranthuses to make them branch freely.

It is possible that Brompton stocks and forget-me-nots from the Late-June sowing may also be far enough advanced to prick out in the same manner. If they are not, the work should be done at the first favourable opportunity that comes along.

Take cuttings of shrubs A great many hardy shrubs, and also shrubby alpines, such as helianthemums and penstemons, can be increased during July and August by cuttings prepared from firm young side shoots and the ends of non-flowering stems. Select pieces from 1 in to 4 in in length, according to the nature of the plant. Prepare them by cutting the base of each cleanly through just below a joint and removing the lower leaves. Then insert them firmly in a mixture of equal parts moss peat and sand.

The cuttings must be prevented from flagging either by keeping them in a very still, moist atmosphere or by spraying them with water frequently. This second method is the one most used by nurserymen but it involves the use of special equipment to provide the overhead spraying as required. This may be electrically or hydraulically controlled and small mist propagation units are available for amateur use.

A close, moist atmosphere can be provided in a propagating case, and many small models are available – some with electric soil warming which improves the speed and certainty of rooting. Alternatively, many cuttings can be rooted very efficiently simply by inserting them in pots filled with the peat/sand mixture and then slipping each pot inside a polythene bag which can be sealed with one of the wire ties that are supplied with bags sold for deep freezing.

Prune mock oranges and weigelas Most mock oranges (philadelphus) and weigelas (diervilla) will have finished flowering by now, and you can prune them if you do not want the bushes to get very big. The method is to cut out all the stems that have just flowered, leaving younger shoots from lower down to take their place.

Mist propagators prevent cuttings wilting by spraying them with a fine mist of water controlled by means of an electronic leaf. Best results are obtained by using mist in conjunction with soil-warming cables

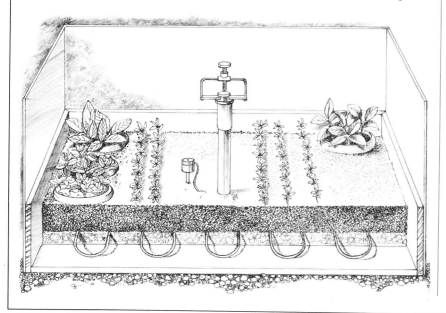

Blanch celery by tying thick paper collars round the stems to prevent soil getting into the hearts of the plants. This could, in time, cause the growing tips to rot

Then draw soil up round the collars with a hoe to ensure that all light is excluded

Summer-prune wisterias
Wisterias that have filled their allotted space can be induced to flower freely year after year without making a lot of new growth by summer and winter pruning. Now is the time for the first of these operations. Shorten all side growths formed on the main branches to about six leaves.

VEGETABLES AND FRUIT
Mulch and spray runner beans
Runner beans will benefit from a fairly thick mulch of well-rotted manure or compost spread on the ground for a distance of a couple of feet on either side of the row if possible. When the plants begin to flower, spray them every evening with tepid water. This will help the flowers to 'set' and so ensure a good crop of beans. Keep this up all through the month and on into August.

Sow and thin Chinese cabbage
Thin seedlings from the Mid-June sowing and make a further sowing for succession (see page 85).

Sow spring cabbage This is the time to make a first sowing of cabbages for use in the spring and early summer. Do not sow all the seed now, however, but keep some for a further sowing during Early August, as sometimes the later seedlings do best in the long run. Choose a suitable variety, such as April, Avoncrest, Durham Elf, Offenham-Flower of Spring or Harbinger. Scatter the seed thinly in a bed of finely broken soil and cover lightly. Water freely if the weather happens to be dry.

Start to earth up early celery If you want to have some sticks of celery for a late August show, you must start to earth up now. This is not a task that can be completed in one operation. At first content yourself by drawing 3 to 4 in of soil round the base of each plant. Remove basal off-shoots as a preliminary, and tie the stems together with raffia so that soil does not find its way into the hearts of the plants. Then, about ten days later, draw up a further 4 in or so of soil, and keep on in this manner at short intervals until only the blades of the leaves can be seen. A further method of ensuring that the plants are kept clean and that soil does not percolate into their hearts is to tie brown paper collars round them before earthing up.

Spray apples against codling moth Repeat application of one or other of the sprays recommended in Mid June (see page 108).

Under Glass
FLOWERS AND SHRUBS
Pot primulas, calceolarias and cinerarias Greenhouse primulas sown in Late June will now need pricking off exactly like the earlier batch in Late May (see page 94). These first primulas will also in all probability require a shift. Do not let them get crowded in their trays, but move them on singly into 3-in pots, using John Innes No. 1 or soil-less potting compost. Return the plants to the frame after potting and give a little shade from strong, direct sunshine.

Calceolarias and cinerarias sown in June (see pages 109 and 113) are almost certain to be forward enough for pricking off in exactly the same manner as the primulas, except that the cinerarias should be spaced a good 2 in apart each way.

In the Garden

FLOWERS AND SHRUBS

Layer border carnations Border carnations can be increased by cuttings like perpetual-flowering carnations, but it is much more satisfactory to increase them by layers. This means that you select young non-flowering shoots that can readily be bent down to soil level and make an incision with a sharp knife through a joint near the base of each. Then the slit portion of stem is bent down to open the slit, covered with fine sandy soil and held firmly in position with a wooden or wire peg. If the layers are kept well watered, roots will soon be formed from the sides of the cut. Early in September the rooted layers can be cut completely from the parent plant and be planted elsewhere or potted up.

Take early-flowering chrysanthemum buds This term requires

Layer border carnations by partially cutting through a joint. Hold the cut area down in the soil with a piece of bent wire

some explanation. It is the chrysanthemum grower's equivalent to disbudding. It means that the flower buds required for producing big blooms are retained, while all smaller buds or shoots surrounding or below them are rubbed out. It is only necessary to do this if you want big flowers borne singly on long stems. If your object is to have sprays of comparatively small flowers, let the plants grow on naturally. In any case you will not be able to complete all the disbudding at once, but look over the plants now, for some at least should be showing flower buds.

Start to feed chrysanthemums It is a mistake to begin to feed chrysanthemums of any type too early, but you can start now with safety using any good chrysanthemum fertilizer applied strictly in accordance with the manufacturers' instructions.

Lift daffodils and bulbous irises Daffodils and narcissi, also the various bulbous irises, will now have completed their growth and may be lifted and cleaned off if they are overgrown or you need

the ground for something else. Otherwise leave them undisturbed for another year. They do not gain anything by annual lifting and drying, as do tulips and hyacinths. If you do lift them, get them replanted as soon as possible and certainly before the end of September.

Plant autumn crocuses You should also plant colchicums, autumn-flowering crocuses and sternbergias if you can obtain supplies. General bulb merchants rarely have them so early, but specialists will be able to supply. Plant the crocuses 3 in deep and 3 in apart; the colchicums and sternbergias 4 in deep and 4 in apart. All should be in well-drained soil and a rather sheltered but sunny position.

Plant Madonna lilies This is the ideal time to plant *Lilium candidum*, the Madonna lily. It differs from almost all other lilies in making quite a lot of new growth in late summer, and it should be planted before this starts. Another peculiarity is that the bulbs grow practically on the surface. You should plant them 8 in apart and only cover them with 1 in of soil. After a while they will probably work themselves out until they show; make no attempt to cover them again. This lily prefers a sunny position and reasonably good, but not freshly manured, ground.

Cut back helianthemums Sun roses tend to get rather straggly if left to their own devices, but if cut back a little each year at about this time they can be kept

quite neat and tidy. You can do the work with a large pair of scissors or the garden shears.

Summer-prune roses Bush and standard roses of the large-flowered type will pay for a light summer pruning now that the first flush of flowers is over. Cut back to about two leaves or a sturdy young-growth all stems that have flowered but have no promising buds on them at the moment. Then give the beds a dusting of any good compound flower-garden fertilizer and water this in if the weather is dry.

VEGETABLES AND FRUIT
Lift and store onions Autumn-sown onions should now have completed their growth and

Changes of level and materials add interest to a patio area

Lift autumn-sown onions that are ripe with a fork and leave them in the sun for a few days to dry off thoroughly before storing

ripened their bulbs, so you may just as well lift them and have the ground free for some other crop such as winter greens. Lift the onions carefully with a fork and lay them out in a sunny place for a few days to dry off. Then shake the soil from them and store in shallow boxes in a cool dry place.

Sow parsley for autumn Make a final sowing of parsley for autumn and winter use. If you sow the seeds in a very sheltered place, you can leave some of the plants undisturbed and keep on

cutting from them as long as possible, but a portion of the seedlings will have to be transplanted into a frame in September if you wish to have a Christmas supply.

Make an outdoor mushroom bed
In sheds or other suitable buildings mushrooms can be grown throughout the year, but unprotected outdoors they are only satisfactory in late summer and early autumn. Now is the time to make such a bed.

First you will need to get a good quantity of fresh stable manure. This you must turn and shake with a fork two or three times, at intervals of a day or so, until the first heat of fermentation has died down and the manure is decaying steadily. Then build it up into a ridge-shaped heap in the open, or a more or less flat-topped bank against a wall. An alternative to stable manure is clean straw rotted with one of the special mushroom compost chemical preparations sold for the purpose. These must be used according to manufacturers' instructions.

Beds made against a north wall at this time of the year are usually very satisfactory. Tread the manure or compost firmly layer by layer as you build it up into the mound. When finished, the bed should be 2½ ft deep; it can be of any width, but 3 ft is usual and convenient. Plunge a soil thermometer into the bed and, when the temperature falls to 21°C (70°F), insert sterilized mushroom spawn in small pieces at intervals of 10 in all over the bed. Simply make a hole about 1 in deep in the manure or compost, push a piece of spawn in, and cover it with manure. Then cover the whole bed with a 1-ft layer of straw.

Crops in Season

In the garden Globe artichoke, beetroot, broad beans, French beans, runner beans, broccoli (calabrese), shorthorn carrots, cauliflower, lettuce, marrows, mustard and cress, onions, peas, early potatoes, radish, spinach, turnips.

Apples, black currants, red currants, white currants, gooseberries, loganberries, pears, plums, raspberries, strawberries.

Under glass Cucumbers, tomatoes.

Apricots, grapes, nectarines.

After two or three weeks scrape away a little of the manure and see how things are getting on. If there are white filament-like growths penetrating the bed freely, the spawn is 'running' and the bed is ready for casing. This is done by covering the manure evenly with a 1-in layer of loam, beaten smooth with the back of a spade. Then replace the clean dry straw to keep the bed at an even temperature. If the weather is dry, the bed must be watered occasionally with tepid water, but too much moisture is not desirable.

Strawberries in pots If you want to grow some early strawberries in the greenhouse, lift a few of the most forward rooted runners now and pot them singly in 6-in pots in John Innes potting compost No. 2. The plants can stand in a frame or a cool position outdoors and must be watered regularly.

Start to bud fruit stocks Stocks of various fruit trees, such as apples, pears, plums and cherries, can usually be budded about this time. You can apply the same tests to the stocks as those suggested for roses (see page 113). Of course, there are no thorns by which you can test the shoots selected as scions, and as it is most important that they should be in just the right condition, you must examine them carefully. You should be able to peel the bark easily from the wood. If it tears, growth is either too young or too dry. The buds should be well developed and clearly visible. The actual details for budding are almost the same as for roses (see page 57). The only difference is that instead of inserting them as low down on the dwarf stocks as possible, they should be put in about 8 in above soil level. It is desirable that the union of rose stock and scion should be covered with soil, but this is not advisable with fruit trees, for the scions might then make roots of their own, which would upset the particular effect, dwarfing or otherwise, of the stock chosen.

Buds can only be inserted into stocks that have thin, supple bark. Some form of grafting in spring (see pages 56 and 57) must be used for old, hard-barked trees that are being reworked.

Start to summer-prune apples and pears You can now start to shorten the laterals of apples and pears exactly as I described for cherries and plums earlier in the month (see page 121). The method is worth applying to all trained specimens, and also to small bushes, pyramids and half-standards, but involves too much labour with full standards or very big bushes.

Lighting in the garden

Lighting in the garden can serve two purposes, not necessarily incompatible but certainly distinct and therefore in need of careful consideration. One is the very straightforward provision of illumination for anyone using the garden after dark, most likely for barbecues and other entertainments. The other for spotlighting particular plants or garden features to make them more dramatic.

Plain illumination may involve nothing more complex than some strategically placed outdoor lights, maybe old street lamps or reproductions of them if the genuine article is not available. Mains electricity is clearly the most convenient source of power but gas, either from mains or bottles, or even paraffin or candles, perhaps in traditional-style hurricane lanterns, are all possibilities that can add an attractively rural atmosphere to a party. Whatever the method of lighting, it is likely that the lamp holders will be part of the decorative scheme and as such they will need to be chosen with care and good taste to suit the style of the garden.

By contrast spotlighting will almost certainly involve concealing the lights as much as possible, the

An unobtrusive lighting fixture can illuminate a potential hazard such as a flight of steps

A concealed spotlight can be used to pick out a statue or specimen plant and add interest to the garden at night

purpose being to concentrate attention on whatever is being illuminated. Electricity will almost certainly be the power source and special equipment, made for outdoor use and fully waterproofed, must be used. Some manufacturers use low voltage lamps to increase the safety factor; the current is usually stepped down to 12 volts from mains voltage by a transformer which should be installed indoors or at any rate in a fully covered and protected place. If no mains supply is available it would be possible to use this low voltage equipment from batteries. Since the current is so low the actual siting and connection of lamps can be done by amateurs, which makes it easy to change things about to suit the seasons or provide some welcome variety. However, the installation of transformers and their connection to mains supplies should be done by a qualified electrician. Usually a variety of coloured lenses is available but, if not, coloured low-voltage lamps can be purchased from most dealers in electrical equipment. If you require a greater degree of illumination than low voltage can supply and so opt for mains supply throughout the garden, the whole work should be entrusted to an expert in this kind of outdoor work. It is all too easy to have serious accidents with electrical equipment outdoors which has been imperfectly insulated or not protected from the weather.

August

*'If the twenty-fourth of August be fair and clear,
Then hope for a prosperous autumn that year'*

General Work

In the Garden

THIS IS the month when you should be reaping the rewards for all the hard work carried out earlier in the year. The garden and greenhouse will be in full production, but even while enjoying the fruits of your labour you must continue to watch out for the gardener's enemies; the ever-present pests and diseases.

Most of my July General Work notes on this subject (see page 114) apply with equal force. One pest that is likely to be on the increase is the earwig. These can be trapped in small flower pots which have been filled with hay or straw and inverted on sticks among dahlias, chrysanthemums and other plants commonly attacked. Examine the traps every morning. Earwigs will hide in them by day, for they dislike the light. Alternatively, you can dust HCH or derris over and around their nests or water them with trichlorphon.

FLOWERS AND SHRUBS

'Take' chrysanthemum buds Continue to take early-flowering chrysanthemum buds – that is, to secure the good buds you need for flowering and to remove all shoots and buds below them, as I explained in my notes for Late July. A little later in the month exactly the same process must be applied to late-flowering chrysanthemums that are being grown for large blooms. Exhibition varieties are usually needed about the middle of November and it is desirable that they should show their buds from the middle to the end of August. However, if some do show up early you must keep them now, for it is too late to remove

Earwigs can be trapped in small pots filled with straw and inverted on sticks. Examine the traps every morning for any of these insects hiding from the light

them and wait for others to appear. Sometimes early buds can be retarded quite a bit by leaving the side shoots to grow up around them for a week or so before pinching them out, but you must not overdo this or you may starve the bud too much.

Continue to remove any faded flowers and runners Throughout the month continue to cut off faded flowers from all bedding and herbaceous plants and roses too. Also remove runners from violets. Disbud dahlias if you require some big flowers (see page 114).

Complete trimming hedges Evergreen shrubs grown as hedges or topiary specimens can still be trimmed during August, but it is wise to complete the work for the season by the end of the month. Late trimming may result in soft autumn growth which will get damaged by frost.

Continue to bud roses You can continue to bud rose stocks throughout the month provided the stocks work well (see pages 56, 57 and 113). As a rule, however, it is wise to complete rose budding as early in the month as possible, as late buds do not give such good results.

Examine the early buds put in during June and July and loosen any ties that are cutting into the bark. It is advisable to replace such ties with new ones, as the buds may not yet have made a very secure union.

VEGETABLES AND FRUIT

Thin vegetable seedlings Do not neglect to thin out seedlings of lettuce, spinach and other sowings made last month. Do the work as soon as you can conveniently handle the seedlings and water those you leave if the soil is dry.

Make successional sowings There are still a few successional sowings to be made. Mustard and cress and also radishes should be sown as before. A small sowing of stump-rooted carrots made early in the month in a very sheltered place will continue the supply of young roots well into the autumn, while endive and lettuce sown about the middle of the month, also in a sheltered border, will provide you with seedlings some of which can be left undisturbed, while others are transferred to a frame.

Lift early beetroot Beetroots do not improve by getting very big, so lift the early globe varieties rather before they average the size of tennis balls – which will probably be about this time. Twist off the tops without injuring the skin of the beetroot in any way (bleeding is very easily caused and, if severe, may spoil the colour of the roots) and store them in any cool shed, cellar, or room. They will keep better if surrounded by sand that is just moist.

Lift second-early potatoes When you come to the end of the first-early potatoes make a start on the second-early or mid-season varieties such as Maris Peer and Wilja, but only lift a few roots at a time as you require them.

Carefully twist off the foliage of beetroots to avoid 'bleeding' and store the roots in moist sand

Endives are easily blanched by covering them with inverted flower pots. The drainage holes should be covered to exclude light. Only blanch a few heads at a time

Start to blanch endive By this month endive from the first sowing made in Late April should be ready for blanching. Only do a few plants at a time, however, as blanching stops growth. There are several ways of accomplishing this task, but none, I think, better than the very simple plan of covering each plant with an inverted plant pot or a saucer. If you use plant pots, you must be careful to cover the hole in the bottom of each to secure perfect blanching. It usually takes about a fortnight to get a complete blanch.

Continue to blanch leeks This work must be continued as I have already described in June General Work (see page 100) until a sufficient length of blanched stem, usually about 1 ft is obtained.

Feed and train tomatoes In the main, treatment of tomatoes this month is exactly the same as during June and July (see page 105). As soon as the outdoor plants have made four trusses of flowers, stop them from growing further by pinching out the tips of the main stems.

Make a new strawberry bed Strawberry runners that were pegged down early last month should now have made good roots and can be severed from their parent plants. A few days later you can lift them carefully and plant them in new beds. Choose a good open position and soil that has been deeply dug and well manured. Plant the strawberries 1 ft apart in rows 2 ft apart. After the first year alternate plants can be removed if the bed has become overcrowded.

Kill woolly aphid on apples This is a suitable time to take steps to destroy woolly aphid (sometimes known as American blight) on apples. This is an insect pest which infests cracks in the branches and twigs and protects itself with a white, cotton-wool-like covering. Go over the trees carefully and brush methylated spirits or a solution of HCH into the woolly patches.

Young strawberry plants should have made good roots by now so, after severing the runners attaching them to their parent plant, move them to a permanent bed

For larger attacks overall, spraying with dimethoate, formothion or malathion may be carried out.

Pick and summer-prune apples and pears During this month and also throughout September you should be picking apples and pears as they ripen. The test for ripeness with apples is to lift a typical fruit without actually wrenching or twisting it off its branch. If it comes away easily with its stalk it is ready for picking, but if it parts unwillingly, tearing off part of the spur or breaking in the middle of its stalk, it is not yet ripe. With pears the best test is to press one or two of the fruits very gently near the stalk; they are ready if they yield. You should also continue to summer-prune the trees (see page 128), but try to complete the work by the end of the month.

Treatment of vines Outdoor vines will be in various stages of growth and should be treated as described in my notes on pages 78, 101 and 117.

Under Glass

General greenhouse management All the remarks in the June and July General Work notes on this subject still apply with as much force as ever. Ventilation will be needed both day and night; top and side most days, but top only at night unless conditions are exceptional. Always be ready with shading at the first sign of scorched foliage, and damp down paths, stages and walls with increased freedom if red spider mites or thrips put in an appearance. August is generally the peak month for these drought-loving pests.

The earliest batches of achimenes, begonias and gloxinias will have finished flowering by this time, and their water supply should be very gradually reduced so that they ripen their growth and go to rest. Similar remarks apply to early hippeastrums, which will also be coming towards the close of their season of growth.

Take pelargonium cuttings You can take cuttings of both zonal and ivy-leaved bedding pelargoniums (geraniums) at any time during the month. Choose shoots, 4 to 5 in long, that are not carrying flowers. Sever them cleanly just below a joint and insert the cuttings around the edge of well-drained 4- or 5-in pots filled with sandy compost. The cuttings will root most rapidly if you stand them in a frame and shade them from direct sunshine, but they can also be rooted in any reasonably sheltered place indoors or out. Water moderately until the cuttings start to grow, after which they will need increasing supplies.

If you want a batch of greenhouse zonal pelargoniums for late spring and summer flowering, take a batch of cuttings now and treat them in exactly the same way as the bedding varieties.

Continue to take shrub cuttings You can continue to take shrub cuttings during the month, as described in my notes for Mid July (see page 124). Hydrangeas usually root very freely during this month, and do best if inserted singly in $2\frac{1}{2}$-in pots, so that there need be no subsequent root disturbance. They must be kept in a shaded frame without ventilation until rooted and should be watered very freely.

FLOWERS AND SHRUBS

Sow stocks Make sowings of both Beauty of Nice and Brompton stocks for flowering in pots in the greenhouse. The former will bloom from Christmas until February or March, while the Brompton stocks will follow on in late spring. Sow very thinly in well-drained pans or trays filled with John Innes seed compost or a soilless equivalent and germinate in a frame, shading until the seedlings appear, but thereafter giving full light and free ventilation. Prick off or pot the seedlings separately into $2\frac{1}{2}$-in pots as soon as they have two true leaves each.

Keep an eye on the cuttings of shrubs and other plants taken last month and as soon as these start to grow remove them very carefully from the pots or propagating frames and pot them up separately in $2\frac{1}{2}$-in pots, using the John Innes No. 1 or an equivalent soilless compost. Keep them in a frame or cool greenhouse for the time being, shading them from strong, direct sunshine and spraying them with tepid water every day. As they get hardened and root out into the new soil, accustom them to outdoor conditions, and eventually, after a few weeks, remove them to a plunge bed in a sheltered place outdoors. Plant them in a sheltered nursery bed in October or March.

VEGETABLES AND FRUIT

Clear out spent cucumbers It is probable that the early cucumbers will not be worth keeping any longer, especially if you have a good supply of plants in frames. Clear them out when they cease to bear

Choose succulents such as mesembryanthemums and echeveria to enliven any dry hot area of the garden

freely, and take the opportunity to give the house a thorough clean out and scrub down. If you have been troubled with thrips and red spider mites, spray with derris or diazinon for both or fumigate with HCH smoke generators or pellets for thrips only. Manu-facturers' instructions should be followed.

Management of fruit under glass There is nothing to add to my remarks on this subject in the notes for July General Work (see page 119), except that ventilation can be even freer and, once cleared of fruits, trees should be sprayed with water more thoroughly than before.

Treat vines according to growth Indoor vines will be in various stages of growth, according in part to the time at which they were started and in part to the variety. Regarding actual treatment, there is nothing to be added to my former remarks (see General Work for May, June and July). Early vines from which you have gathered the crop should be ventilated freely and sprayed with water fairly frequently if there are any signs of red spider mites on the leaves.

In the Garden

VEGETABLES AND FRUIT

Ripen off onions Onions from the January and March sowings will now be approaching ripeness, and you can hasten this by bending over the leaves just above the neck of each bulb.

Sow spring cabbages Make a second sowing of spring cabbages now in the same way as in Mid July. The reason for this is that in some seasons the earlier seedlings run to seed instead of forming hearts. If you also want to have some big red cabbages for pickling next year, sow a few seeds in exactly the same manner.

Under Glass

FLOWERS AND SHRUBS

Sow cyclamen It is possible to raise cyclamen from seed sown very early in the year and flower the plants the following winter, but better results are usually obtained by sowing about the middle of August and keeping the seedlings growing steadily,

The ripening of onions sown early in the year will be hastened if the stems are bent over gently, so slowing down the passage of food

but slowly throughout the following autumn, winter, spring and summer so that they make fine big corms for flowering the following autumn and winter. Sow in well-drained pans in soil- or peat-based seed compost and space the seeds individually $\frac{1}{2}$ in apart each way. Cover with $\frac{1}{4}$ in of the same soil and then lay a pane of glass and a sheet of paper on top. Germinate in a frame or greenhouse, where a steady temperature of 16°C (60°F) or rather more can be maintained. Very high temperatures are unnecessary.

Repot and start arum lilies The arum lilies that have been resting during the summer since Early May should now be started into growth. If they have been more than one year in their present pots, repot them first. Shake the old compost off the tubers and place them in 6-, 8-, or 10-in pots, according to their size. If they have made any sturdy offsets, these can be detached and potted separately in John Innes potting compost No. 1. Stand the pots in a sheltered place in the open and water very moderately at first, but gradually give more as growth proceeds.

Pot winter-flowering begonias If you were able to root cuttings of winter-flowering begonias in April, the plants should now be about ready for potting on into their flowering pots. These should be 5- to 6-in in diameter. Use John Innes potting compost No. 1. Place the plants on a shelf in the greenhouse and shade from direct sunshine.

Pot freesias Provided the corms are properly ripened, the earlier freesias can be potted the better. The beginning of August is usually about as soon as one can purchase the corms, so if you want a supply of flowers for Christmas, pot up some now in 5- to 6-in pots. You can place six corms in a 5-in pot or ten in a 6-in pot in John Innes No. 1 or a peat-based potting compost. Bury the corms 1 in deep in this and then stand the pots in a frame. Water moderately and shade from direct sunshine, but do not use the lights as yet. Old corms from last year that have been resting during the summer since Early May should also be shaken out and repotted now.

Pot lachenalias For late winter or spring flowering in the greenhouse, lachenalias should also be potted. Alternatively they can be placed in hanging baskets, a very delightful method of growing these beautiful South African bulbs. The method of culture in pots is exactly the same as for freesias (see above). If to be grown in hanging baskets, the latter must be well lined with moss and then some of the bulbs should be placed at the bottom and around the sides of the basket, as well as on top. Use the same compost as for freesias in pots and cover the top bulbs to a depth of $\frac{1}{2}$ in. Hang the baskets up in a cool place for the time being and water moderately until growth starts when the plants will need more to sustain them.

Watering

Holidays can be a problem time for pot plants if they are not normally kept on any kind of automatic system. Nevertheless there are ways of getting round the difficulty. Wicks can be inserted through the drainage holes in the bottoms of the pots and allowed to hang down into a water container – preferably one that is large but shallow so that a number of plants can be stood over it on a suitable slat support which will hold them just above the water. This will be drawn up into the pots as necessary by capillary attraction. At least one firm markets rigid plastic wicks, like little sticks, which can be pushed well up into the soil in the pots. Alternatively ordinary wicks, such as those used for paraffin lamps, will do or wicks can be made of the glass wool used for insulation.

Outdoors it is possible to have sprinklers turned on automatically and controlled by a time switch. Such systems are fairly expensive to install but cost little to run and, if sensibly adjusted, are economical in their use of water. All watering outdoors is best done by sprinklers and these should not deliver the water too quickly since there will then be less tendency for it to run off wastefully or puddle the surface soil. An average delivery of $\frac{1}{2}$ in of water per hour will be excellent.

Wicks poked through drainage holes will take up water from a reservoir and so keep plants moist over several days

Sprinklers are of several different types. There are rotaries which throw the water over a circular area and have the merit of simplicity of construction, oscillators covering a rectangle which can usually be adjusted for size, and impulse sprinklers. These latter produce a spray, usually adjustable for density, which moves around slowly and can be made to cover a full circle or any arc of a circle. Each has advantages and drawbacks but for small garden use probably the oscillating type will be found most satisfactory.

Above left: Rotary sprinklers throw the water over a circular area. *Left:* Oscillating sprinklers cover a rectangular area. The spray area can usually be adjusted in both types

Plants for August

Many of the flower colours in August are strong. It is the season for phloxes, kniphofias (though not all varieties deserve the popular name red hot pokers), alstroemerias, sunflowers (helianthus) of various kinds as well as the nearly allied and equally rich yellow heliopsis and rudbeckias, scarlet lobelias, magenta lythrums and yellow lysimachias, heleniums and hypericums as well as zonal and ivy-leaved pelargoniums, better known as bedding geraniums, scarlet salvias, marigolds and many more brilliant bedding plants.

Amongst all this gaiety one can do with plenty of silver and grey to cool things down and there is no shortage of good plants that can be at their best in August. The grey-leaved shrubby *Senecio greyi* can provide its own quota of bright colour, for it is in summer that it produces its clusters of yellow daisy flowers, but it is also an excellent foliage plant well worth planting on that score alone. There are numerous artemisias, some with leaves so finely cut that they resemble lace, others simpler in design and more upstanding in habit. Anaphalis is always a useful plant to have for the coolness of its grey leaves is accentuated by the little clusters of silvery 'everlasting' flowers. Then there is lavender, which will be flowering in August, and various thymes, some grey-green and others covered in close grey down. These are all lime lovers as also are sages and Jackman's rue, each bringing its own highly personal foliage colour to the garden.

Helichrysum splendidum, a plant better known in gardens as *H. trilineatum*, is a great sprawler if one does not keep it in check but that is easy enough to do with shears or secateurs whenever it spreads too far. Ballota is softer and more downy and almost equally vigorous, but unhappily it is more tender and untrustworthy outdoors in winter except in the mildest or most sheltered places. There is nothing in the least tender about *Stachys lanata*, affectionately known as lamb's ears, but its very woolly leaves do get rather bedraggled in winter when it can be a sorry sight.

A bed of grey foliage plants includes rosemary, variegated ivy, sage, lavender, thyme, senecio and ballota

Above: Summer bedding in a small garden
Above right: A shady pergola hung with gaily-planted baskets surrounds a patio
Below right: Hypericum olympicum

Herbaceous plants Acanthus, achilleas, aconitums, alstroemerias, anaphalis, Japanese anemones, anthemis, *Artemisia lactiflora*, aster, astilbes, buphthalmum, campanulas, centaureas, chelones, chrysanthemum, dierama, echinacea, echinops, gaillardas, geums, gypsophilas, heleniums, helianthuses, heliopsis, hemerocallis, hollyhocks, hostas, inulas, kniphofias, liatris, ligularias, limoniums, lychnis, lysimachias, lythrums, monardas, nepetas, oenotheras, penstemons, phloxes, physostegias, platycodons, polygonums, romneyas, rudbeckias, *Salvia superba*, scabiosa, sedums, sidalceas, solidagos, stokesias, thalictrums, *Tradescantia virginiana*, veratrums, verbenas, veronicas.

Bulbs, corms and tubers Amaryllis, crinum, crocosmias, curtonus, *Cyclamen europaeum*, gladioli, liliums, montbretias, tigridias.

Annuals See page 46 and 33.

Bedding plants See page 123.

Deciduous shrubs Abelia, *Aesculus parviflora*, *Buddleia davidii*, calycanthus, caryopteris, *Ceanothus delinianus*, ceratostigma, clerodendrum, *Clethra alternifolia*, colutea, *Escallonia virgata*, fuchsias, *Genista aetnensis*, *Hibiscus syriacus*, hydrangeas, hypericums, indigoferas, *Itea virginica*, *Leycesteria formosa*, perovskia, potentillas, roses, *Rubus odoratus*, *R. ulmifolius bellidiflorus*, sorbarias, *Spartium junceum*, stuartias.

Deciduous trees *Aralia chinensis*, eucryphia, koelreuteria, *Sophora japonica*, *Tilia petiolaris*.

Hardy climbers See page 123, also campsis, tropaeolum.

Mid August

In the Garden

FLOWERS AND SHRUBS

Cut back pelargoniums Show and regal pelargoniums that were stood outdoors last month should now be cut back. Shorten all growths to about 1 in and then begin to spray the plants with tepid water, continuing this daily throughout the month. The shoots that you cut off can be inserted as cuttings if you need some more plants. The method of preparing and rooting the cuttings is the same as for pelargoniums (see page 134).

Cut back violas and pansies for propagation It is an excellent plan to cut back a few plants of any good violas and pansies one may have with a view to encouraging basal growth which will provide cuttings next month. Cut off the present flowering shoots to within 1 in of the roots. Then scatter a little fine soil mixed with sand and sifted leaf-mould over the plants.

VEGETABLES AND FRUIT

Sow winter spinach and spinach beet Choose a fairly sheltered place and make a sowing of prickly-seeded spinach to stand the winter. Sow the seed thinly in drills 1 in deep and 1 ft apart.

You can also sow spinach beet for use in winter and spring. This variety of beetroot is grown for its leaves, which are used as a substitute for spinach. Sow the seeds in small groups 8 in apart, in drills 1 in deep and 15 in apart. Later, you can single out the clusters of seedlings.

Prune summer-fruiting raspberries By this time the summer-fruiting raspberries will have quite finished cropping, and the sooner they are pruned the better. Cut out, right to ground level, all the canes that have just fruited, and train in the young canes in their place. This treatment will also suit the variety Lloyd George, for though this raspberry is sometimes described as perpetual-fruiting, any late summer or autumn fruits it may carry will be on the current year's canes, not on last year's canes.

Under Glass

FLOWERS AND SHRUBS

Sow schizanthus In order to have really large plants of schizanthus in 7- to 8-in pots for spring decorations in greenhouse and conservatory you should sow now. Sow seeds thinly in well-drained seed boxes, using a soil- or peat-based seed compost, and germinate in a frame. Keep the lights on and the frame shaded until the seedlings appear, then remove the shading and begin to give a little ventilation, increasing this until after a week or so the lights are only used to keep off heavy rain. The cooler the conditions under which the plants are grown the better, for schizanthus get drawn very easily.

Pot calceolarias and cinerarias As soon as greenhouse calceolarias begin to touch in the boxes in which they were pricked off in Mid July, they must be pricked off a second time. Leave 3 in between plants or pot them up singly in 2½-in pots in John Innes No. 1 or a soilless potting compost. Return the plants to the frame, treating them as before and being careful to keep them cool by ventilating and shading. Also, keep an eye on cinerarias in frames. The first batch sown in Early May is likely to require a move on into 5-in pots, while the later batch, pricked off in Mid July, will certainly soon require potting into 3-in pots. For this use John Innes potting compost No. 1 or a soilless equivalent. Spray the plants daily with clear water.

Start nerines Give a little water to nerines that have been resting all the summer and increase the amount as soon as growth appears. Stand the pots on the staging in a sunny greenhouse. Ventilate freely and do not shade.

Restart cyclamen Old cyclamen tubers that have been resting in a shady frame since Early May may now be repotted and started into growth. Clean off all the old foliage, shake most of the soil from the roots and repot in the smallest pot that will accommodate the tubers comfortably. Use John Innes potting compost No. 1 and keep the tubers about half exposed. Return the plants to a shady frame for a few weeks, ventilate rather sparingly, water very moderately at first, but spray the corms daily with tepid water to encourage them to make new growth.

Late August

In the Garden

FLOWERS AND SHRUBS

Prune hydrangeas Most hydrangeas will have finished flowering and will benefit from a little pruning. Cut off each faded flower truss as far back as the first plump-looking growth bud, and remove any thin, weak-looking stems. Of course, if some of the branches are still producing good blooms leave these unpruned.

VEGETABLES AND FRUIT

Start to earth up maincrop celery It is now time to begin to earth up the maincrop celery. The process is exactly as described for early celery (see page 125) except that with these bigger plants more soil will be required. It is quite a good plan to draw the stems together with raffia or soft string before starting to earth up, so that both hands are free for working the soil around the plants.

Lift spring-sown onions Onions sown in January under glass and

Prune hydrangeas by cutting off the faded flower heads to the first plump-looking bud

in March outdoors should now have completed their growth, and there is no point in leaving them in the ground any longer. Lift them carefully with a fork and spread the bulbs out on the surface of the soil to dry. It is a good plan to cover the bulbs with a row of cloches or lay them in an empty frame to dry if there is any likelihood of rain. If there is sun they will dry even quicker this way than when left in the open. After a few days you can shake any soil from the bulbs and store them, either on shelves or in shallow boxes in a dry, frost-proof shed or room, or else strung together in ropes.

Sow onions This is the time to sow onions, both for use as small salading in the spring and also to provide early bulbs before the spring-sown crop. For the former purpose White Lisbon is the best variety as it is very mild in flavour, but for bulb-making choose Express Yellow, Kaizuka Extra Early, Senshyu Yellow or some other variety known to do well when sown at this time. Select a fairly sheltered place and ground that has been well cultivated but not recently manured. Sow the seeds thinly in drills $\frac{1}{2}$ in deep and 9 in apart.

Under Glass

FLOWERS AND SHRUBS

Pot early narcissus bulbs If you want narcissi by, or even before Christmas, pot tazetta hybrids such as Soleil d'Or, Paper White and Scilly White now. Place the bulbs almost touching in pots of

It is a good plan to cover onions that have just been lifted with a few cloches to ensure they dry out thoroughly

John Innes potting compost No. 1 and leave the tips of the bulbs exposed. Place the pots in a light greenhouse or frame but do not use any artificial heat yet.

Crops in Season

In the garden Globe artichoke, broad beans, French beans, runner beans, beetroot, broccoli (calabrese), cabbage, carrots, cauliflower, celery, ridge cucumbers, endive, kohl rabi, lettuce, marrows, mustard and cress, onions, peas, potatoes, radish, spinach, sweet corn, tomatoes, turnips.

Apples, blackberries, cherries, red currants, white currants, black currants, gooseberries, grapes, loganberries, melons, mulberries, pears, plums.

Under glass Aubergines, capsicums, cucumbers, tomatoes.

Apricots, figs, grapes, melons, nectarines, peaches.

September

General Work

In the Garden

HARVEST TIME has come and while the gardener is lifting vegetables and picking fruit, his thoughts will be turning to next year. Spring bulbs must be planted and the new lawn prepared and sown.

As autumn comes the days may still be warm but the nights are cool and the mornings dewy. These local humid conditions encourage powdery mildew, the disease most to be feared during September. It may appear on roses, peas, delphiniums, chrysanthemums, gooseberries, plums and a variety of other plants and fruits. In all cases it covers leaves and stems with a whitish powdery growth. As a preventive, spray with benomyl or dinocap and repeat a fortnight later.

FLOWERS AND SHRUBS

Plant bulbs and corms Narcissi (including the trumpet daffodils), crocuses, Spanish, English and Dutch irises, snowdrops, muscari, scillas and also all lilies, with the exception of *Lilium candidum* (see page 126), can be planted at any time during the autumn, but the best results are obtained by early planting. If you can complete this work before September is out, so much the better. Tulips and hyacinths, however, may wait a little longer, even until Late October.

All bulbs should be planted on fairly rich, well-worked soil, but preferably not ground that has been recently dressed with animal manure. Fertilizers of the right type are quite a different matter. A dusting

Planting depth for bulbs

Plant	Depth	Distance apart
Chionodoxa	2½ in	3 in
Crocus	2 in	3 in
Crown imperial	6 in	1 ft
Dog's tooth violet	2 in	6 in
Hyacinth	6 in	8 in
Iris, Dutch, English and Spanish	4 in	6 in
Lilies (stem rooting)	8 in	12 in
Lilies (not stem rooting)	6 in	12 in
Muscari	3 in	4 in
Narcissus	5 in	8 in
Scilla campanulata	4 in	4 in
Scilla sibirica (squill)	2½ in	2 in
Snowdrop	3 in	3 in

A bulb planter facilitates the job of naturalising bulbs; just put the bulb in the hole and replace the plug of turf

Stem-rooting lily bulbs should be planted deep enough to allow room for the upper roots to develop

of bonemeal, at 4 oz per square yard, makes an excellent finish to the preparation of any bulb bed. The actual depth of planting should vary a little according to the nature of the soil, being rather deeper on light than on heavy land, but a fair average is given in the chart. The depths refer to the hole prepared and not to the soil actually covering the top of the bulb. On the important point of whether a lily is or is not stem rooting, the catalogue of any specialist bulb firm will give you full information.

It matters because lilies that make roots from the base of the flowering stem as well as from the base of the bulb benefit from being planted a little deeper than the others so that there is plenty of scope for these stem roots to develop. The list is too long to be printed here (see page 146 for lilies in pots).

Do all the planting with a bulb planter, trowel or spade rather than a dibber. The latter tends to make a pointed hole in which the bulb hangs suspended, with a space beneath it.

Take cuttings of evergreen shrubs Many hardy evergreen shrubs can be propagated quite readily from cuttings taken during September and rooted in a frame or a sheltered border. The process is similar to that which I have described for summer cuttings (see page 124) except that, on the whole, larger shoots are selected. They may be from 6 to 9 in in length and should be pulled off with a 'heel' or cut closely beneath a joint. Insert them firmly 2 to 3 in deep in very sandy soil. If in a frame keep the light on, but only shade from strong direct sunshine. Water sufficiently to keep the soil moist but not sodden. Privet, *Lonicera nitida*, laurel, aucuba, rosemary and lavender will all root readily in this way, and so will some herbs, such as thyme and sage.

THE LAWN

Sow grass seed Grass seed will germinate well enough at any time during September, though the sooner it can be sown the better, for then it will be well established before the winter. Full details of sowing and turfing a lawn are given on page 147.

VEGETABLES AND FRUIT

Plant spring cabbage Cabbages from the Mid-July sowing will be ready for moving to the plot in which they will mature. You could not do better than follow them on after onions that have just been lifted or place them on the ground that has recently been cleared of potatoes. Rake it clean, give it a dusting of superphosphate of lime at the rate of 1 oz per square yard, and plant the cabbage about 1 ft apart in rows 18 in apart. Later in the month the seedlings from the Early-August sowing should be treated in the same way.

Continue to earth up celery and leeks From time to time during the month continue to draw more soil around celery plants and leeks, as described on pages 125 and 100 respectively.

Continue to blanch endive During the month you should continue to blanch a few endives as they reach a fair size (see page 133).

Complete planting of strawberries There is still time to plant rooted strawberry runners in their fruiting quarters, as I explained last month (see page 133), but the sooner the work is completed the better. If for some reason you cannot get them all planted out in September, leave the rest of the plants undisturbed until Mid March.

Continue to pick apples and pears Keep a sharp eye on apples and pears and continue to pick them as soon as they are ripe. With certain varieties of pear, such as Beurré Hardy, Dr Jules Guyot and Williams' Bon Chrétien, it is even advisable to pick a little before they are ripe and to complete the ripening process in a dry, fairly warm shed or room.

Treat vines according to growth Many fruits will be ripe enough to be gathered this month. The same remarks as those I made in July General Work notes still apply with equal force (see page 134).

Under Glass

General greenhouse management Nights now begin to get much colder and one must be watchful with ventilation. The aim should still be to maintain an average day temperature of close on 16°C (60°F), with a night minimum not much below 10°C (50°F). Side ventilators are not likely to be needed, and even the top ventilators should be closed early in the afternoon if the weather is cold. Shading can be washed off the glass about the middle of the month for all except the most shade-loving plants – some ferns, for example. Spraying and damping down should also be discontinued gradually. There will soon be too much moisture in the air for most greenhouse plants.

Continue the ripening of early hippeastrums, achimenes, begonias and gloxinias (see page 134). Some of the later batches will also need less water if they have finished flowering, but at no time need hippeastrums be kept completely dry. It is an advantage if the main roots remain plump and not actually dormant.

FLOWERS AND SHRUBS

Take cuttings of bedding plants Throughout September you can take cuttings of a variety of plants, notably bedding calceolarias and penstemons, verbenas, mesembryanthemums, violas and pansies (cut back last month), zonal pelargoniums (including the bedding varieties), antirrhinums and violets. With the exceptions of violets, violas and pansies, the method is to prepare cuttings 3 to 4 in long from firm, non-flowering shoots. Violet cuttings are prepared from the ends of the runners; pieces about 3 in long

This is the month to lift maincrop potatoes (see page 153)

are ideal. Viola and pansy cuttings are made from young, non-flowering shoots coming from the base of the plant or directly from the roots. Frequently these can be pulled out with a few young, white rootlets attached. Zonal pelargonium cuttings should be rooted in pots, as I have already described (see page 134), and must be accommodated in a frost-proof greenhouse from late September onwards, but the others are better inserted directly into a bed of sandy soil prepared in a frame. Dibble them in a few inches apart, water freely, and keep the lights on and shaded until the cuttings are rooted. Then ventilate freely throughout the winter, only keeping the frames closed when frost threatens and removing the lights altogether when the weather is mild.

Pot lilies for the greenhouse I have separated lilies from other bulbs for the greenhouse because their treatment is rather different and also because it is not so essential to pot early. If you can buy all the bulbs you need at the beginning of September, by all means get them potted, because lilies gain nothing by being out of the ground. But a good many bulbs come from abroad – some from America and the Far East – and these do not usually arrive until later, so you may have to wait awhile if you need any of these until around Early January.

Lilies are best grown singly, in pots 6 to 7 in in diameter according to the size of the bulbs. Set the stem-rooting kinds (see page 144) well down in the pots and only just cover them with soil now. Then,

later on, as the stem grows, you can add topdressings of soil until the pot is almost full. Non-stem-rooting bulbs are potted nearer the surface and are not top-dressed. Use John Innes compost No. 1 or a peat-based potting compost. The pots are not plunged under ashes like narcissi but are stood in an unheated frame or greenhouse to form roots. Do not use any artificial heat until top growth is several inches in length.

VEGETABLES AND FRUIT

Make successional sowings These can no longer be made outdoors as in former months, unless you live in a particularly mild district. However, it is a good plan to make yet another sowing of lettuce and endive in unheated frames and also to sow radishes and mustard and cress in the same way.

Ripen off melons Melons in the greenhouse are likely to be finished, or nearly so, by this time, but plants in frames should be ripening their fruits and the atmosphere must be kept dry. Do not spray the leaves with water at all and reduce the water supply to the roots, giving only sufficient to keep the leaves from flagging. Stand each fruit on an inverted flower pot to expose it to the sun as much as possible, and cover the frames at night with sacks or mats.

Ripen fruit tree growth Late peaches and nectarines under glass may still be carrying fruits, if so the treatment recommended in earlier months must still be carried out. However, the main effort during September is likely to be directed towards the thorough ripening of growth. This means plenty of ventilation when possible without lowering the temperature too much. The day minimum should be 13°C (55°F) and the thermometer should not fall lower than 10°C (50°F) at night if possible. Ordinary feeding should be discontinued altogether and there should be a gradual reduction in water supply. If growth tends to be excessive give a dressing of sulphate of potash at 1 oz per square yard.

Treat vines according to growth Many grapes will be sufficiently ripe to be gathered some time during September, after which ventilation can be increased and syringing resumed as described in August, General Work. Late-ripening grapes will need a rather drier, warmer atmosphere and steps to prevent mildew will need to be taken (see page 119).

Making a lawn

There are numerous different lawn grasses and as a rule they are used in mixtures rather than in isolation. A creeping grass will be mixed with a tufted grass to give a better cover and bind the turf together, so making it more resistant to wear. Alternatively broader-leaved grasses, such as perennial rye or smooth-stalked meadow grass, may be mixed with narrow-leaved fescue and agrostis species to give a stronger turf that will withstand rough treatment and need little attention. Every seedsmen offers a choice of mixtures of these kinds.

A great deal of subsequent time and expense will be saved if the ground is completely cleared of weeds before it is sown. Digging will get rid of weeds already there but not of the weed seeds. However, if the lawn site is then levelled and raked ready for seeding but allowed to lie fallow for two or three weeks most weed seeds sufficiently near the surface to germinate will do so and can be immediately destroyed by spraying with herbicides such as paraquat or glyphosate which leave no harmful residues in the soil. Then the grass seed is sown without further soil disturbance and covered with a sprinkling of clean sifted soil. It is usually recommended that lawn seed should be sown at 2 oz per

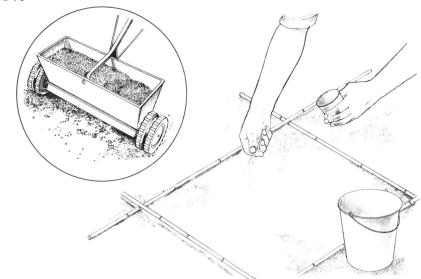

Sow seed by hand, 2 oz per square yard. Alternatively, use a spreader to apply seed at the correct rate

square yard but half this will do if the ground is clean and sowing is even.

An alternative to seed is turf which can be laid directly on the soil after all growing weeds have been dug out since it will itself smother most weed seeds especially if it is cut $1\frac{1}{2}$ to 2 in thick. Stagger the turves in alternate rows. Use whole turves, either 3 ft by 1 ft or 1 ft square at the edges and, if any filling in is necessary, use smaller pieces on an inside row. Beat turves firmly but gently on to the soil so that they lie snugly. Fill in any cracks left in between by scattering some fine sifted soil over the surface and brushing it in.

Beat the turves gently in place and brush soil into any gaps that may be present

Early September

In the Garden

FLOWERS AND SHRUBS

Sow hardy annuals A number of hardy annuals may be sown outdoors now to stand the winter and flower in May and June next year. Sow them thinly where they are to flower and cover lightly with soil. Thin the seedlings out to 3 or 4 in apart as soon as they can be handled, but leave any further thinning until March or April. Among the best varieties for sowing in this manner are annual alyssum, calendula, candytuft, clarkia, annual coreopsis, cornflower, godetia, larkspur, nigella, Shirley and cardinal poppies, annual scabious and viscaria. Antirrhinums can also be sown now, but unless your garden is exceptionally sheltered I advise you to make this sowing in a frame. Give free ventilation, but use the lights to protect the seedlings against frost.

Plant anemones Make a first planting of anemones of the St Brigid and de Caen types. If these are put in in successional batches, it is possible to extend the flowering season. The tubers should be planted 3 in deep and 6 in apart.

VEGETABLES AND FRUIT

Sow cauliflowers In a sheltered place make a small sowing of cauliflowers. Scatter the seed thinly broadcast and cover with ½ in of fine soil.

Start to gather mushrooms If you were able to make a mushroom bed in the open early in Mid July you should draw back the straw covering and examine it now for the first mushrooms. Gather the 'buttons' (young mushrooms) as they form. The bed should continue to bear well into the autumn.

Fix grease bands Now is the time to fix grease bands around fruit trees. They are particularly serviceable on apples, but it is advisable to have them on all the tree fruits just for safety. These grease bands are actually strips of grease-proof paper tied round the trunk or main branches, and also any supporting stakes, at least a couple of feet above ground level, and covered with a tacky substance. You can buy both paper strips and tacky compound from your local dealer in horticultural sundries. Keep the bands sticky until next March. They will catch all manner of insects that try to crawl over them, and are particularly

Fix grease bands round fruit trees and their stakes (if they have any) to trap winter moths and other pests

useful against the winter moth, March moth and woolly aphid.

Under Glass

FLOWERS AND SHRUBS

Sow annuals As I have already explained in Early March (see page 45) many annuals make first-rate pot plants for the cool greenhouse. If sown now they will start to flower in early spring and continue until May. Sow thinly in well-drained seed trays or pans and germinate in a frame or unheated greenhouse. Shade until the seedlings appear, but subsequently give them plenty of light and air.

Pot freesias Make a further potting of freesia corms, if you wish, as described in the notes on page 136. If these are placed in a frame, and are protected from frost with lights but no attempt is made to force them, they can be introduced to the warm greenhouse a few at a time from November onwards and will supply a succession of flowers in winter and early spring.

Pot hippeastrums Pot specially prepared 'Christmas-flowering' hippeastrums. Plant one bulb in a 4- or 5-in pot of John Innes potting compost No. 1 or a peat-based equivalent and place the pots in a light room or greenhouse with a minimum temperature of 10°C (50°F).

Pot on primulas and calceolarias There may be quite a lot of potting on to be done if growth during August has been fairly good. Greenhouse primulas from the Late-April sowing should be about ready for their final pots, 5-in in diameter, while the Late-June-sown primulas are also likely to need potting singly into 3-in pots of John Innes potting compost No. 1 or a peat-based potting compost. After potting, the plants can go back into the frame for a few weeks, but will not need much shading now, and they must be ventilated more sparingly.

Greenhouse calceolarias which were given more space in Mid August must also be moved into larger 3½-in pots before they get starved. All other cultivation details are the same as for primulas.

VEGETABLES AND FRUIT

Make a mushroom bed under cover As I explained in Mid July, mushrooms can be grown at any time of the year but are easier to manage at certain seasons. Just as July is the ideal time for making outdoor beds, so Early September is the best for beds in frames, outhouses or sheds.

These beds will start to crop about the middle of October, just as the outdoor mushrooms are coming to an end, and with a little care will continue well into the winter. The method of forming the beds is exactly the same as before (see page 128), except that in frames the whole area is covered with manure to a depth of 2 ft. Also it is particularly important to cover frame beds with an extra thick layer of straw. The frame lights may also be covered with thick mats or sacking for mushrooms do best in the dark, and the extra covering will help to keep the bed at an even temperature.

Storing vegetables

Freezers are admirable for storing many green vegetables including peas, beans of all types, Brussels sprouts, broccoli (especially the sprouting calabrese varieties) and cauliflowers split into quite small sections. Sweet corn also freezes well on or off the cob and there are many other vegetables that can be tried but for root crops and bulbs the old-fashioned methods of storing are still the best.

Potatoes can be bagged in hessian or thick paper sacks (never in plastic sacks) and stored in any dark, frost-proof place. A well built garage may be quite satisfactory if the potato sacks are themselves well covered with more sacking, old rugs, quilts or anything else that will keep out the cold but they must not be allowed to freeze or even become severely chilled. An alternative is to build a clamp. Spread a thick layer of dry straw on the ground and pile up the potatoes in a steep cone or ridge. Cover them with a lot more straw and then throw soil on top and beat it firmly and smoothly with the back of a spade to form a layer several inches thick. It is a good idea to allow some ventilation by drawing some wisps of straw up through the top of the cone or ridge like a little chimney so damp, musty air can escape.

Carrots and parsnips can be stored in the same way. However parsnips are so hardy that they can be left in the ground all winter if preferred. The main advantage of storing them is that it makes it easy to collect them even when the soil is frozen.

Onions store well in boxes in a dry, cool but frost-free place or they can be plaited together with raffia or fillis in 'ropes' which can then be suspended from the rafters in a dry shed.

A clamp for potatoes showing layers of straw and earth

Plants for September

This is the season of change when the hot colours of summer are giving way to the generally much cooler shades of autumn. It is the month when Michaelmas daisies take over. Outdoor chrysanthemums can bring some distinctively autumnal shades of copper and bronze as well as pure yellows, pinks and rich crimsons and dahlias, too, can be used to maintain brightness in the garden continuing to flower until the first really hard frost brings them to a halt. Pampas grass now begins to unfurl its silken plumes and hydrangeas gradually exchange their summer pinks and blues for the more unusual shades of metallic green and purple which some varieties assume before they finally turn brown.

Many bedding plants will still be flowering freely, the more so if they have been well looked after, fed and watered when necessary and relieved of their dying flowers. This is also the month for montbretias (crocosmia) which have been wonderfully improved by clever breeding so that the new varieties such as Lucifer and Spitfire and the fine species *Crocosmia masonorum* are not only much more effective in flower but have no inclination to ramble all over the place as the common old montbretia can so easily do.

Roses, such as *Rosa moyesii*, *R. setipoda*, *R. rugosa* and *R. villosa* will begin to show their large scarlet heps and there will be other fruits, including many berries, to ensure that this is anything but a dull season in the garden.

Herbaceous plants See page 139, also *Achillea ptarmica*, *Aconitum carmichaelii*, cimicifugas, eupatorium, liriopes, phygelius, *Polygonum campanulatum*, rudbeckias, schizostylis.
Hardy bulbs, corms and tubers Amaryllis, colchicums, crinums, crocosmias, curtonus, autumn-flowering crocus, *Cyclamen neopolitanum*, *Leucojum autumnale*, *Lilium auratum*, *L. speciosum*, montbretias, *Nerine bowdenii*.

Below: Cortaderia selloana (Pampas grass)
Below right: The delicate lacecaps of hydrangea last well into the autumn

Above: An autumn border containing crocosmia, heliopsis, heleniums and *Salvia splendens*
Below right: The huge glossy heps of *Rosa rugosa rubra*

Annuals and bedding plants See page 123.
Evergreen shrubs *Abelia grandiflora*, desfontainea, ericas, hebes, *Hypericum calycinum*, vincas, yuccas.
Deciduous shrubs Abelia, *Buddleia davidii*, caryopteris, ceanothus, ceratostigma, clerodendrum, fuchsias, *Hibiscus syriacus*, hydrangeas, hypericums, indigoferas, leycesteria, perovskia, potentillas, roses, spartium, *Tamarix ramosissima*.
Deciduous trees *Laburnum anagyroides autumnalis*.
Hardy climbers Campis, clematis, *Polygonum baldschuanicum*, *Rosa bracteata*, *Solanum crispum autumnale*.

Mid September

In the Garden

FLOWERS AND SHRUBS

Plant rooted carnation layers
Carnation layers pegged down in Late July should be well rooted by this time. Scrape away a little of the soil and see how things are. If there are plenty of fibrous roots around the cut area sever the layers from the parent plants and, a few days later, lift them – each with a good ball of soil – and transfer them to their flowering quarters or, alternatively, pot them in 4- to 5-in pots, place them in a frame, and plant them out in Late March. The soil should be good and loamy, with a scattering of crushed chalk or limestone chippings and a sprinkling of bonemeal.

Prune rambler roses Most rambler roses will have finished flowering and may be pruned. If they have made a great deal of new growth, much of it from

Carnation layers should have rooted and can be severed and transferred to their permanent flowering positions

near ground level, you can cut out all the old canes that have just borne flowers, but if there is not much young wood you will have to keep the best of the old and simply remove that which is obviously worn out or diseased. If you have to do this you must be careful to cut back all faded flower trusses, together with any heps they may be bearing. Weeping standard roses are pruned at the same time and in a similar manner. After pruning, train the long shoots round the umbrella-shaped training frames, which should be securely fastened to the stakes supporting the plants.

Start to plant evergreen shrubs
From now until mid October is usually the ideal time for planting hardy evergreen shrubs lifted from the open ground. Of course, you cannot do this work if the weather happens to be hot or the ground is dry, but neither condition is likely to continue for long at this time of the year. Plant firmly and stake all big specimens at once. Later on, if winds are very cold and drying, erect temporary shelters of hurdles, evergreen boughs, fine-mesh plastic netting or sacking strained

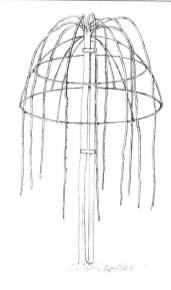

Weeping standard roses are pruned in a similar manner to ramblers. The long growths are trained round the frame

between or around stakes to protect the shrubs, particularly on the north and east sides.

VEGETABLES AND FRUIT

Lift maincrop beetroot The main crop of beet sown in Early May should also be lifted and stored at about this time (and, in any case, before the roots get old and coarse) as described for early beet (see page 132).

Lift maincrop carrots Lift the maincrop carrots sown in Mid April. If they are left in the ground any longer the roots are liable to crack. Dig them up carefully with a fork, cut off the tops and store the roots in a heap in any shed, cellar, or other frost-proof place. They will keep better and be less likely to shrivel if they are covered with sand or sifted ashes.

Lift potatoes for storing The exact date at which maincrop

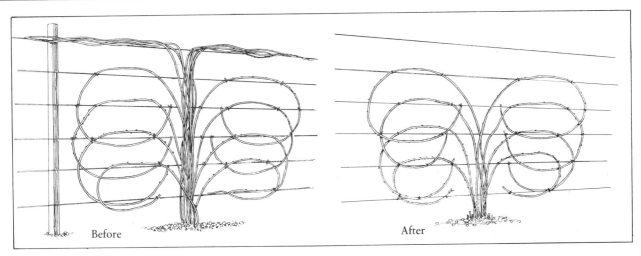

Prune loganberries by cutting out the old canes that have fruited and train in the new growth

---

and late potatoes should be fit for storing cannot be decided entirely by the calendar as it depends to some extent upon disease and also the weather. If much disease appears, it is wise to lift the tubers at once, before they get badly affected. Similarly, if August is very dry at first and then wet later, tubers may begin to make second growth and must be lifted before they have dissipated themselves in a multiplicity of small potatoes. But,

---

Prune rambler roses by cutting out canes that have flowered and any weak growth or diseased wood that may be present

given average weather and freedom from disease, lifting commonly becomes general about this time. There is no necessity to wait until haulm dies down if the tubers are a good size and the skin holds really firmly to them. You can easily satisfy yourself on these two points by lifting a sample root. If you decide to lift the whole crop, put aside any damaged tubers for immediate use and store the rest in thick, preferably brown, paper sacks in a frost-proof shed or cellar.

An alternative is to make a clamp in the open. This is done by placing a layer of dry straw on the ground, heaping the potatoes on it in a steep-sided bank, covering with more straw and then a good coating of soil beaten down with the back of a spade. It is a wise precaution to

draw a few wisps of straw through the soil at intervals along the ridge to allow warm, damp air to escape.

Prune loganberries By this time loganberries will have finished fruiting and they should be pruned as soon as possible. Simply cut out to the base of the plant all canes that have just borne fruit and train the young canes to the wires in their place.

Under Glass

FLOWERS AND SHRUBS

Prick off schizanthus Schizanthus seedlings from the Mid-August sowing will be in need of pricking off. This should be done at the earliest possible moment so that they have no chance of becoming leggy. Prick off the seedlings 2 in apart each way into deep, well-drained seed trays filled with the same compost as that used for seed sowing.

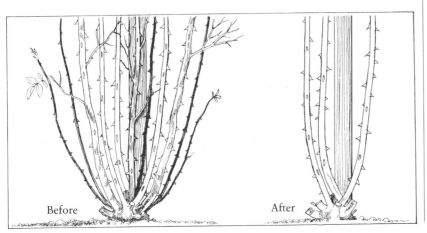

Heather and Conifers

Though a great many heathers are low growing, mat-forming plants, some kinds are much taller and bushier. It is, therefore, possible to plant quite a varied garden entirely with heathers, but there will be a similarity of leaf shape. The monotony produced by this can be completely broken by introducing small conifers. Both heathers and conifers thrive in porous, humus-rich soils which neither dry out rapidly in summer nor become waterlogged in winter. Many heathers need acid soil and this also suits most conifers though these are more tolerant and some kinds, particularly junipers, actually prefer alkaline soils.

HEATHERS

Calluna vulgaris H. E. Beale, double pink flowers, 24 in, Sept–Nov; Kinlochruel, double white flowers, 10 in, Aug–Sept; Silver Knight, grey leaves, pink flowers, 12 in, Aug–Sept.
Daboecia cantabrica Alba, white, 24 in, June–Oct; Atropurpurea, purple, 24 in, June-Oct.
Erica australis Mr Robert, white, 5 ft, April–June.
Erica carnea Foxhollow, yellow leaves, 10 in, Feb–March; Springwood Pink, pink flowers, 10 in, Jan–March; Springwood White, white flowers, 18 in, Jan–March; Vivellii, bronze leaves, carmine flowers, 10 in, Feb–March.

Below left: Calluna vulgaris and dwarf chamaecyparis
Below: Erica carnea aurea with *E. vagans* Mrs D. F. Maxwell and *Chamaecyparis pisifera filifera rogersii* and *C. lawsoniana minima aurea*
Bottom: Chamaecyparis pisifera Boulevard with *Calluna vulgaris* Gold Flame and *Erica cinerea* Pink Ice

154

Erica ciliaris Corfe Castle, pink flowers, 12 in, July–Oct; David McClintock, grey leaves, white flowers, 12 in, July–Oct.

Erica cinerea C. D. Eason, deep pink flowers, 12 in, July–Sept; Windlebrooke, deep yellow leaves, purple flowers, 10 in, July–Sept.

Erica darleyensis Arthur Johnson, rose pink, 30 in, Nov–May.

Erica mediterranea (*erigena*) Brightness, purple flowers, 36 in, March–May; W. T. Rackliff, white flowers, 24 in, March–April.

Erica tetralix Con Underwood, grey leaves, crimson flowers, 10 in, June–Oct; Pink Star, grey leaves, pink flowers, 10 in, June–Oct.

Erica veitchii Exeter, white, 5 ft, March–May.

Dwarf Conifers

Abies balsamea Hudsonia: Dark green, 12 in.

Chamaecyparis lawsoniana Ellwood's Pillar: Blue-grey, 3 ft.

Chamaecyparis obtusa Nana Gracilis: Flat sprays of green leaves, 75 in.

C. pisifera plumosa Aurea Nana: Feathery yellow leaves, 24 in.

Juniperus chinensis Kaizuka: Curling branches, 3 ft.

J. communis Compressa: Erect grey columns, 15 in.

J. media Old Gold: Yellow leaves, wide habit, 3 ft.

J. sabina tamariscifolia: Low wide mounds of grey, 24 in.

J. scopulorum Blue Pyramid: Silver blue leaves, pyramidal, 7 ft.

J. squamata Blue Carpet: Semi-prostrate, silvery blue leaves, 24 in.

Picea abies Frohburg: Weeping habit, green leaves, 7 ft.

P. glauca albertiana Conica: Bright green, conical, 3 ft.

P. pungens Globosa: Silvery-blue leaves, 24 in.

Pinus mugo Mops: Grey-green needles, 15 in.

Taxus baccata Standishii: Narrow gold column 4 ft.

Thuja occidentalis Rheingold: Coppery-yellow, 4 ft.

Mixed heathers and conifers give interest throughout the year

Late September

In the Garden

FLOWERS AND SHRUBS

Shelter tender plants It will be necessary to give some shelter to all tender greenhouse plants that have been outdoors during the summer months. This includes pelargoniums of various kinds (not forgetting the cuttings that have been rooted in pots), marguerites, perennial mesembryanthemums, tender fuchsias, double tropaeolums, tender hydrangeas, heliotropes, Indian azaleas, camellias, genistas, arum lilies and *Agapanthus africanus* (African lily). Any of these that have been used for summer bedding should also be lifted and potted if you wish to save them for another year. *Agapanthus campanulatus* and the Headbourne Hybrids are sufficiently hardy to overwinter outdoors in all but the coldest parts of Britain.

The blue *Salvia patens* and dahlias and begonias used for bedding may be left outdoors until the frost first blackens their foliage. If you have no room for the other bedding plants as they are, you can cut back growth severely so that they do not take up so much space.

A good frame will provide sufficient protection for all these plants for a while if you cover the lights with sacks on frosty nights, but by the end of October it will be safer to have most of them inside the greenhouse, where you can use a little artificial heat to exclude frost.

Perpetual-flowering carnations that have been stood out for the summer should also be moved inside before they are injured by frost. Stand them in a light greenhouse with plenty of ventilation and just enough artificial heat to keep out frost and prevent the atmosphere from becoming damp and stagnant.

Plant violets in frames Long-stemmed and double-flowered violets that have been growing outdoors and are required to provide cut flowers in winter should now be lifted and removed to frames for winter flowering. The frames must stand in a sunny sheltered position and be filled with good loamy soil to within 8 in of the glass.

Plant the violet clumps almost touching one another. Water them in freely, but do not close the frames as yet. Later on, if frost threatens, put the lights on; but throughout the winter give the plants free ventilation whenever the weather is mild.

VEGETABLES AND FRUIT

Thin out vegetable seedlings Spinach beet, winter spinach, lettuce, and endive, from the sowings made in Mid August will need thinning out. Leave the plants of spinach beet about 15 in apart and the spinach itself about 4 in apart. The lettuces should be from 8 in to 1 ft apart, according to variety, and the endive 1 ft apart.

The seedlings of endive and lettuce can be transplanted carefully, either to a very sheltered border or, better still, to a frame. Water them in freely and they will provide a succession to those plants left undisturbed. An alternative method with endive is to thin out the plants now to about 4 in apart and then lift the bigger plants at the end of October and transfer to a frame. They stand transplanting well and by means of this late shifting one can sometimes make use of a frame that is filled with cucumbers or melons at the moment.

Transplant parsley to a frame Lift some of the parsley seedlings from the Late-July sowing and transplant them carefully into a frame filled with good soil with which you have mixed some leafmould and a little old manure. Set the plants about 6 in apart each way and water them in freely. They will provide a crop throughout the winter if you use the lights just for frost protection.

Pick all tomatoes Outdoor tomatoes are not likely to ripen any more on the plants now, so it is as well to pick all the fruits that are showing some trace of colour and stand them in a sunny window to finish ripening. Absolutely green fruits can be made into chutney. The summer crop of tomatoes under glass will also be coming to an end and, in view of the fact that every inch of greenhouse space is likely to be required in the next few weeks, it will be as well to clear these also, treating them in the same way as the outdoor fruits.

Under Glass

FLOWERS AND SHRUBS

Pot cyclamen seedlings Some cyclamen seedlings from the

Outdoor tomatoes will finish ripening if laid on a sunny window sill indoors

sowing made in Early August may be ready for pricking off or potting. Often the seed germinates very irregularly, so, if some of the seedlings are too backward for potting at the moment, leave them in the seed pans, lifting the more forward ones with a sharpened wooden label. The ideal time for potting is when the seedlings have two or three leaves each. Pot singly in 2½-in pots, using John Innes potting compost No. 1. Keep the tiny corms well up on the surface of the soil. After potting, stand the pots on a shelf or staging in the greenhouse, giving them a good light place but shading them for a while from any very strong direct sunshine. Maintain an average day temperature of 13°C (55°F) and 7°C (45°F) at night. Similar remarks apply if you decide to prick off into boxes instead of potting singly.

House late-flowering chrysanthemums It is wise to bring in all chrysanthemums that are to flower in the greenhouse now before frost damages their tender buds. Pot plants should be carried in and set on a hard bottom of ashes or gravel, or be arranged on staging, while plants that have been grown outdoors since Late May for lifting must be dug up with as much soil as possible and either be planted in the greenhouse borders or else be dropped into suitable boxes and tubs. Give the plants sufficient room for air to circulate between them and light to reach their leaves, otherwise you are certain to have trouble with mildew. Ventilate very freely while the weather is mild, but at any threat of frost close the house early in the afternoon and even use a little artificial heat if necessary.

Plant bulbs Hyacinths and narcissi that are to be grown in undrained ornamental bowls should be obtained as soon as possible. Special bulb fibre containing oyster shell and charcoal must be used for these. Put a few good lumps of charcoal in the bottom of the bowl, then spread a little fibre over it, set the bulbs firmly in position, allowing 1 in between each, and only just cover them with more fibre. Water freely and stand in a cool, dark place under cover or they may be flooded by rain (a cupboard will serve admirably) until the shoots are about 1 in in length. Then the bowls must be arranged in as light a place as

When planting in ornamental bowls without drainage holes, spread the bulb fibre over a little charcoal

Place the bulbs on the fibre so they are close together but not touching each other

Pack more fibre round the bulbs leaving the tips exposed. Water and stand them in a cool dark place until they shoot

cover to a depth of $\frac{1}{2}$ to $\frac{3}{4}$ in. Then stand all the containers in the coolest place available. This can be outdoors at the foot of a north-facing wall if the containers are drained. It helps to cover the pots with a 3- to 4-in layer of moist peat, sand, or well-weathered ash as this helps to keep the temperature below 9°C (48°F) which is what is required for the first eight to twelve weeks.

VEGETABLES AND FRUIT

Sow French beans for forcing
French beans are easier than most vegetables to force, and, if you have space at your disposal in a greenhouse that can be heated to a temperature of about 16°C (60°F) you may make a sowing now for a winter crop. The method is exactly the same as for early spring crops (see page 21).

possible. Keep the fibre moist throughout.

Lose no time in potting or boxing all the hyacinths, tulips, narcissi, ixias, gladioli of the *Gladiolus nanus* type, and bulbous irises, including those suitable for forcing, such as Wedgwood, that are required for flowering in the greenhouse or

Topiary, kept trim in summer, is a source of interest throughout the year

house during winter and spring. If the containers are provided with drainage holes use either John Innes potting compost No. 1 or a peat-based potting compost.

Place the bulbs of tulips and narcissi almost touching one another and barely covered with compost. Space the smaller bulbs and corms about 1 in apart and

Bulbs planted in pots with drainage holes can be plunged in the garden and covered with moist peat

Crops in Season

In the garden Globe artichoke, French beans, runner beans, beetroot, broccoli, cabbage, carrots, cauliflower, celeriac, celery, ridge cucumbers, endive, kohl rabi, leeks, lettuce, vegetable marrow, mushrooms, mustard and cress, parsnips, peas, potatoes, radish, spinach, sweet corn, tomatoes, turnips.

Apples, apricots, blackberries, cherries, figs, grapes, melons, nectarines, peaches, pears, raspberries.

Under glass Aubergines, capsicums, cucumbers, tomatoes.

Apricots, figs, grapes, melons, nectarines, peaches.

Opposite: In the greenhouse grapes will continue to ripen and tender plants must be moved inside and tidied up

Tree surgery

Trees require pruning for three reasons. Firstly because they are taking up too much room, secondly because their branches are overcrowded or badly balanced, or thirdly because some parts of them are diseased or otherwise damaged. In all cases the pruning should be done in such a manner as to preserve as much as possible of the natural shape and character of the tree. The only exceptions to this general rule are when trees are deliberately pollarded, as common willow often is to make it produce many strong young shoots as withes, or eucalyptus trees may be to ensure that they produce juvenile rather than adult foliage. Also when trees are trained, as lime trees often are when they are used to form pleached alleys.

For pollarding and pleaching it may be essential to leave stumps of branches which will produce the necessary thicket of long, flexible stems that can be cut or bent and trained in any desired direction. However, for all other purposes this should be avoided, branches either being removed completely close to the main trunk or to the larger branches from which they grow, or being shortened to a point at which they fork so that another stem remains to continue, as nearly as practicable, the natural branch pattern of the tree.

Most of this kind of pruning must be done with a saw or strong lopping shears. Use the latter for the stems up to about 1 to $1\frac{1}{4}$ in in diameter and a saw for the thicker branches. Lopping can be done in one swift operation precisely where the stem is to be removed. However sawing, especially if the branch is heavy or at all awkwardly placed, always needs at least two separate amputations. Make the first 1 to 2 ft away from the final cut; the object of this being to reduce the weight and thus lessen the risk of branch splitting. Even with this precaution an undercut should be made before the branch is sawn off from above. This undercut should be 1 to 2 in nearer the base of the branch than the top cut and should be to a depth of about one sixth of the diameter of the branch. This is to ensure that, when the two cuts are almost parallel, the branch snaps off cleanly with no bark tearing. After the final cut close to the trunk or fork, there will remain a small step of branch to remove leaving a clean straight cut. All branches must be pruned back to completely healthy and undamaged wood.

For most tree pruning the best type of saw is one with a curved blade and cutting teeth on the inner side only. A tapered bushman's saw is also useful for

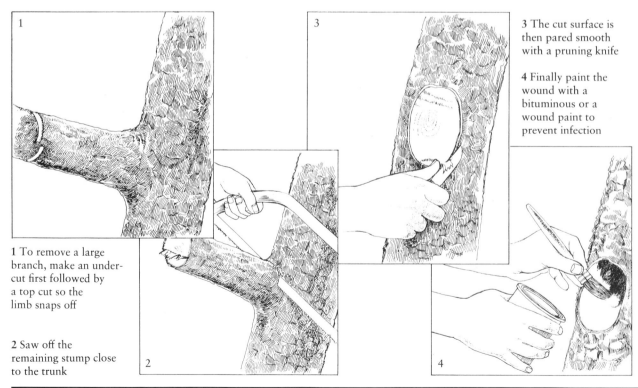

1 To remove a large branch, make an undercut first followed by a top cut so the limb snaps off

2 Saw off the remaining stump close to the trunk

3 The cut surface is then pared smooth with a pruning knife

4 Finally paint the wound with a bituminous or a wound paint to prevent infection

Support low spreading
branches with
strong forked posts

large branches and a small chain saw for cutting
really thick branches that can be reached from ground
level and also for cutting into logs for the fire later.
Only trained persons wearing a proper harness
should attempt to use a chain saw high up in trees.

It is customary to paint all large wounds with a
bituminous or plastic paint that is both weather and
germ proof but if radial cracks develop further
applications may be necessary to prevent fungal
spores getting in. Some tree surgeons also like to
dress small cuts while others think that these heal
more rapidly if left untreated. There is little hard
evidence to indicate which view is correct.

There is no such disagreement about the necessity
to fill large cavities in main trunks due to branches
being torn off by wind or by old age and decay. All
such cavities should first be thoroughly cleaned, all
debris being removed and dead or rotting wood cut
or scraped out. Then the exposed wood can be
painted with a wound dressing and the cavity filled
with cement mortar or a plastic filler itself sealed
with bituminous or waterproof paint.

The branches of trees with a naturally spreading
habit tend to get pulled down by their own weight as
they age and may eventually either break off or lie on
the ground where they form roots and produce fresh
branches so forming a thicket where originally there
was only one tree. This can be prevented in a number

of ways: by shortening and so lightening the branches,
by supporting them on forked posts well bedded into
the soil or by linking them with chains or wire cable
to the main trunk much higher up the tree. If chains
or cable are used steps must be taken to prevent them
cutting into the branches by placing sections of old
car tyre or something equally resilient yet tough
between them and the bark. All such supports require
annual inspection so that they can be renewed or
adjusted as necessary.

Branches can be supported by
chains or cables cushioned
by pieces of old car tyres

October

'Hail, old October, bright and chill
First freedman from the summer sun!'
CONSTABLE

General Work

In the Garden

AUTUMN COLOUR is usually at its most glorious at this time of the year. Unfortunately the richly-tinted leaves will be falling thick and fast so be careful to sweep them all up from time to time during the month. They are a particular source of danger in the rock garden, for if they lie thickly upon the plants they may kill them. All healthy leaves can be built up into a heap in some out-of-the-way corner and left to rot to provide valuable leafmould. Similar remarks also apply to any other soft refuse such as old pea and potato haulms, the tops of carrots, beetroots and other vegetable crops. But if there has been any disease in the plants from which leaves or refuse have come, do not keep them in this way but burn them without delay.

Apply bonemeal and lime October is a good month during which to use bonemeal, which acts slowly and supplies phosphates, and lime. The herbaceous border may have bonemeal applied at 4 oz per square yard, and this will also do a lot of good to bulb beds and to bulbs that are naturalized in grass.

Lime can also be applied now but not where compost or manure has recently been applied. All parts of the vegetable garden can do with a dose every third or fourth year, unless the ground happens to be naturally impregnated with lime or chalk. Use about 8 oz per square yard of hydrated (air-slaked) lime. On light sandy soils ground chalk is really better, but must be given more freely – about 2 lb per square yard. In all cases the fertilizers or lime need only be scattered over the ground. Rain will wash them in,

and if the ground is to be dug or forked later on this will further incorporate them with the soil.

FLOWERS AND SHRUBS

Lift half-hardy flowering plants Begonias, dahlias, cannas and *Salvia patens* that have been growing out of doors during the summer months must be removed to a frost-proof store just as soon as their foliage is blackened by frost. Precisely when this will happen no one can say. Very often it is early in October, but there have been seasons when these plants have continued unharmed until November. So keep a sharp look-out and be ready to dig the tubers up as soon as frost puts a stop to their display. Cut off the dead growth just above the tubers and store the latter in trays and boxes according to their size. It is a good plan to pack them round with dry moss peat as this is a protection and keeps them from drying out too much. Do not water at all, but place the boxes in any dry, fairly cool, but frost-proof place. A good outhouse or garden shed will do well.

Plant herbaceous perennials On light, well-drained soils, October is quite a good month for planting most herbaceous perennials, but it is better to do the work in spring (see page 38) on all heavy or wet soils. Details of planting are exactly the same in either case. Perennials and biennials raised from seed in Early June may also be planted now.

Plant spring bedding As soon as you are able to clear beds of their temporary summer occupants, such as pelargoniums, marguerites, scarlet salvias, begonias and dahlias and have cleared out all annuals that have finished flowering, lose no time in planting out the spring occupants. These may include wallflowers, *Cheiranthus allionii*, forget-me-nots, double daisies, polyanthuses and coloured primroses, together with various bulbs, particularly tulips and hyacinths. May-flowering tulips can be planted together with forget-me-nots or wallflowers, but the early-flowering tulips and hyacinths are not sufficiently tall to stand above these and so, if you wish to have a groundwork beneath them, use double daisies, arabis or aubrietas. Wallflowers and cheiranthuses should be planted from 9 to 12 in apart, according to the size of the plants; forget-me-nots, double daisies and polyanthuses, 6 to 8 in apart. I have given distances for bulbs by themselves on pages 144 and 176, but if they are planted with a groundwork of other plants they may be spaced out more: 12 to 15 in apart will be a good average. The only preparation that the ground will need is a dressing of manure or compost, well forked in, and a topdressing of bonemeal applied at the rate of 4 oz per square yard.

Insert hardwood cuttings Many shrubby plants, both ornamental and useful, including gooseberries, currants and rambler roses, can be increased at this time of the year by means of what the gardener calls hardwood cuttings. These differ from summer cuttings in being prepared from much riper and firmer wood. Select shoots of the current year's growth from 6 to 12 in in length according to the nature of the plant. They can either be cut immediately below a joint, exactly like the summer cuttings, or else pulled off the parent plant with a thin strip of older wood (gardeners call these heel cuttings, but many amateurs refer to them as slips). If you adopt the latter method, and it is a good one, trim off the thin piece of bark close to the knob of wood at the base of the cutting. In the case of gooseberries nick out all the lower growth buds to prevent sucker shoots from being formed below the soil. Insert the cuttings to a depth of 3 to 4 in in sandy soil, in a sheltered place outdoors. These hardwood cuttings root slowly and will not be ready for removal to their permanent quarters until the following autumn. If desired these cuttings can be dipped in hormone rooting powder or solution.

Prepare sites for trees and shrubs All new rose beds and the sites for any new fruit or deciduous trees and shrubs of all kinds should be prepared as early in October as possible. The ideal time for planting these is in November and it is all to the good if the ground can have a few weeks in which to settle between digging and planting. Dig the ground at least 2 ft deep, and, unless it is already very rich, work in plenty of well-rotted animal manure or decayed vegetable refuse in the second spit, but keep it away from the surface for it will do no good to freshly-planted roots. Finish off with a surface dusting of bonemeal at the rate of 4 oz per square yard. If you can also dig or trench any other vacant ground during October so much the better, for, though this work can be done at any time during the winter when the ground is not very sticky, considerable advantage is gained by early soil cultivation. Leave the surface quite rough so that a large area is exposed to the weather.

A fork or spiked roller can be used to aerate lawns that have become compacted

THE LAWN

Turf and repair lawns This is an excellent time to lay new lawns from turf or to repair worn patches in old ones. Cut out the turf from the worn places with an edging tool and lift with a sharp spade or special turf-lifting tool, making all sides straight. It is a difficult task to fit a patch neatly into a curved hole.

When laying a number of turves side by side, stagger them like the bricks in a wall so that the joints do not come together in both directions. This will give a better 'bind' until such time as the turves have rooted into their new soil, (see page 147 for full details).

If your lawn has been used a lot for games during the summer, it will also benefit from a thorough aeration, either with a spiked roller or a fork thrust in at frequent intervals. Mowing will not be necessary anything like so frequently from early October onwards. An occasional raking with a spring-toothed grass rake will remove moss, and you should also use a birch broom frequently to distribute worm casts. If these are allowed to lie on the grass, they will kill it in small patches.

VEGETABLES AND FRUIT

Protect cauliflowers The curds of cauliflowers are liable to be damaged by frost, so look over the bed occasionally and bend some of the outer leaves over any hearts that are forming. This will give them all the protection they need.

Continue to blanch endive Similar instructions to those given in my August and September General notes still apply (see page 133).

Take hardwood cuttings of bush fruit Cuttings of black currants and gooseberries can now be taken. Details of taking hardwood cuttings are given on page 164.

Cut out and replace any areas of badly worn turf using an edging iron

Protect cauliflowers throughout the winter by bending a few outer leaves over the curds

Cox's Orange Pippin and any other apples or pears still on the trees must be gathered in this month and put into store

Prepare sites for fruit trees See details given on page 164.

Under Glass

General greenhouse management Nights are now likely to be sufficiently cold to necessitate the use of artificial heat for the majority of greenhouse plants. The ideal temperatures to be aimed at are about 10°C (50°F) by day, rising to 18°C (65°F) with direct sun heat and never falling below 7°C (45°F) even on the chilliest nights. Damping down and spraying with water are not likely to be needed, except for hothouse plants in temperatures 18°C (65°F) or over. Supply water to plants in growth in sufficient quantity to keep the soil moist right through, but avoid splashing unnecessarily and be careful to keep water off the leaves and crowns of primulas. Air should be admitted through top ventilators rather than those at the side, and it is unlikely that any ventilation will be needed at night for most of the plants. Chrysanthemums, however, must be kept as hardy as possible or they may contract mildew. If this disease does appear, dust the leaves with flowers of sulphur, space the plants out as much as possible to let in light and air and use a little artificial heat to dry the atmosphere.

FLOWERS AND SHRUBS
Disbud perpetual-flowering carnations Young plants rooted as cuttings in the winter should now be forming flower buds, and to get the best results these must be thinned out. Leave only the central terminal bud on each flower stem and remove all others at as early a stage of development as possible. See that the long, slender stems are properly staked. There is nothing better for this purpose than the circular supports made specially for the purpose.

Pot hardy plants for indoors Several hardy perennial plants commonly grown out of doors also make good pot plants inside. They include herbaceous astilbes in a great number of varieties, Solomon's seal and *Dicentra spectabilis*. Pot these now in the smallest pots that will accommodate the roots and then stand them in a frame or plunge them in ashes or sand in a sheltered place outdoors until you need them. They can be brought into the greenhouse in successive batches from January onwards, and if kept in a temperature of about 13°C (55°F) will grow rapidly and soon come into flower.

VEGETABLES AND FRUIT
Ripen fruit growth Your aim should still be to ripen any soft green growth that remains on peaches, nectarines and apricots under glass. Keep the air as dry as you can by free ventilation and, if possible, the occasional use of artificial heat if the air outside is very damp and stagnant; do not spray with water at all unless red spider mites are still about, and maintain a temperature of 7 to 10°C (45 to 50°F).

Similar remarks apply to vines. With late vines that are still carrying bunches it is a good plan to remove some of the foliage so that berries are exposed to the light and relieved from the danger of drips of water from the leaves.

Opposite: Boston ivy (*Parthenocissus tricuspidata*) is a fast-growing, self-clinging climber which will soon cover a wall. During autumn it turns from green to a wonderfully rich crimson

Early October

In the Garden

FLOWERS AND SHRUBS

Protect outdoor chrysanthemums
If any of the early-flowering border chrysanthemums are still flowering well, it will be advisable to rig up some kind of temporary shelter over them. Quite an effective method is to drive a few stout stakes, about 5 ft in length, into the bed at convenient points, join them across the top with a few horizontal bars nailed or tied in position, and then throw some sacking or fine mesh plastic netting over them on frosty nights, making it secure at the corners with string. It does not take much to keep off the light frosts that are otherwise quite capable of ruining all the chrysanthemum flowers and buds.

VEGETABLES AND FRUIT

Plant spring cabbages Plant as many as possible of the spring cabbages from the Early-August sowing. Any seedlings that remain in the seed beds after the middle of the month are best left undisturbed until February.

Complete earthing up of celery and leeks Complete all earthing up of celery as soon as possible. I have already given full particulars in the notes for Mid July and Late August. Sometimes rust appears on the leaves at this time of the year. Prompt removal of affected plants, followed by immediate spraying with Bordeaux mixture, will check it.

Leeks should also be earthed up for the last time. The longer

Earthing up celery should be completed

the length of fully blanched stems obtained the better.

Under Glass

FLOWERS AND SHRUBS

Bring in flowering pot plants If you want to have some arums to cut for Christmas, you must bring them into the greenhouse now. Arrange them in a light place not too far removed from the glass and maintain a night temperature of 13°C (55°F), rising to 18°C (65°F) by day and water freely.

You may also bring in some more freesias, if you wish. Arrange them on the staging and maintain a temperature of 16°C (60°F) by day and 10°C (50°F) by night. Lachenalias potted in Early August may also be brought inside now. There is no need to hurry them at all unless you want early flowers so any temperature above freezing point will serve for them. Both these plants like plenty of light and air.

Rest summer-flowering pot plants Tuberous-rooted begonias, gloxinias and achimenes will be going to rest and can be finally dried off during this month, after which the begonias may be shaken out of their soil and stored in dry peat. Gloxinias

Early-flowering chrysanthemums which are still flowering should be given some protection from frost

are sometimes treated in the same way, but are really better in the soil in which they have been growing. Tap the dry balls of compost out of the pots, heap them together, and cover them with sacks. Of course, both these and the begonias must be in a dry, frost-proof place, but a high temperature is not desirable. Something around 10°C (50°F) is ideal.

Hippeastrums are allowed to get nearly but not quite dry in their pots, after which they can stand in any out-of-the-way place. Similar remarks apply to cannas which are grown in pots.

Vallotas are never dried off to quite this extent, but their water supply is greatly reduced during the winter. It is quite sufficient to keep the soil just moist. Reduce the temperature to about 7°C (45°F) if possible. Similar remarks apply to clivias. This is a good time to purchase and pot new bulbs of vallotas and plants of clivia. Use the ordinary potting compost and the smallest pots that will hold them comfortably.

Pot on cinerarias and stocks
Cinerarias sown in Late June are likely to be in need of a move into larger containers. Give them 5-in pots and the same compost as before. You can still keep them in a frame for a few weeks if you are very careful to close it up early in the afternoon and cover with sacks on cold nights, but they will soon have to go into the greenhouse.

The same remarks apply to stocks sown in Early August and intended for winter flowering.

Pot freesias This is the time to make a last potting of freesias to flower in the spring. Details are as before (see page 136) except that now you will have to keep the frame closed more, especially at night, for there will be increasing danger of frost from now on.

Composting

All soft refuse, leaves, green stems, damaged fruit and grass clippings can be rotted down into a good substitute for animal manure which will enrich the soil with useful chemicals as well as with humus to improve its texture and promote healthy bacterial activity. Decay will be more rapid if the weather is fairly warm, there is plenty of moisture, a reasonably free passage of air, an ample supply of readily available nitrogen and sufficient lime to neutralise acids produced by decay.

Refuse is best built up in layers, each about 6 in thick, the first layer sprinkled lightly with sulphate of ammonia, the next with powdered chalk or limestone and so on alternately until the heap is complete. Alternatively one of the proprietary compost accelerators can be used according to maker's instructions. Heaps should not be more than 3 ft high or across so that some air can penetrate right through them but they can be of any length convenient. If made in bins these should have open slat or wire-mesh sides, again so that air can penetrate easily.

After a few weeks the heap should be completely turned, the outer parts being buried inside and the inner part brought outside. If any of the rotting material appears dry it should be well wetted while turning. At this stage there are likely to be a lot of white filaments, the mycelium of fungi, in the heap and the inner parts may be very hot. This is natural and indicates that decay is progressing normally. The compost is ready for use when it is well rotted, brown and of even spongy texture throughout.

A compost heap should be no more than 3 ft high and should be completely turned after a few weeks so the outermost material goes into the centre of the new heap and vice versa

Plants for October

Now it is definitely autumn colour that becomes dominant in the garden; first the rich leaf colour of early maturing cherries such as *Prunus sargentii*, and also of the sumachs, then the ripening berries and other fruits of many trees and shrubs. It is at this time that one realises how wise it was not to choose all the crab apples for their richly coloured flowers but to include some, such as John Downie, Golden Hornet and Veitch's Scarlet, that look much like ordinary apples when they are in bloom in the spring but are now brilliant with innumerable little fruits which may be anything from rich yellow to brightest crimson or scarlet according to variety.

Japanese maples will be improving in leaf colour daily and *Fothergilla major* will be another less familiar shrub quick to show the effect of shortening days and falling temperatures on its leaves which can produce some of the richest colour of its kind in the whole great autumn display. The foliage of *Euonymus europaeus*, the spindle tree, turns crimson before it falls. Its fruits are bright red, but beware for they are poisonous.

Some sedums, most notably Autumn Joy, will enchant by their slow change of colour from rose to russet red and *Physalis franchetii* will be expanding the bladder-like receptacles which will later become skeletonised to reveal the orange-red fruits within. These are favourites for cutting and drying for winter decoration indoors.

The spectacular autumn foliage of *Fothergilla monticola*

Above: Euonymus europaeus and *Phormium tenax variegatum*
Top right: Physalis franchetii
Centre right: Sedum Autumn Joy and the fronds of *Osmunda
regalis* beginning to change colour
Bottom right: Acer palmatum

Herbaceous plants *Aconitum carmichaelii*, Japanese anemones, asters, helianthus, kniphofias, liriopes, scabiosa, schizostylis, sedum, solidago, verbena.
Hardy bulbs, corms and tubers Colchicum, autumn-flowering crocuses, *Cyclamen neopolitanum, Galanthus nivalis reginae-olgae, Nerine bowdenii*, sternbergias.
Evergreen shrubs *Abelia grandiflora, Arbutus unedo*, calluna, *Coronilla glauca, Erica ciliaris, E. cinerea, E. darlyensis, E. tetralix, E. vagans, Fatsia japonica*, hebes.

Deciduous shrubs *Abelia schumannii*, ceratostigma, fuchsias, perovskia, roses, *Teucrium fruticans*.
Evergreen trees *Arbutus andrachnoides*.
Deciduous trees *Alnus nitida*.
Hardy climbers *Clematis flammula*, roses.
Fruiting trees, shrubs and climbers *Aucuba japonica*, berberis (mainly deciduous), callicarpas, celastrus, *Clematis orientalis, C. tangutica, C. vitalba*, cotoneasters, crataegus, *Euonymus europaeus, E. latifolius, E. yedoensis, Lycium chinense*, malus, pernettyas, pyracanthas, *Rosa moyesii, R. multibracteata, R. rubrifolia, R. rugosa, R. setipoda, R. villosa, Sambucus canadensis, S. nigra*, skimmias, sorbus species and vars., symphoricarpos, *Viburnum betulifolium, V. davidii, V. opulus, Vitis vinifera*.

Fencing

There are many different types of fencing from simple horizontal wires strained between posts to quite expensive and very permanent pre-cast concrete fencing available in various finishes to suit the surroundings. In between these two extremes one has the choice of traditional closeboard vertical fencing, horizontal closeboard, open ranch-type fencing which can suit country gardens well, palisade fencing, again very suitable in some country settings especially for cottages, and interwoven fencing which has the merit of being light, quickly erected and giving immediate protection from wind, which may be important for newly-planted shrubs. No doubt cost of material and erection will be important considerations in choosing the most suitable fencing but the style of the garden and house which it will

protect should also be taken very carefully into account.

All fencing requires good support and the more solid the fencing the more robust and well bedded in the soil the posts must be. Palisade and ranch-type fencing do not offer anything like so much wind resistance as, say, closeboard or interwoven fencing. Concrete or wooden posts may be used, the former having the longest life but usually presenting more initial work since it may be necessary to attach fillets of wood to them to take nails or screws.

All wooden posts should be thoroughly impregnated with preservative especially if they are to be buried directly in the soil. An alternative is to use short concrete posts in the soil and bolt wooden posts to these above ground level. This can be a convenient way of repairing old fences where posts have rotted in the soil but are still sound above ground level.

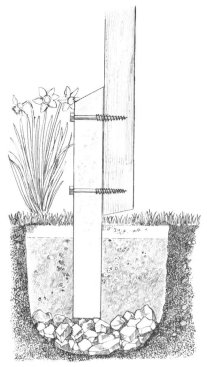

A wooden post that has rotted at soil level can be supported by a concrete spur set into cement on a foundation of rubble

A wide variety of fencing is available so your choice should be governed by the function you wish your fence to perform
1 Mesh netting offers little privacy or wind resistance
2 Lapped boards are more of a wind barrier; the trellis on top allows plants to trail through
3 Weather boarding is widely used for boundary fencing
4 Hurdles make a less formal partition

If posts are to be set in concrete, as is usually best, it may be wise to leave the concrete filling until the main fencing panels or rails are fixed in case some adjustment is necessary. The posts can be held in place temporarily with battens placed at cross angles and lightly tacked to the uprights so that they can be easily removed later. Then, when it is quite certain that the posts are correctly spaced and aligned, the concrete can be poured in around them and left to harden completely. Whether set in concrete or merely well bedded in soil, all posts should rest on a secure base of broken bricks, stones or other hardcore that will allow water to drain away freely.

One merit of open paling and ranch-type fencing is that climbing plants can wind around them or be attached to them with string. Closeboarded and interwoven fences may require nails or vine eyes to be driven into them for direct tying or to support wires to which plants can be attached.

Above: A strong fence post can have vine eyes driven in to support wires for training plants. Note the coping on top of both fence and post to shed water and so prevent rotting

Fencing held in position by means of an arris rail and a wooden post

Alternatively, fencing panels can be slotted into a specially-designed concrete post

Left: Arris rails can be used to form an open boundary fence or to divide off a utility area. If plants are trained through an attractive screen will be formed *Below:* A picket fence still looks best round a small cottage-style garden

Mid October

In the Garden

FLOWERS AND SHRUBS

Lift gladioli and montbretias All gladiolus corms will be better out of the ground now. Dig them up carefully with a fork, cut the leaves off just above the corms and place the latter in shallow boxes, in which they can be stored in any dry, cool but frost-proof place. Remove any small corms and keep these for growing on in a reserve bed. They may not flower next year, but they can be fattened up for the following season. Tiny cormels (spawn) can also be kept and grown on, but this is more of a specialist's job, and is only worth carrying out with new and expensive varieties. Pull off and throw away the old, shrivelled corms that adhere to the bases of the new ones.

Choice montbretias are also better out of the ground for the winter, but there is no need to move the common or hardier kinds, for these will look after themselves outdoors. Some people store the choice varieties exactly like gladioli, but I prefer to replant them, close together, in a frame and keep them nearly, but not quite, dry until March, when they can be started into growth once more. The lights can be kept on most of the time, but it is a good plan to remove them occasionally for a few hours on mild days, just to give the frame an airing.

VEGETABLES AND FRUIT

Cut back asparagus and globe artichokes The growth of

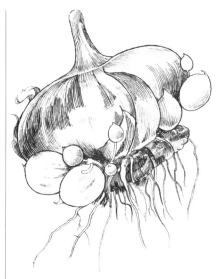

Gladioli should be lifted and the old shrivelled corm and the tiny cormels removed. The latter can be grown on into corms of flowering size

asparagus will have turned yellow and the sooner it is removed the better. Do this with a pair of garden shears and cut off all the tops close to the soil. All rubbish should then be raked together and burned.

The yellowing leaves and stems of globe artichokes should also be cut down. Then fork between the plants lightly and cover the crowns with some sharp dry ashes or a thin layer of leaves as a protection against frost.

Gather all remaining apples and pears It is wise to complete the gathering of all apples and pears now as it is not advisable to let them hang once the weather gets really wintry. Bring them all into store. Apples keep very well if each fruit is wrapped in paper and carefully packed in boxes deep enough to hold three or four layers. These should be stood in a cool but frost-proof place preferably with a slightly moist atmosphere. A shed with an earthen floor is ideal, because there is usually a little moisture rising up. Pears, however, keep more satisfactorily in a rather dry atmosphere; indeed, with them it is really a slow ripening process rather than keeping. Lay

Apples can be successfully stored if individually wrapped in paper and stored in a box in a cool frost-proof place

Allow plants to grow through wooden palings to create an attractive screen

them out thinly in a room or cellar with an average temperature of about 10°C (50°F). Never pile them one on top of the other. Watch carefully for the ripening period as pears spoil quickly.

Under Glass

FLOWERS AND SHRUBS

Stop feeding chrysanthemums It is rarely wise to continue the feeding of exhibition chrysanthe-mums after this date. If feeding is carried on too long, buds tend to decay in the centre. From now on supply them with plain water only.

Sow sweet peas The best exhibition sweet peas are obtained from sowings made at this time of the year. Some growers sow outdoors where the plants are to bloom, but a far better method in most districts is to sow in pots – about five seeds in a 3-in pot – and to germinate them in an unheated frame. Once the seedlings are up they can be ventilated very freely; indeed, the lights will only be needed in very frosty or windy weather. The great advantage of this method is that the seedlings are much more under control and can be protected from excessive cold or wet if necessary.

VEGETABLES AND FRUIT

Prick off cauliflowers Cauliflowers sown in Early September in the open must now be transferred under cover. Prepare a bed of finely broken soil in a frame and dibble the seedlings straight into it 3 in apart each way. Ventilate freely and only close when there is danger of frost.

Late October

In the Garden

FLOWERS AND SHRUBS

Plant lily of the valley This is a good time to make a new bed for lily of the valley. Choose a cool, semi-shady place and good rich soil with plenty of humus. Plant the crowns separately, 3 in apart in rows 6 in apart. The simplest method is to nick out shallow trenches with a spade, lay the roots in these, and just cover the crowns.

Plant tulips and hyacinths

Unlike many other hardy bulbs, tulips and hyacinths do benefit from a thorough drying off and ripening out of the ground, and there is nothing to be gained by planting before Late October. This is also convenient, because they can then be planted in the ground just cleared of summer bedding and annuals. Give the soil a dusting of bonemeal at the rate of 4 oz per square yard, fork this in and then plant the bulbs; hyacinths 6 in deep and 8 in apart, early tulips 3 in deep and 8 in apart, May-flowering tulips 4 in deep and 8 in apart.

VEGETABLES AND FRUIT

Lift and store turnips Lift a good supply of turnips of reasonable size and store them in a frost-proof place for the winter. They will keep quite well in a heap in any dry shed or outhouse, but are all the better for a light covering of dry sand or ashes. Cut off the tops first. If you leave some of the roots in the ground they will supply a useful crop of turnip tops later on.

Crops in Season

In the garden Jerusalem artichokes, broccoli, cabbage, carrots, cauliflower, celeriac, celery, endive, kohl rabi, leeks, lettuce, mushrooms, parsnips, peas, spinach, turnips.

Apples, cobnuts, figs, filberts, grapes, medlars, pears, plums, raspberries, walnuts

Under glass French beans, cucumbers, mustard and cress, radish, tomatoes.

Figs, grapes.

Under Glass

FLOWERS AND SHRUBS

Pot annuals Annuals sown in Early September for flowering in the greenhouse in spring should now be ready for potting singly in 3-in pots. Use John Innes potting compost No. 1 or a peat-based equivalent, and after potting arrange the plants in a frame or cool greenhouse. Water moderately and ventilate freely whenever the weather is mild, but be careful to exclude all frost. Pinch out the points of clarkias so the plants branch.

Similar remarks apply to schizanthus seedlings pricked off in Mid September. Pinch out the growing tip of each plant, as advised for clarkias.

With certain annuals grown for greenhouse display, a better effect is obtained by placing three or four plants in a pot than by potting singly. Examples are coreopsis, limnanthes, mignonette, nemophila, phlox and saponaria.

Pot on greenhouse plants Right at the end of October it is a good plan to finish off any greenhouse potting there may be to do before getting really busy with outdoor planting. It is probable that June-sown primulas and calceolarias will be ready for a move into 4- or 5-in pots, while the early cinerarias, sown at the beginning of May, will require their last shift into the 7- or 8-in pots in which they will flower. John Innes potting compost No. 1 will do admirably, but the loam passed through a larger mesh sieve for the cinerarias than for the other plants. It is no longer really safe to have any of these plants in frames, and you should remove them to a light airy greenhouse in which you can maintain an average temperature of 13°C (55°F).

Any roses or deciduous shrubs in pots such as lilacs, deutzias, forsythias and cherries, that are to be flowered early in the greenhouse, may also be repotted now if they need it; but do this work with as little root disturbance as possible. Simply transfer the unbroken root ball to a larger receptacle and work some fresh compost such as John Innes potting compost No. 2 around it. After this treatment return the plants to a frame or to a plunge bed in a sheltered position outdoors.

VEGETABLES AND FRUIT

Lift and box mint A supply of young mint shoots is usually very welcome at Christmas and the

New Year, and can be obtained very easily by lifting a few roots now, laying them thinly on any fairly light compost spread in deep seed trays, covering them with a further inch of the same compost and bringing them into a warm greenhouse. Any temperature over 10°C (50°F) will secure growth – the higher it is the quicker the roots will grow. Keep just moist at first, but when shoots begin to appear, water more freely.

Lift a few roots of mint and lay pieces on compost in a seed tray, covering with more moist compost

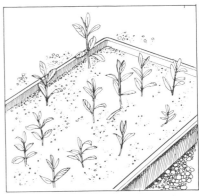

Fresh young mint shoots will soon be produced if the trays are kept in a warm greenhouse

Seed and potting composts

Different mixtures of soil, peat, sand, etc., are required for germinating seeds, rooting cuttings and potting established plants. The simplest are those for seeds and cuttings for which little plant food is necessary and the essentials are porosity combined with reasonable ability to retain moisture. Peat plus coarse sand, perlite or vermiculite satisfy these requirements, are light to handle and are normally free of weed seeds and disease-causing organisms. A suitable seed compost for many plants can be made with equal parts medium grade peat and either sharp sand, perlite or horticultural grade vermiculite. This will also suit many cuttings but for some it may be better to reduce the quantity of peat so making the compost even more porous.

For growing on plants some gardeners prefer composts containing soil since it is then possible to mix in more base fertilizer without running the risk of scorching growth. The basic John Innes potting formula is seven parts by bulk loam, three parts medium grade sphagnum peat and two parts coarse sand. To every eight gallons (roughly four bucketfuls) of this mixture is added $\frac{3}{4}$ oz of ground limestone or chalk and 4 oz of John Innes base fertilizer. These quantities of lime and fertilizer are doubled for J.I.2 and trebled for J.I.3.

However, because of the difficulty of obtaining loam as fibrous as intended by the John Innes research workers, many gardeners now prefer to alter the ratios to two parts loam and one part each of peat and sand or even to equal parts loam, peat and sand. There is also a tendency to use modern fertilizers, such as Vitax Q4, Phostrogen or En Mag, which contain trace elements to make up for the poor quality loam. Manufacturer's instructions should be followed when using any of these proprietary fertilizers. Composts sold as 'John Innes' do not always conform accurately to the original J.I. requirements and it is not easy to find out precisely what formula they do follow. The term 'John Innes' has come to be used loosely for any soil-based compost.

Peat or peat and sand composts containing fertilizers can be purchased ready for use. Alternatively a soilless compost can be made with equal parts peat and coarse sand or perlite to every two-gallon bucketful of which is added $\frac{1}{20}$ oz potassium nitrate, $\frac{1}{20}$ oz potassium sulphate, $\frac{1}{2}$ oz superphosphate, $1\frac{1}{2}$ oz finely-ground magnesium limestone and $\frac{1}{2}$ oz finely-ground calcium carbonate. However, this compost will run short of food after four to eight weeks when supplementary feeding must start. A richer compost can be made with the same ingredients plus from $\frac{1}{2}$ to 1 oz of hoof and horn meal to each two-gallon bucketful but this must not be added more than one week before use. The compost without hoof and horn meal can be stored indefinitely. Yet another alternative is to use the peat and sand or perlite mixture plus a small quantity of Vitax Q4, Phostrogen or En Mag but in rather smaller amounts than would be used in a soil-based compost. When preparing composts at home, it is essential to mix them thoroughly by turning them over eight to ten times as small pockets of fertilizer remaining imperfectly distributed can cause much harm.

November

'November's sky is chill and drear,
November's leaf is red and sear'

SCOTT

General Work

In the Garden

THE EVENINGS are long and dark now and winter is nearly here, but there is still plenty to do outside. Most important is to get the ground dug before the bad weather really sets in. The soil should be workable and when dug can benefit from the action of the weather. Full details of how to dig the ground are given on pages 180 and 181.

As I have explained in the notes for October General Work, the earlier in the autumn ground can be turned over roughly the better. By this time a great deal of the vegetable garden should be free for digging or trenching. The latter is simply deep digging to a depth of two or even three spade blades (almost 3 ft). Very deep trenching can only be practised on rather good soil, but there are few gardens that would not benefit from periodic trenching two spades deep, especially if care is taken to keep the first and second spits (a spit is the depth of a spade blade) separate, and not bring the lower and less fertile soil to the top. Do as much of this work as you can now, and make no attempt to break up the surface as yet. The rougher it is left the greater will be the surface exposed to the beneficial action of wind and frost.

Manure or rotted garden compost can be worked in at the same time if required, or alternatively you can apply slow-acting fertilizers or lime, if not already given. It is unwise to apply manure and lime at the same time, as the latter liberates and wastes ammonia from the manure, but they can be used at a few weeks' interval, one way or the other, without ill effect.

FLOWERS AND SHRUBS

Tidy up herbaceous borders By this time most herbaceous perennials will have finished flowering, and the borders may be tidied up for the winter. Cut off all dead or dying stems and leaves, but leave evergreen foliage such as that of kniphofias. Give the ground a dusting of bonemeal if you have not already done this. Prick over the surface of the border with a fork, but be careful not to disturb roots or to dig up bulbs accidentally. It is wise to mark the positions of the latter clearly when planting.

Gather rose heps If you have made any special rose crosses and wish to try your hand at seed raising, gather the heps now. Lay them thinly in seed trays, cover with a little silver sand, and place outdoors in an exposed position for the winter. It does not matter if the heps get frozen, because this will prepare the seeds for germination in Early March. The process is known as stratification, and is necessary to aid germination of many berries and tree or shrub seeds.

Prune roses The pruning of almost all bush and standard roses can begin as soon as all the leaves have fallen, and be continued as convenient until March. Full details are given on pages 192 to 193.

Pot shrubs for the greenhouse November is a good month during which to purchase and pot deciduous

Digging

Digging is done to increase the depth of fertile soil, to bury, and hopefully destroy, weeds and to mix bulky organic material such as animal manure and garden compost with the soil. It can be done at any time of the year with spade or fork, the former being better if the soil is light and crumbly, turf is present on the surface or a lot of weeds or spent crops need to be turned in. A fork makes lighter work of heavy land and may be preferred where the surface is already fairly clean. Persistent weeds such as couch grass and bindweed should be picked out, not buried.

Plain or single spit digging means breaking up and turning over the soil to the full depth of a spade blade or the tines of a fork, usually from 10 in to 1 ft. It is done by opening a trench one foot deep and about 9 in wide across one end of the plot, turning the soil over into this, spadeful by spadeful, until it is filled and another similar trench has been opened. Continue working in the same way to the far end of the plot where the soil displaced from the first trench is used to fill up the last. Alternatively the plot can be divided lengthwise into two equal parts one half being dug as already described and the other half dug in the opposite direction so that the soil at each end is available for filling the last trenches instead of having to be transported from one end to the other.

Double digging means digging to twice this depth and is a little

Handling the spade correctly will make digging far less tiring. Drive in the spade to the depth of the blade and move it to and fro before lifting the clod out and throwing it forward

shrubs for early flowering in the greenhouse. Hydrangeas, lilacs, brooms, deutzias and roses are all suitable. After potting, stand the hydrangeas in a frame and protect from frost, but plunge the others to the pot rims in a sunny, sheltered place outdoors. Make no attempt to force these shrubs in a high temperature the first winter, but you can bring them into a cool greenhouse in December or January to get flowers a few weeks ahead of the normal season. You can also purchase Indian azaleas in bud now, either in pots or with their roots wrapped in hessian or polythene, and the latter have only to be potted up in a suitable compost to be ready for gentle forcing.

Prune deciduous hedges All deciduous hedges, such as hawthorn, blackthorn, myrobalan plum, sweet briar, beech and tamarisk may be pruned during November. This is a good time to do any hard cutting that may be necessary to keep growth within bounds. The base of a hawthorn or sweet briar hedge sometimes gets bare, but can be kept well furnished with growth by bending down a few long branches and pegging them into position. If the hawthorn branches refuse to bend, half-slit them near the base with a billhook.

Plant trees and shrubs This is the best month of the year for planting all deciduous trees, shrubs and climbers, both ornamental and fruiting which have been lifted from the open ground. The sooner the

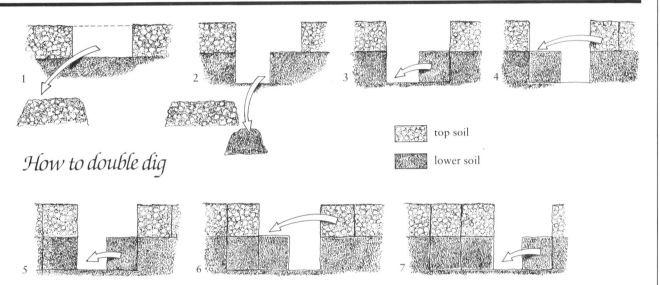

How to double dig

top soil

lower soil

more complicated. The first trench opened is 1 ft deep and 2 ft wide. In the bottom of this a second trench is opened 1 ft wide and going a further foot down. All the soil from these two trenches is thrown out but kept separate so that the soil can be used for filling in the same order when digging is completed. The first wide trench will now have a narrower step in it and the soil forming this is turned over into the deeper part of the first trench. Now another strip of top soil is marked out, but only 1 ft wide. The top soil from this is thrown well forward onto the second

spit soil in the first trench. This exposes another 1 ft wide strip of lower soil which is turned over into the deeper part of the first trench. So the work proceeds across the plot, breaking all the ground to a depth of 1 ft 8 in to 2 ft but keeping the top soil on top and the lower soil below.

Trenching is only likely to be necessary to improve the drainage of very heavy land. The work proceeds much as for double digging except that when each lot of lower (second spit) soil has been turned forward the soil exposed below is broken up with a fork as deeply as possible so

giving nearly a 3-ft depth of cultivation.

Ridging is a method of exposing a large surface of soil to the beneficial effects of wind and frost in winter. The land is divided into $2\frac{1}{2}$-ft-wide strips each of which is dug lengthwise, but instead of the soil being kept as level as possible it is worked into steep ridges. This is done by throwing the middle spadeful forward, the left-hand spadeful to the right and the right-hand spadeful to the left. It is a good method to use on clay soils in the autumn.

The bright clusters of berries on *Cotoneaster* Cornubia provide welcome colour as winter advances. This and other trees are best planted during November

work can be completed once the leaves have fallen the better, but if you have much to do it will almost inevitably be necessary to spread the planting over several weeks, because it is not possible to work either when the ground is frozen or when it is very wet. However, if you cannot finish it all by the beginning of December, I advise you to postpone the remainder until early in February rather than to do it when the ground is very cold and wet.

In almost all cases the details of planting are the same. Protect the roots from sun and drying winds until you are quite ready to plant. Prepare a hole wide enough to accommodate all the roots spread out as they grew formerly and without bending, and deep enough to permit the uppermost to be covered with a clear 3 to 4 in of soil. Cut off any broken or bruised root ends. Then hold the tree or bush in position in the middle of the hole (it is easier if you have someone to help you in this), and throw back the soil a little at a time while gently jerking the plant up and down, so that the fine particles of soil work

down between the roots. When the hole is almost full, tread the soil down really firmly. Then return the rest of the soil, but leave this loose and level on the surface.

All standard trees and large bushes should be made secure to strong stakes driven firmly into the soil immediately before planting, while trained fruit trees must also be tied to their supports without delay. There is nothing that will delay rooting so much as constant disturbance by wind.

Deciduous climbing plants such as honeysuckles, clematises, *Polygonum baldschuanicum* (Russian vine), jasmines and ornamental vines are usually supplied in containers, and this is a great advantage, as it means that one is practically certain to get the roots intact and undamaged. If they are at all dry on arrival, soak them in a bucket of tepid water for a few minutes, then stand them out to drain for an hour or so. When you are ready to plant, carefully tap the plant out of its pot or slit the polythene sleeve, loosen the roots in the pot ball a little and work some of the new soil around them. Be sure to make them really firm in their new surroundings and to tie the shoots up to a support at once.

Ornamental trees and shrubs differ greatly in growth so no hard and fast rules can be given, but as

Planting a tree

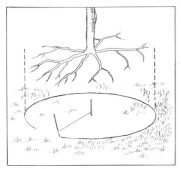

1 Measure the widest spread of the roots and scratch a circle, slightly wider in diameter, to mark the size of the hole

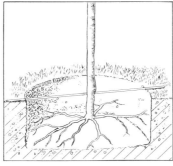

2 To ascertain the hole is the correct depth, lay a rod across the centre and hold the tree in position; the old soil mark should be just below the rod

3 Fork some well-rotted manure into the bottom of the hole and bang in a strong supporting stake before planting

4 Work the soil in well between the roots with the fingers and by gently moving the tree up and down

6 (right) Attach the tree to its stake after planting with a tree tie fastened firmly but not too tightly. The tie should have a pad of rubber or rope to prevent the tree rubbing against the stake. It is important to check the tie at regular intervals and loosen it when it feels tight. Also ensure that all lower branches are well clear of the top of the stake to avoid rubbing, and in consequence, damage to the tree

5 When the hole is almost full tread the earth down really firmly. Then return the remaining soil leaving it loose on the surface

Crop rotation plan

Whilst digging the ground over, think ahead to the crops you plan to grow next year and prepare the ground accordingly. Divide the vegetable plot into sections and move the crops round in rotation each year. For example, potatoes are grown in section B in the first year, section A in the second year and section D in the third year and so on.

A Cabbages, cauliflowers, brussels, sprouts, kale, savoys, and other brassicas. Preceded by, or inter-cropped with lettuces, radishes, and other small salads.
Plot dressed with rotted manure or compost and limed (not at the same time).

B Potatoes. Followed by broccoli, spring cabbage, leeks.
Plot dressed with rotted manure or compost, but *not* lime.
Complete artificial fertilizer, such as National Growmore, applied just prior to planting potatoes.

C Carrots, parsnips, turnips, and beetroots.
Peas and beans intercropped with summer spinach and lettuces.
No manure or compost except in pea and bean trenches. Wood ash or bonemeal forked in. Complete fertilizer (low nitrogen ratio) applied just prior to sowing.

D Onions.
Plot dressed with rotted manure or compost and bonemeal or any wood ash.

a general guide I would suggest that most of the smaller shrubs should be planted 3 ft apart and the bigger kinds 5 to 6 ft apart, and that no trees should be closer than 15 ft. Most climbing plants, including roses, should be at least 6 ft apart. Bush roses must be from 1½ to 2 ft apart each way, while standards should be at least 4 ft apart.

VEGETABLES AND FRUIT

Protect cauliflowers The curds of the early cauliflowers will be forming now and it is as well to protect them from frost by bending some of the outer leaves over them.

Lift and blanch chicory Dig up roots of chicory as required, pack them quite close together in pots or boxes filled with moist peat and bring them into a warm, dark place. New growth will be made quickly and can be cut when 6 in in height for use as a salad.

Plant fruit trees and bushes Full details of planting are given above, the spacing is as follows. Bush apples, pears, plums and cherries should be planted 15 ft apart, but standards of these same trees must be allowed from 25 to 30 ft each. Espalier-trained apples and pears and fan-trained plums, cherries, peaches, nectarines and apricots must be about 12 ft apart. Cordon apples and pears are planted 2 ft apart, and, if there is more than one row, the rows must be at least 6 ft apart and should run north to south for preference. Bush currants and gooseberries must be at least 4 ft apart each way – it is really wise to allow black currants 5 ft, as they grow very vigorously. Raspberry canes should be 15 in apart and in rows 6 ft apart, while loganberries, blackberries and other vigorous bramble fruits need nearly twice that amount of space.

Prune fruit trees November is the best month for doing any hard pruning of fruit trees and bushes that may be necessary (full details are given on pages 196 to 197).

Under Glass

General greenhouse management During November lack of light and a damp coldness in the atmosphere are two of the principal obstacles that one usually has to overcome in the greenhouse. If the glass is at all dirty, wash it thoroughly, both inside and out. Ventilate very cautiously. Open the top ventilators a little for a few hours during the day when the weather is mild and reasonably clear, but keep them shut if it is very cold or foggy.

Keep a sharp look-out for decayed leaves and remove these at once. Dust the plants with flowers of sulphur to prevent the disease from spreading. Avoid splashing water about. Damping down and spraying with water will only be required by a few exceptional things, such as tropical foliage plants and winter cucumbers, as these also require a much higher temperature than the general run of greenhouse plants. Where such plants as primulas, cinerarias, calceolarias and cyclamens are growing together with pelargoniums, marguerites and other stored bedding plants, a day temperature of 13°C (55°F) will serve now, but it should not be allowed to fall below 7°C (45°F) at night.

FLOWERS AND SHRUBS

Attend to plants in frames From now on until the early spring plants in frames will require very careful handling. Some, such as rooted viola, pansy and violet cuttings, sweet pea seedlings and also violet clumps, are quite hardy and only in need of protection from hard frost or heavy rains, which might disturb the small cuttings and seedlings or prevent the clumps from flowering. These need very free ventilation. Lights may be removed altogether during the day when the weather is mild, but should be placed on the frames again before the sun sets.

Antirrhinums from late-summer cuttings and seeds, bedding calceolarias and penstemons need just a little more protection, but are almost hardy. They should always be fully exposed on warm, sunny days and ventilated freely whenever there is neither frost nor very cold wind.

Pelargoniums, marguerites and choice fuchsias are liable to be damaged severely by even a few degrees

of frost, and must be well protected with sacks at night. Ventilate the frames on favourable days, but be careful to get the lights back in time to trap heat against the night.

In all cases, take advantage of a warm day now and then to have the lights off and examine all plants carefully. Remove and burn any decayed or yellowing leaves. Also stir the surface of the soil with a pointed stick to aerate it.

Water sufficiently to prevent the soil from getting dry, but reduce the amount during frosty weather, especially for the tender plants.

VEGETABLES AND FRUIT

Successional sowings The only successional sowings to be made are mustard and cress and radishes, all in a warm greenhouse or frame with soil-warming cables. A temperature of 10 to 16°C (50 to 60°F) is necessary to ensure germination and quick growth. If it is 5°C (10°F) higher, so much the better for them.

Blanch endive Most, if not all, endive plants will be in frames, and you can blanch them as described previously (see page 133), or, if you want a lot at once, by the even simpler process of covering a whole frame so thickly with sacks that all light is excluded.

Ventilate and prune fruit trees All the fruit trees under glass must now be pruned in exactly the same way as those outdoors (see pages 196 to 197). No artificial heat will be required unless some growth is still unripened and ventilation can be really free through both top and side ventilators, the house only being closed completely when the thermometer falls much below freezing point.

Ventilate vines according to growth The latest-fruiting vines may still be carrying bunches of grapes and will need very careful ventilation and heating. The latter will be used to keep the air dry rather than to maintain a high temperature; 10°C (50°F) will be a sufficient average. Ventilation must be given with the same object. In a damp, stagnant, cold atmosphere berries will crack and mould will appear on them. All fallen leaves must be swept up and removed daily. Vines that have finished fruiting are much easier to manage. They can be ventilated freely and will need no artificial heat while they remain dormant.

Early November

In the Garden

FLOWERS AND SHRUBS

Place glass over alpines Some choice alpines, and especially woolly-leaved plants such as many of the androsaces, suffer badly during the winter from excessive wet, which lodges in their leaves and makes them rot. Plants such as these can be completely protected by covering them now with pieces of glass supported well above the plants on notched sticks or bent pieces of wire. Make no attempt to close in the sides of the shelter. Free circulation of air is essential.

Lift early-flowering chrysanthemums Border chrysanthemums are quite hardy in many gardens, but sometimes they rot off during the winter, so to be on the safe side it is advisable to lift a few plants of each variety now and place them close together in a frame, or in boxes which can be stood in a cool greenhouse.

Protect woolly-leaved plants from winter rains with a sheet of glass

Early-flowering chrysanthemums can be lifted and packed into boxes to provide cuttings later on

Simply pack a little light soil between them; that left over from seed trays will do well. Cut off the stems 2 to 3 in above soil level. No artificial heat will be necessary, and only enough water to keep the soil from drying out. Later on, early next year, these 'stools' as they are called, will furnish plenty of good cuttings.

Complete planting of tulips and hyacinths There is still time to plant tulips and hyacinths (see page 176), but the sooner the work is completed the better.

VEGETABLES AND FRUIT

Sow broad beans There can be no doubt that the very best way to grow early broad beans is to sow seeds in boxes in Early February and germinate them in a warm greenhouse. But if you have no such greenhouse it is worth making an outdoor sowing now in a sheltered place. Choose a longpod variety and sow the seeds 4 in apart in drills 2 in deep and 18 in apart for dwarf, or 30 in apart for tall kinds.

Sow hardy peas Some people are very successful with culinary peas sown now outdoors where they are to mature. A rather sheltered position and well-drained soil are essentials for success, and you must also use an absolutely hardy variety, such as Pilot Improved or Meteor. Other details of sowing are the same as in the spring (see page 46).

Opposite: The bright *Hedera helix* Buttercup and *H.h.* Aureovariegata contrast sharply with the dark upright *Chamaecyparis lawsoniana* Fletcheri

Under Glass

FLOWERS AND SHRUBS

Bring in early bulbs Examine the bulbs that were boxed or potted in Late September and placed in a plunge bed outside. A few of the most forward may now be brought into a moderately heated greenhouse, but do not attempt to force them too fast at first. An average day temperature of 16°C (60°F), falling to 10°C (50°F) at night, will be ample to begin with, but may rise to 21°C (70°F) once the flower buds are well formed. Another important point is to make quite certain that the bulbs have made plenty of roots before bringing them into the greenhouse. You can tap one or two out of the pots carefully without disturbing them, or alternatively examine the drainage holes in the bottoms of the pots and boxes. When the soil begins to get full of roots they will start to grow through these drainage openings.

From this time onwards it is advisable to keep an eye on the plunge bed and either to remove forward boxes and pots of bulbs to the greenhouse, or, if you are not ready for them, to place them in an unheated frame, preferably with a north aspect. Here growth can be retarded for a number of

Tools

Many amateur gardeners buy tools that are too large for them. Professionals, trained to use spades and forks and with muscles attuned to work with them, can progress more rapidly with spade blades that measure about $7\frac{1}{2}$ in by $11\frac{1}{2}$ in but most home gardeners will fare better and be less likely to suffer back strain with a blade of from $5\frac{1}{2}$ to $6\frac{1}{2}$ in by 9 to $9\frac{1}{2}$ in. It also helps to have a rather long handle, say 32 in against the more usual 28 in as this means less bending and more leverage. Exactly the same applies

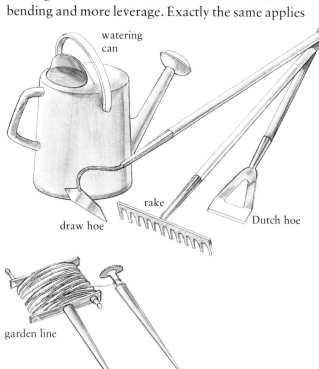

watering can

wheelbarrow

spade

fork

draw hoe

rake

Dutch hoe

garden line

to forks, the tines of which should cover an area approximately the same as the spade blade.

Long-handled hoes of either the Dutch or draw types are essential in large gardens but in small gardens much weeding and surface cultivation can be done more conveniently with a trowel, handfork or short-handled onion hoe. This does mean getting down on one's knees but this need not be arduous if a proper kneeling stool is used complete with waterproof cushion. Turned up the other way this kneeler and cushion makes a little stool on which to sit while pruning roses, tying plants and doing many other jobs.

weeks without any harm coming to the bulbs.

Cut back chrysanthemums As chrysanthemums in the greenhouse finish flowering, cut them back to within 2 or 3 in of ground level. This will make more room in the house and will also encourage the roots to throw up sucker shoots which will make ideal cuttings later on in December.

Start to force flowering shrubs If you want some really early flowers on Indian azaleas, bring the plants into a slightly warmer temperature now – 18°C (65°F) will do admirably – and spray them lightly every morning with slightly tepid water. Various other early-flowering shrubs, such as forsythias, ornamental cherries, *Viburnum carlesii*, *Jasminum primulinum*, and even lilac can also be brought into the greenhouse now if you wish, but do not subject them to temperatures above 16°C (60°F) unless they are really well established in pots.

The same applies to a hand fork.

Some kind of spraying machine is sure to be needed and for most purposes a pneumatic type, holding about one gallon, will be adequate and convenient. In tiny gardens it may well be sufficient to have one of the little trigger operated sprayers that can be held and operated by one hand, leaving the other free to draw branches into reach or hold a card behind to prevent spray drifting where it is not wanted.

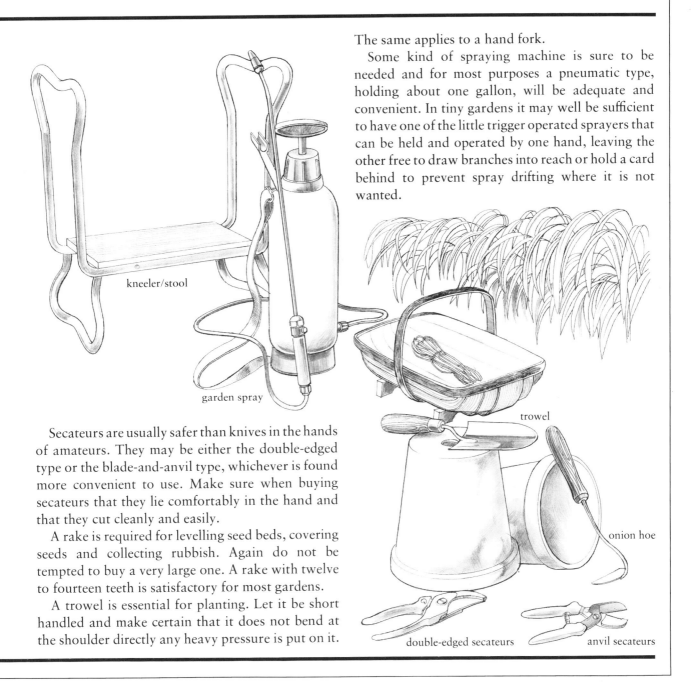

kneeler/stool

garden spray

trowel

onion hoe

double-edged secateurs

anvil secateurs

Secateurs are usually safer than knives in the hands of amateurs. They may be either the double-edged type or the blade-and-anvil type, whichever is found more convenient to use. Make sure when buying secateurs that they lie comfortably in the hand and that they cut cleanly and easily.

A rake is required for levelling seed beds, covering seeds and collecting rubbish. Again do not be tempted to buy a very large one. A rake with twelve to fourteen teeth is satisfactory for most gardens.

A trowel is essential for planting. Let it be short handled and make certain that it does not bend at the shoulder directly any heavy pressure is put on it.

Plants for November

As the leaves fall from deciduous trees and shrubs, evergreens of all kinds assume a new importance in the garden, standing out conspicuously among the bare branches and making new patterns and colour schemes that went unnoticed before. Particularly welcome are all those with golden leaves or variegations for on a sunny day they can seem every bit as cheerful as flowers.

Shrubs that hold their fruits well, as many pyracanthas do and also the sea buckthorn and some, but not all, cotoneasters and barberries (berberis), are also particularly valuable at this time of the year.

Yet even at this late date there can still be fine flowers in the garden, one of the most distinguished being *Nerine bowdenii*. This lily-like bulb from South Africa is far hardier than most gardeners imagine and will grow well in any sunny sheltered place provided it is planted with the tips of its big bulbs just exposed so that they get well ripened by sunshine in summer. *Schizostylis coccinea* is another South African plant that will thrive in sunny places

Pernettya mucronata, with its brightly coloured berries, is one of the showiest dwarf evergreen shrubs around during the winter months and it is completely hardy

Colchicum daendels

Pyracantha atalantioides flava

in all the southern and western counties and many sheltered gardens elsewhere. Colchicums and autumn flowering crocuses can still be in bloom, as can that most beautiful of hardy cyclamens, *C. neopolitanum*, and the dainty gentians, *G. farreri*, *G. macaulayi* and *G. sino-ornata*.

Although interest in the garden may not be all it was earlier in the year, the greenhouse can hold a number of delights. Many of the winter-flowering begonias, such as *B. fuchsioides* and those of the Lorraine, de Sceaux and Optima types, will be coming into flower. *Primula obconica*, and *P. sinensis* are beginning their winter-long flowering period and *Kalanchoe blossfeldiana* will be showing its clusters of bright red flowers.

Herbaceous plants *Aster grandiflorus, Helianthus atrorubens, Helleborus niger altifolius, Hosta tardiflora, Iris unguicularis, Liriope muscari.*
Hardy bulbs, corms and tubers *Colchicum agrippinum, C. autumnale* and vars., *C. byzantium, C. decaisnei, C. speciosum* and vars., *Crocus banaticus, C. biflorus, C. cancellatus, C. kotschyanus* (*zonatus*), *C. medius, C. nudiflorus, C. ochroleucus, C. pulchellus, C. speciosus* and vars., *Cyclamen africanum, C. neopolitanum, Galanthus nivalis reginae-olgae, Nerine bowdenii, Schizostylis coccinea* and vars., *Sternbergia clusiana, S. lutea.*
Evergreen shrubs *Buddleia asiatica* (sheltered places only), *Camellia sasanqua* vars., *Elaeagnus macrophylla, E. pungens, Erica carnea* vars., *E. darleyensis, Fatsia japonica,* hebes, *Viburnum tinus.*
Deciduous shrubs *Arbutus unedo, Buddleia auriculata* (sheltered places only), *Hydrangea macrophylla* (autumn colour on flowers of some varieties), *Hamamelis virginiana.*
Evergreen trees *Arbutus andrachnoides.*
Deciduous trees *Prunus subhirtella autumnalis.*
Hardy climbers *Jasminum nudiflorum.*
Fruiting trees, shrubs and climbers See page 171.

Nerine bowdenii

Rose pruning

Roses are shrubs which have a natural tendency to replace old growth with new. In the wild they do this by allowing the oldest stems to die and decay. In gardens we hasten and tidy the process by removing some of the older stems every year, long before they have reached the dying stage, and encourage sturdy new growth by retaining only the most promising stems. These are shortened to concentrate the rising sap on a few of the best growth buds and this quite drastic reduction should be supplemented by generous feeding.

Ramblers, the pruning of which is described on pages 152 and 153, show this natural tendency for renewal in a most marked degree but it is present to some extent in all roses, climbing, shrub or bedding (bush). So pruning falls into two distinct operations usually carried out concurrently. The first is designed to cut out as many as possible of the oldest stems that are carrying little good new growth, or to cut each back to a

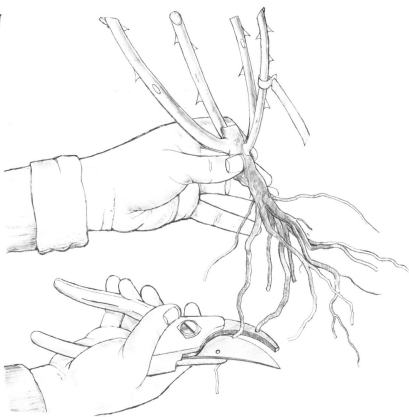

When planting a rose, prune each strong growth down to two or three buds, remove any damaged roots and the old snag of the stock

point at which there is a sturdy young stem. At the same time any diseased or damaged stems are also removed. Old wood can

be recognised by its dark coloured and usually rather rough bark in contrast to the green or reddish, smooth bark of the young growth. Disease shows as brown, purple or black patches on the bark often accompanied by splits or cankers.

When all this useless or

When pruning a bush rose first remove any dead or diseased branches

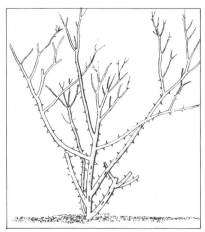

Then cut out any worn out branches and shorten new growths

The bush rose after the final pruning in the spring

second-rate growth has been removed there should still be a lot of young stems but some may be so thin and weak as to promise little hope for the future. These should either be cut out or shortened so as to leave only one or two growth buds to each. That leaves the really good new stems, many of which will have grown the preceding spring and summer. They can be shortened a little or a great deal according to circumstances; a little if there is room for a big bush bearing a lot of medium size flowers or for a climber that has plenty of space to fill; or a lot if one wants the largest possible individual flowers maybe for cutting or for exhibition. In this context 'a little' means removing a few inches from the end of each stem and 'a lot' means cutting each stem back so that it retains only three or four growth buds. Every kind of intermediate between these two extremes can be

applied to meet particular needs, fill available space or suit the growth patterns of different varieties of rose.

In the spring roses start to grow at the top and the buds lower down frequently remain dormant. If stems are pruned very severely it may be that all remaining buds will break into growth. Should these young and tender shoots be damaged by frost or accident there will be

nothing left to grow. So this kind of hard pruning is usually left until March or even early April when the danger of frost damage is receding. Stems that are only lightly pruned will have plenty of dormant reserve buds left even if the first to grow are lost, so pruning can commence much earlier thus spreading the work and also reducing the risk of wind damage to long stems.

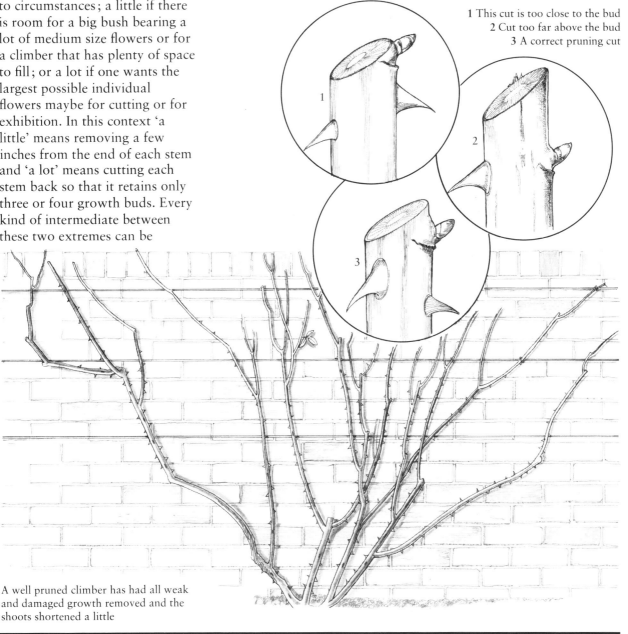

1 This cut is too close to the bud
2 Cut too far above the bud
3 A correct pruning cut

A well pruned climber has had all weak and damaged growth removed and the shoots shortened a little

In the Garden

VEGETABLES AND FRUIT

Lift and store Jerusalem artichokes, parsnips, horseradish and salsify Jerusalem artichokes will have completed their growth, so cut off all the tops and lift the tubers with a fork. Store the larger tubers in exactly the same way as potatoes (see page 153), and put the smaller tubers on one side in a dry shed or room for planting next year if you are sure they are free from virus disease.

Parsnips and horseradish are perfectly hardy, and will not suffer any harm if left in the ground all the winter; indeed, the parsnips are actually improved in flavour by frost, but as it is well-nigh impossible to lift these long roots when the ground is frozen hard, it is as well to dig up a few now and store them in a shed or cellar as a standby. Simply cut off the tops, pile up the roots, and cover them with a little dry sand, ashes or soil.

At least a portion of the crop of salsify should also be lifted and stored in exactly the same way as the parsnips and horseradish. If you wish, however, you can leave a portion of the bed undisturbed, so that the roots may produce flowering stems in spring. These young shoots are boiled and eaten like asparagus.

Lift seakale for forcing The top growth of seakale should have died down by this time, and the roots will be ready for lifting in preparation for forcing. Dig them up carefully, cut off the side roots and lay these in bundles in

Cut any grapes still on the vine and store them in a cool place with their stems in a bottle of water

a sheltered position outdoors in readiness for planting out in Early March. Then stand the stout central roots, each provided with a crown from which growth will come, against a shady wall or fence and heap ashes or sand around them until only the crowns are visible. They will keep safely like this all the winter, and you can pot up and force a few at a time as you require them.

Start to force rhubarb Rhubarb may also be forced from now onwards throughout the winter. The method of forcing is different from that of seakale. Strong roots are lifted and allowed to lie on the ground unprotected for a day or so. If the weather is frosty so much the better; growth will be all the quicker for this exposure. Details of forcing are given below.

Prune vines Outdoor vines may

be pruned as soon as they have shed their leaves. The method is the same as for those grown under glass and details are given on the opposite page.

Under Glass

Force seakale Pot three or four roots in a 6- or 7-in pot, using any old potting or seed compost, bring them into a warm greenhouse and cover with another empty pot, blocking up the drainage hole in the bottom of this with a piece of slate or turf. The crowns must be in absolute darkness. Water moderately. In a temperature of about 16°C (60°F) growth will be rapid. When the blanched shoots are about 9 in long you can cut them. The forced roots are useless and should be thrown away.

Force rhubarb After rhubarb roots have lain outdoors for a few days, exposed to the cold, take the roots into a warm greenhouse, stand them quite close together in deep boxes or on the floor under the staging, pack soil between them and keep them absolutely dark by fixing up a screen of sacking, linoleum or boards. Water moderately and maintain a temperature of 13 to 24°C (55 to 75°F). A few more roots should be brought in every fortnight or so.

Roots started at once and kept in a temperature of about 20°C (68°F) will give good sticks at Christmas.

Cut and store grapes There is not much point in trying to keep

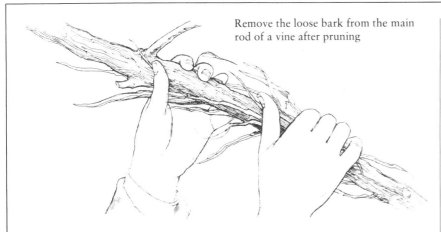

Remove the loose bark from the main rod of a vine after pruning

the bunches of late grapes hanging on the vines any longer, especially if you have a cool, dark and dry room in which you can store them. Cut each bunch with 9 in or more of the ripened lateral from which it is hanging, insert the lower end of this into a bottle nearly filled with clean, soft water and containing a few pieces of charcoal to keep it sweet, and then stand the bottle in a rack or on a shelf tilting it sufficiently to prevent the berries

Lower the rods of grape vines so they hang horizontally during the winter

from coming into contact with it, or, for that matter, anything else.

Prune early and maincrop vines
By this time the leaves should have fallen from early and maincrop vines, and the sooner most of them are pruned the better. Outdoor vines may also be pruned. For both types pruned at this time the method is the same. Cut back every lateral (side) growth to within one, or at most two, dormant growth buds of the main rod or spur. Then rub or pull all loose shreds of bark from the main rods and

paint the latter thoroughly with a mixture of equal parts of soft soap and flowers of sulphur with added water to make it the consistency of paint. Be particularly careful to work this in to all rough, gnarled places round the spurs where insects may be hiding.

After pruning and cleaning, cut the ties holding the main rod and lower it on long pieces of cord so that it hangs more or less parallel with the floor. This will discourage sap from rushing up to the top when the vine is restarted and will ensure an even 'break' all over.

Crops in Season

In the garden Jerusalem artichokes, Brussels sprouts, cabbage, cauliflower, celeriac, kohl rabi, leeks, parsnips, spinach.

Under glass French beans, cucumbers, endive, lettuce, mustard and cress, radish.
  Grapes.

Fruit tree pruning

The pruning of fruit trees falls into two broad classes – one known as renewal pruning and the other as spur pruning. Raspberries and blackberries are examples of renewal pruning at its most extreme since, of their own accord, these fruits lose all their old canes (those that have already carried a crop) each winter leaving it to young canes to carry on the following summer. All that the gardener does is to anticipate this natural process by a few weeks, cutting out the old canes as soon as possible after the crop has been gathered and at the same time thinning out the young canes, if there are a lot of them, to a reasonable number that can be trained to the wires or other supports.

A modified version of this kind of pruning is used for black currants which do not actually lose their old growth naturally but do bear all their best fruits on young stems made the previous summer. So to help this natural process and encourage the sturdiest possible new growth, the old fruiting stems are removed annually as soon as convenient after the crop has been gathered. Wherever possible they are cut out at a point where a good young stem is growing from them but if there is no young growth on a particular branch it is cut to within an inch or so of the base in the hope that this will force it to make new growth the following year.

A further modification of renewal pruning is used for peaches, nectarines and Morello cherries all of which fruit best on young side growths formed from the main branches the previous year. So again the old fruiting side growths are cut out when the crop has been harvested and the young ones are retained to crop the following year. However, in their case this simple autumn or winter pruning is usually supplemented by summer thinning to reduce the young stems to a number that can be accommodated without overcrowding. When these trees are fan trained, as they often are, this, in practice, usually results in three young stems being retained for each currently fruit-bearing stem. One near or at its tip to draw sap through it, another near the middle, partly for the same purpose partly as an insurance against accidents, and the third as near the base as possible. This latter will be the one retained to replace the fruiting stem when it is cut out in the autumn or winter.

Spur pruning is used for apples, pears, plums, sweet cherries, gooseberries and red and white currants, all of which fruit on stems that are two years or more old. Moreover the fruit buds usually proliferate, forming quite large clusters in time which are known as spurs, or they may be produced on short side shoots. Therefore the aim of pruning is to maintain a plentiful supply of healthy growth of medium age well supplied with fruit buds and spurs. Very old branches that are losing vigour are cut out and so are branches that are either growing so tall that they are out of convenient reach or have been so weighed down by years of cropping that they are dragging on the ground or making it difficult to work beneath the trees.

Renewal pruning of a peach involves removing the old fruited wood and leaving a replacement shoot that is trained in to bear fruit during the coming year

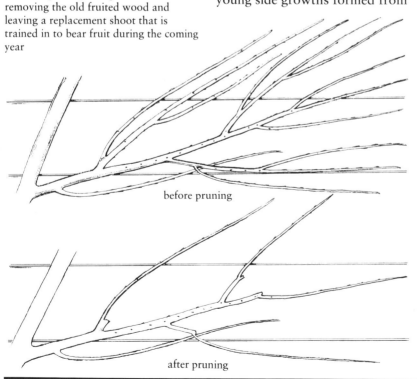

before pruning

after pruning

before pruning

after pruning

Pruning an established black currant bush using the renewal system. The old wood that has borne fruit is cut out leaving new fresh growth to produce fruit in the summer

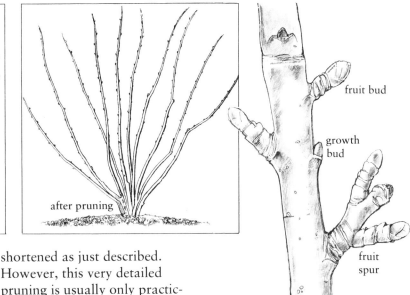

fruit bud

growth bud

fruit spur

A shoot of apple showing a fruit spur and the different buds

Fruit bud and spur formation are encouraged by shortening side growths (known as laterals) quite a lot, usually eventually to 1 or 2 in. Ideally this is done in two stages, the first between June and August when side shoots are shortened to about five well developed leaves each and the second in autumn or winter when they are further shortened as just described. However, this very detailed pruning is usually only practicable on small trees, espaliers, fans or cordons. Larger bushes and standards are simply given a good thinning out of branches to prevent overcrowding, particularly in the centre of the tree. The multitudinous side shoots are left more or less unpruned to form fruit buds naturally but this is largely conditioned by time and feasibility. If it is possible to summer and winter prune side growths of large spur-bearing trees there is no reason why it should not be done.

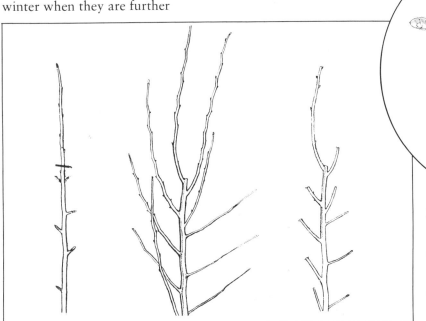

Establishing a spur system by pruning involves cutting back the leader to encourage side shooting. These side shoots are shortened to produce more fruit buds
Far left: Shorten second-year leader
Centre: Third-year growth before pruning
Left: Third-year growth after pruning
Circled: An established spur

December

'In a drear-nighted December,
Too happy, happy tree,
Thy branches ne'er remember
Their green felicity'

KEATS

General Work

In the Garden

One of the most enjoyable activities of this month is to settle into an armchair in front of the fire with the new season's catalogues and plan what you are going to grow next year. However, if you still have any trenching or digging still to be done this may be continued throughout December, as and when the weather allows. But it is unwise to do this work when there is snow on the ground or when it is frozen or very wet.

Sterilize infected soil This is a task which can be done at any time of the year, but it is essential that the soil should have no plants growing in it. Any ground which has been sterilized by chemical means should remain unused for a month or so after treatment, so December is often the most convenient month for this work. The purpose of sterilization is to rid the soil of all harmful organisms, including insect pests, their eggs and the spores of fungi, which cause diseases. There is no point in treating soil that is in good order, but if diseases or pests have been rampant, the work involved in sterilization may be well repaid.

Chemical sterilization is commonly carried out either with formaldehyde or cresylic acid but various proprietary formulations are available. Formalin, which has a formaldehyde content of 38 to 40%, is diluted with forty-nine times its own bulk of water and the soil is then soaked thoroughly with it. Soil can be treated in situ, but a more effective method is to spread it out on a hard floor, soak it, and then immediately draw it into a heap and cover with

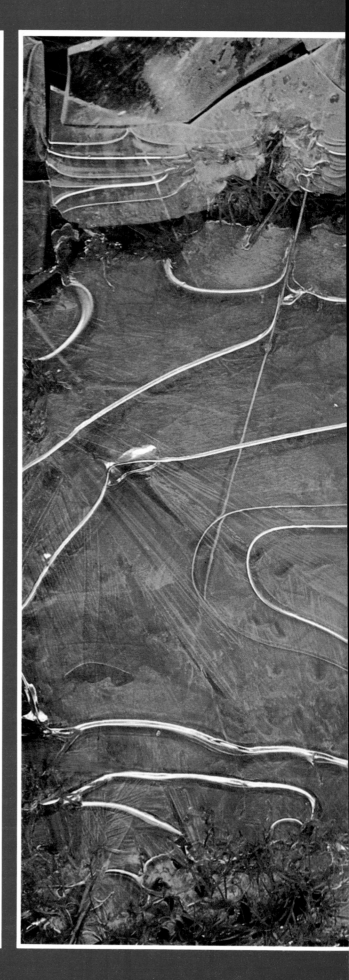

Chemical sterilization of soil is a relatively easy operation. The soil is spread out on a hard surface outside. The sterilant is applied with a watering can and the soil covered with polythene sheeting or tarpaulin and left for the required period of time

sacks or polythene sheeting to trap the fumes. You must not use the soil until it has lost all smell of the chemical.

Similar methods are adopted with cresylic acid. This you can purchase in various strengths, but that

Greenhouse cleaning

In winter light is as critical as warmth for the health and well-being of many plants grown under glass. It is also the time when grime and green slime are most likely to accumulate on the glass so it is important to clean it off, the simplest way usually being to use warm water containing a little detergent applied to the glass with a long handled mop or squeegee.

It is as necessary to clean the inside of the greenhouse as the outside and here it may be wise to add a little disinfectant to the water to kill any insects, insect eggs or germs of any kind that may be harbouring there. Be careful to clean the interspaces where one pane of glass overlaps another for these are often filled with dirt. It is not easy to do but a thin plastic plant label can be a

useful aid if slipped between the panes and worked backwards and forwards to dislodge the grime.

Woodwork and metalwork should be thoroughly cleaned at the same time and, if necessary, woodwork can be treated with a preservative such as copper naphthenate that is harmless to plants. Do not use creosote, even if the greenhouse is empty, as fumes may be given off later when the house gets hot and they can be deadly to plants.

If possible all soil in borders should be changed annually to a depth of at least 10 in. It is almost certain to contain some harmful organisms probably including eelworms. Replace with the best garden soil available or with good loam if any can be found. It is a commodity in short supply nowadays.

Whether it will be possible to overhaul heating apparatus in winter depends on whether the house is being used or is empty. If the former it will be better to leave the work until much later when artificial heat can be

Clean the area where panes of glass overlap with a thin plant label

known as 'pale straw-coloured carbolic acid' is most suitable. Dilute it with thirty-nine times its own bulk of water.

Another method of sterilizing soil is by heat. Steam can be used for supplying this and is the best medium, since it will neither char the soil nor make it too wet. The amount of soil treated at any one time must be sufficiently small to allow the temperature to reach 100°C (212°F) in about thirty to forty minutes. This temperature is maintained for ten minutes, when the soil is removed immediately and allowed to cool down rapidly by being spread out thinly. The soil, unlike that which has been chemically treated, can be used for any purpose as soon as it has cooled, but as the treatment results in a reduction of fertility for a while, it is advisable to counteract this by adding suitable chemicals such as John Innes base fertilizer.

Small and large proprietary steam sterilizers can be obtained but it is also possible to sterilize soil in a saucepan using boiling water. The soil should be fairly dry to start with and for a 5-pint saucepan, about $\frac{1}{2}$ pint of water is sufficient. As soon as it boils, fill the saucepan with soil to within $\frac{1}{2}$ in of the top and boil for seven minutes with the lid on. Leave it to stand for seven minutes, then spread it out to cool.

You should note that soil fumigation is a rather different matter from sterilization as it is directed solely at insect pests, for example, wireworms, leatherjackets and millepedes, and has no effect upon diseases. Flaked naphthalene is commonly used for the purpose, and is dug into any vacant ground at the rate of 4 oz per square yard. There are also a number of proprietary soil fumigants which must be used strictly in accordance with the manufacturers' instructions.

dispensed with, but an annual check up at some time is desirable to make sure that everything is clean and in good working order. Be particularly careful to check thermostats to make certain that they are working freely and responding correctly to the control knob. After months of disuse they may have become corroded or otherwise impeded so that they do not function properly.

If there are any electrical difficulties it is usually best to take the apparatus to a specialist.

Precisely the same applies to misting apparatus in propagators particularly when solenoid valves become stuck. Moisture sensors can be rendered inoperative by deposits of lime but these are easily removed with very dilute acid. Spray nozzles that are blocked can usually be blown clear.

Pots not in use should be well washed in water with a little detergent and disinfectant but rinse them out well in clear water so that no trace of chemical remains to inhibit growth.

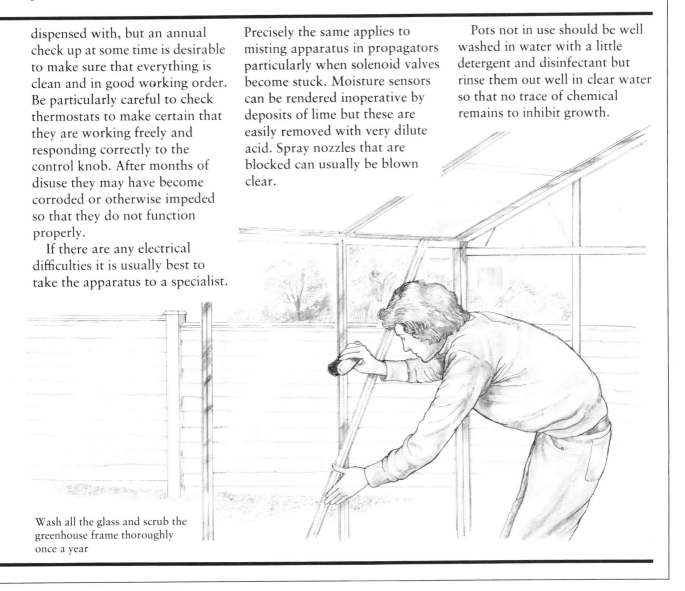

Wash all the glass and scrub the greenhouse frame thoroughly once a year

Protect tender shrubs with a chicken wire frame loosely stuffed with straw or bracken

FLOWERS AND SHRUBS

Protect tender plants Very little damage is done by early autumn frosts to such slightly tender plants and shrubs as gunneras, eremuruses, escallonias, evergreen ceanothuses and crinodendrons. But, as the winter sets in with greater rigour, it is advisable to provide some protection for these if they happen to be growing in rather exposed places. Wall shrubs and climbers which are in any way tender can be protected efficiently and without difficulty by hanging sacking in front of them or fixing wattle hurdles or wire-netting close up to them and then stuffing any intervening space with straw or bracken. The plant must not be entirely shut off from air. Whatever form of protection you use, always leave the top open so that foul air and moisture may escape.

For slightly tender herbaceous plants, the crowns of which may be injured by frost, the best method of protection is to place a piece of fine-mesh galvanized wire netting over each, heap dry leaves, straw, or bracken on this, and cover with another piece of netting pegged down at the corners.

Christmas roses (hellebores) are not in the least tender, but they will be forming their flower stems now and the blooms will benefit from a little pro-

tection to keep off heavy rain and mud splashes. Cover them with spare frame lights supported on bricks at the four corners, or with cloches.

Prune Clematis jackmanii Clematises of the Jackmanii and nearly allied Viticella classes may be pruned. It is not absolutely essential to do the work at once, so long as it is completed before the end of February, but in the interests of tidiness the sooner it is done the better. There are two methods of pruning. One is to cut all growth back to within about 1 ft of the ground every year, so keeping the plants fairly small, and the other is to allow a framework of main vines to form and then prune each side growth back to one joint.

Prune roses Continue to prune bush and standard roses (see pages 192 to 193).

VEGETABLES AND FRUIT

Continue to protect cauliflower From time to time during the month you must continue to bend down leaves over the curds of cauliflower as they form.

Protect celery Late celery may be injured by very hard frosts or heavy rain, so it is good policy to cover the ridges at this time with a little dry straw or bracken held in position with some wire-netting pegged down to the soil, and also to dig a shallow trench on each side of the ridge to allow surplus surface water to run off.

Continue to prune fruit trees Throughout the month you can proceed with the pruning of fruit trees and bushes of all kinds (see pages 196 to 197). It is a mistaken notion that fruit trees must not be pruned when the weather is frosty.

Under Glass

FLOWERS AND SHRUBS

Bring bulbs inside Bring further batches of bulbs into the greenhouse from the plunge bed and frame to ensure a succession of flowers later on.

Opposite: Euonymus japonicus ovatus aureus is a most valuable variegated evergreen. It seems to glow amid the bare frosted branches of its deciduous neighbours

Start to propagate carnations Perpetual-flowering carnation cuttings may be taken from now until the end of March (see page 16).

Continue to cut back chrysanthemums Throughout the month continue to cut back the later chrysanthemums as soon as they finish flowering.

Start to take chrysanthemum cuttings Some growers start taking cuttings of chrysanthemums considerably earlier than the third week of December, but I do not think that the amateur gains anything by being in too much of a hurry. You should start on those varieties that are to be grown for second crown buds, and particularly on November incurves and singles.

The best shoots to select are those that come up through the soil direct from the roots. These should be severed just below soil level when they are a couple of inches or so in length. They are prepared by cutting off the lower leaves with a very sharp knife and trimming off the base cleanly just below a joint; then insert them about $\frac{1}{2}$ in deep in sandy soil. It does not matter much whether they are in boxes, pots, or directly in a bed made up on the staging in the greenhouse so long as there is ample provision for drainage. The cuttings cannot be rooted out of doors at this time of the year. It is possible to manage them in a well-constructed frame, but it is much easier in a greenhouse with just a little artificial heat to keep out frost. Some growers keep the cuttings in a frame within the greenhouse, while others prefer to have them open on the staging. Both schemes work well, but using the latter method rather more watering is necessary, and it is advisable to spray every morning with slightly tepid water.

Take chrysanthemum cuttings from stools when the shoots are about 2 in in height and trim just below a leaf joint. Insert in sandy compost

Remove Christmas plants to greenhouse The sooner pot plants used in the house for decorations during the Christmas festivities can be returned to the greenhouse or conservatory the better. They do not like the over-dry atmosphere and ever-changing temperature of living rooms at all, and quickly deteriorate as a result. Palms, aspidistras and dracaenas will benefit from a thorough sponging down with tepid water into which a few drops of milk have been stirred. After this they should be kept in a rather warm atmosphere for a few days and sprayed daily with clear water. Flowering plants such as cyclamens, primulas, cinerarias and heaths should be given as light a place as possible on the staging in a temperature of 13 to 16°C (55 to 60°F), and be watered very carefully, all excesses one way or the other being avoided. Remove any withered or mouldy leaves. Berried solanums should also be given plenty of light and a rather higher temperature.

Stop sweet peas Mid-October-sown sweet peas should have their growing tips pinched out some time during the winter. It does not matter when it is done, so long as it is before the plants have made shoots more than 3 in in length.

Crops in Season

In the garden Jerusalem artichokes, Brussels sprouts, cauliflower, celeriac, celery, endive, kale, leeks, parsnips, savoys.

Under glass Chicory, endive, lettuce, mustard and cress, radish, rhubarb, seakale.

VEGETABLES AND FRUIT

Successional sowings These are exactly the same as last month, mustard and cress and radishes, all in a warm greenhouse or a frame equipped with soil-warming cables.

Continue to lift and blanch chicory Further roots should be lifted and treated as already described (see page 184).

Continue to force seakale and rhubarb At intervals of about a fortnight bring in further roots of rhubarb and seakale and force them in the greenhouse (see page 194).

Ventilate fruit trees and vines There is really nothing of importance to add to my November notes on the management of these houses. Free ventilation should be the rule right up to the time at which vines and fruit trees are restarted into growth. If the weather is very cold, close up the houses in sufficient time in the afternoon to keep off the worst frost, but a few degrees of frost will do no harm at all.

Saving heat in the greenhouse

Considerable savings in the cost of maintaining a greenhouse in winter can be made by reducing fuel consumption. There are several ways in which this can be done. Efficient thermostatic control will ensure that artificial heat is only used when it is really required. Many small greenhouse heaters, both electric and gas, have built-in thermostats but if a separate thermostat is installed it should be placed in a middle position in the house and shielded from direct sunshine with some bright reflective covering that does not impede the free circulation of air.

Since every 3°C rise in minimum winter temperature can double fuel consumption, con-siderable savings can be made by reducing the minimum to the lowest safe level. For a great many popular plants this can be from 6 to 7°C (43 to 45°F) though a few degrees more will give earlier or more continuous flowering and make management easier.

Very considerable fuel savings can be made with double glazing or interior lining. A few green-house manufacturers offer greenhouses with the option of double glazing and though this adds considerably to the initial cost this capital outlay may be recovered in two or three years of use.

All greenhouses, wood or metal framed, can be lined inside in winter, the most effective material being quilted polythene. This is made by trapping bubbles of air between two thin sheets of barrier coated polythene film. The material is light and easy to

Quilted polythene clipped to the green-house frame provides insulation to conserve heat during the winter months

handle, can be fixed in wooden-framed houses with drawing pins or in metal-framed houses with special clips or adhesive tape or by suspending it from wires. It should be placed with the bubbles towards the glass.

Very considerable heat savings, up to twenty per cent, can be obtained simply by lining from floor to eaves. Even more saving will result if the lining is carried right up to the ridge but this does increase the difficulty of efficient fixing, slightly reduces light transmission and may result in internal condensation and drip. The polythene quilt should be removed in summer but can be used time and again.

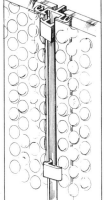

Plants for December

There should still be some berries left in December, particularly many of the yellow and orange coloured kinds including *Sorbus* Joseph Rock and the yellow-berried hollies and pyracanthas which seem to be less attractive to birds than red berries. A notable exception to this rule is *Cotoneaster conspicuus*, the bright red berries of which are seldom eaten and are likely to be still there at the end of the winter. The Christmas rose, *Helleborus niger*, should be coming into bloom in sheltered places, there will still be plenty of flowers on the autumn cherry, *Prunus subhirtella autumnalis* and the witch hazels and winter viburnums will be in flower. As for the greenhouse it can be ablaze with colour including the scarlet bracts of poinsettias if there is sufficient heating to maintain a comfortable temperature.

Ilex aquifolium Golden King is a particularly fine variety having both variegated foliage and plenty of berries

Herbaceous plants *Helleborus niger, Iris unguicularis, Schizostylis coccinea.*

Hardy bulbs, corms and tubers *Crocus imperati, C. laevigatus, Cyclamen coum, Galanthus nivalis cilicicus, G. corcyrensis, G. graecus, G. rhizehensis.*

Evergreen shrubs *Camellia sasanqua, Erica carnea, E. darleyensis, Fatsia japonica, Mahonia lomariifolia, M. media* vars. see page 19, *Viburnum tinus.*

Deciduous shrubs *Arbutus unedo, Chimonanthus praecox, Daphne mezereum autumnalis, Hamamelis intermedia, H. japonica, H. mollis, Lonicera fragrantissima, L. standishii, Viburnum bodnantense, V. farreri (fragrans).*

Deciduous trees *Crataegus monogyna praecox, Prunus subhirtella autumnalis, Salix britzensis.*

Hardy climbers *Jasminum nudiflorum, Lardizabala biternata* (sheltered places only).

Fruiting trees, shrubs and climbers *Aucuba japonica, Berberis hookeri, Celastrus orbiculatus, C. scandens, Cotoneaster conspicuus* and var. *decora, C. frigidus, C. horizontalis, C. microphyllus, C. rotundifolius, Crataegus crus-galli, C. lavallei, Hippophae rhamnoides, Ilex aquifolium, Pyracantha angustifolia, P. atalantioides, P. coccinea, P. crenato-serrata, P.* Orange Glow, *Rosa*

Poinsettia is one of the most popular Christmas houseplants

fargesii, R. moyesii and var. Geranium, *Sorbus* Joseph Rock, *Taxus baccata.*

Some of the other varieties mentioned in November (see page 191) may continue into December but those listed above are particularly reliable. Much depends upon the speed with which birds clear the berries and other fruits.

Below: The stems of *Salix britzensis* should be cut down hard each spring to keep their bright colour
Below right: The beautiful bark of *Prunus serrula*

Chemicals in the Garden

Pests and Diseases

Plants are attacked by various diseases and small creatures, including a number of insects. It is scarcely possible, and certainly not necessary, to have a garden from which pests and diseases are completely excluded, but it is essential to keep them within reasonable bounds. To do this successfully it is not necessary to have a detailed knowledge of pests and diseases but it is necessary to have a general idea of the main groups, suckers or chewers, into which they fall, especially from the standpoint of treatment.

PESTS

Consider the insects first; the two most familiar are the aphids (greenflies, blackflies) which suck and the caterpillars which chew. There are a great many different kinds of suckers and of chewers, which will be found described in detail in books devoted to garden pests, but since the methods of control are very similar for most kinds, the gardener can usually get along with no more knowledge than that which enables him to distinguish a greenfly from a caterpillar.

Aphids These are often referred to as plant lice and it is a good description. They are small and soft skinned and they breed rapidly so that, given favourable conditions, in a few days the young shoots and leaves of plants may become covered with them. They suck the sap, greatly weakening the plant in so doing, and often causing leaves to curl and become sticky. Moreover they act as carriers of disease, principally of virus diseases, and so it is very necessary to keep greenflies under control. They are most likely to be troublesome in spring and early summer, for it is the young shoots and leaves of plants that they like.

Aphids are generally controlled by spraying and there are a number of good insecticides available for this purpose. Some of them, such as menazon, formothion and dimethoate, are absorbed by the plant and are carried about inside it in the sap. This type of insecticide is known as systemic, and it is very useful because it cannot be washed off by rain nor is it likely to do a great deal of harm to those insects that do not damage plants.

The drawback to the systemic type of chemical is that, if it is used on a food plant, a lettuce for example, or an apple, it cannot be removed by wiping or wash-ing. Most systemic insecticides sold for garden use break down fairly quickly in the plant and food crops can be used safely a few weeks after application. However, some gardeners may prefer to reserve this kind of insecticide for the ornamental garden and use non-systemic insecticides for vegetables and fruit. There are plenty of these capable of killing aphids, including HCH, malathion, derris, pirimiphos-methyl, pirimicarb, resmethrin, bioresmethrin and permethrin.

Beetles As a class these are friends rather than foes but two exceptions are the flea beetle and the raspberry beetle. The former attacks the first young leaves of turnips, cabbages, Brussels sprouts and other allied crops, filling them with tiny circular holes. It is very small, lively and black and it is easily killed by dusting or spraying with HCH or carbaryl. The raspberry beetle feeds on the flowers of the raspberry, but it is its little creamy-white grubs that are most troublesome for they eat right into the raspberry fruits. Derris, fenitrothion and malathion are the best chemicals to kill them with and one or other must be applied at the right time – as the first fruits turn pink.

Cabbage root, onion and other flies Fly larvae often attack at or just below soil level. If young cabbage or Brussels sprout plants start to flag and, when pulled up, it can be seen that the roots have been gnawed, it is very likely that the cabbage root fly is responsible. Another fly attacks young onions and a third attacks the young roots of carrots. HCH, pirimiphos-methyl, bromophos or trichlorphon can be used to kill them or 4% calomel dust for cabbage root fly and onion fly.

The grubs of some flies tunnel into leaves and are called leaf-miners. Most insecticides do not get at them because they are protected within the leaf, but trichlorphon, pirimiphos-methyl, diazinon and HCH will kill them.

Capsid bugs These pests bring us back to the suckers as distinct from biters. They feed like aphids but they are larger and usually far less numerous. They do a quite disproportionate amount of damage, causing leaves to pucker and become stunted and flowers to be deformed. Since they are active and hide quickly when disturbed, it is often difficult to find them but the damage they do is very distinctive. HCH, diazinon, fenitrothion and pirimiphos-methyl are effective in killing them.

Caterpillars These are the grubs or larvae of moths and butterflies. Most people have a general idea of what a caterpillar looks like but they sometimes confuse them with large fly larvae, such as leatherjackets; the larvae of the daddy-long-legs. Obvious points of difference are that every caterpillar has short legs and a distinguishable head, whereas the fly larva has not. Derris is a good caterpillar killer and various other chemicals are available including malathion, HCH, carbaryl, pirimiphos-methyl, permethrin, fenitrothion, and trichlorphon.

Caterpillars do not suck sap but bite holes in leaves, fruits and even in stems and branches. So do the many weevils that attack plants and the damage they do may often be mistaken for the work of caterpillars. Weevils look like little beetles and they are so active that it is usually difficult to find them, particularly as most of them feed at night. However, the chemicals recommended for use against caterpillars are also poisonous to most weevils, so if you are doubtful whether it is caterpillars or weevils that are eating holes in the leaves of plants use a spray containing one or other of these chemicals.

Eelworms Microscopic, transparent, eel-like creatures which often infest roots or stems of certain plants in great numbers, causing knots, goutiness and distortion. Much larger, transparent nematode worms are frequently mistaken for them and are allied but are harmless as they feed on decaying matter in the soil and are frequently found in manure, compost, or leafmould.

Eelworms are principally found in phloxes, chrysanthemums, narcissi, tomatoes, cucumbers, potatoes, and onions. Usually there is no satisfactory remedy and plants should be destroyed. Eelworms on potatoes form tiny white cysts on the outside of the tubers and these can be washed off in plain water.

Infected narcissus bulbs can be cleared of eelworms and fly larvae by keeping the bulbs for three hours in water maintained at 43°C (110°F) followed by immediate cooling in cold water but special apparatus is required for this. Infected chrysanthemum stools from which all stems have been cut can be heated in a similar manner but for twenty to thirty minutes only.

For strawberry runners the time is five to six minutes and the water temperature 46°C (115°F). Clean stock of phlox can usually be obtained from root cuttings. It is always advisable to use sterilized soil if practicable in pots, containers and also in greenhouse borders.

Leaf hoppers These are little bug-like creatures which live on the undersides of leaves, sucking the sap and making the leaves become mottled and weak. Like aphids they can also carry virus diseases. They change their skins from time to time and the empty white skin-cases remain attached to the lower side of the leaf, providing a ready means of identification. HCH, carbaryl, fenitrothion, resmethrin, bioresmethrin, permethrin and malathion are effective.

Red spider mites A rather similar grey or yellowish mottling is caused by red spider mites. These are not spiders and they are rust coloured rather than red. They are so tiny that a hand lens is required to see them clearly and they live on the underside of leaves, sucking the sap from them. They thrive in hot, dry weather and hate damp and cold, so that one way to keep them down is to spray frequently with water. Chemicals effective in dealing with them are derris, diazinon, malathion and pirimiphos-methyl.

Sawflies These are not true flies and they produce larvae which look very much like the caterpillars of moths, having legs and a distinct head. Some eat into fruits, for example the apple sawfly, whose white grubs cause the maggoty apple one finds in the early summer. Some eat the surface of leaves, leaving a transparent skeleton, and some cause leaves to roll up. All can be destroyed by spraying with HCH, pirimiphos-methyl, dimethoate, fenitrothion, trichlorphon or derris.

Slugs and snails Slugs and snails can be very troublesome, particularly in wet mild weather. They feed largely at night, eating leaves and young stems, and there are few plants they will not attack. Since they hide by day their presence is not always suspected.

They cannot be killed with any of the insecticides mentioned, since they are not insects. They are very fond of bran and so one way to kill them is to mix a slug poison, such as metaldehyde, with bran and place it near plants that are being attacked. Ready-prepared bait is sold by all dealers in horticultural sundries. Another method is to use a liquid slug killer containing metaldehyde, distributing this from a watering-can fitted with a rose and applying it freely to creeping plants under which slugs and snails may be hiding, or to dead leaves, rubbish and stones. Metaldehyde is most effective in fairly dry conditions. If it is wet, methiocarb is better. It is prepared ready for use to be sprinkled around plants likely to be attacked. But whatever is done, slugs and snails are likely to return and so treatment must be repeated.

Thrips Thrips cause streaky mottling on foliage, usually with a good deal of brown marking. They are very small, long in proportion to their breadth, and they run fast when disturbed. They often attack rose flowers, causing them to become deformed and develop dark markings. If such a bloom is tapped smartly over a piece of white paper the thrips will fall on to it and will be seen running away. They attack a great many other plants and the best way to deal with them is to spray with HCH, derris, resmethrin, bioresmethrin, permethrin or malathion.

Whitefly There are several different species of this pest of which the most damaging is the greenhouse whitefly which attacks a wide range of plants grown under cover. The adults are tiny, white, moth-like insects which, when disturbed, may fly out in a dense cloud so rapidly do they breed. Whitefly lay eggs on the undersides of leaves and these hatch into scale-like larvae attached like minute limpets to the leaves. Sap is sucked from the plants and they are covered with a sticky exudation on which sooty mould usually develops. It is not only unsightly but prevents the leaves from functioning properly causing the plants to be weakened or even killed. Another species of whitefly attacks brassicas outdoors and under favourable conditions can be very troublesome.

Whiteflies have proved difficult pests to control since, though there are several chemicals which will kill adults efficiently, few have much effect on either the eggs or the scales. Repeated treatment at intervals of three or four days is therefore necessary to kill successive broods of adults as they emerge. The most effective chemicals are resmethrin, bioresmethrin, permethrin and pirimiphos-methyl which can be used outdoors and under cover. In greenhouses HCH smoke generators can also be used.

There is also a parasite that can be introduced to greenhouses and at temperatures of 21–27°C (70–80°F) will breed rapidly and greatly reduce, but not entirely eliminate, whiteflies. However, it will not survive low temperatures.

Other pests Cockroaches can be caught in proprietary traps baited with bran. Earwigs may be trapped in inverted flower pots stuffed with hay, hollow broad bean stalks, slightly opened matchboxes, or any other similar dark hiding place. Leatherjackets can be trapped under wet sacks or heaps of damp vegetable refuse laid on the soil. Millipedes and wireworms can be collected from sliced carrots and potatoes buried just beneath the surface of the soil.

DISEASES

If the trouble is due to disease, decide whether this is caused by a fungus or a bacterium or virus. Fungi usually cause dark, dampish spots, or patches of decay or outgrowths of mould or rusty coloured spots. Bacterial and virus diseases usually cause drier spotting or streaking without obvious outgrowth, but are in general more difficult to identify. The common diseases can also be grouped according to their symptoms and treatment, so that the interested gardener can soon acquire a working knowledge of them.

Damping off Seedlings in the greenhouse will often collapse in hundreds, stricken by fungi in the soil which kill their roots or attack their stems near soil level. This is known as damping off and it is most likely to occur when seedlings are overcrowded or when they are kept too wet and insufficiently ventilated. Sterilized soil helps to prevent this disease. Seed can also be dusted before it is sown with captan or thiram as a preventive or watered with Cheshunt Compound or quintozene.

Grey mould One of the most widespread of diseases is grey mould, also known as botrytis. It attacks all manner of plants, causing a soft dark decay and a characteristic is the fluffy white outgrowth which quickly follows this decay. It is a disease that is very prevalent in damp, cool weather and it is very difficult to control. Thiram, captan, benomyl, dichlofluanid and thiophanate-methyl are the most useful chemicals to check it.

Powdery mildew All the powdery mildews make plants look as if they had been dusted with flour. Roses can suffer very badly, especially in dry summers, and so can Michaelmas daisies. There are mildews which attack peas, apples, vines, gooseberries and a great many other plants. All can be tackled with dinocap, carbendazim or bupirimate, but it is necessary to get the treatment started early as it is a means of prevention rather than of cure. Some systemic fungicides, such as benomyl and triforine, will actually kill mildew in the plant.

Rusts Then there are the equally numerous rusts, so called because they produce rust-coloured spots on the leaves, and sometimes the stems, of plants attacked. There is a very troublesome rust disease of hollyhocks and another of antirrhinums. These and most other rusts can be prevented by occasional spraying in summer with thiram or maneb. Triforine may even kill rust after infection has occurred.

Spot diseases There are a great many spot diseases and they are rather diverse in their origin. One of the worst is black spot of roses, which produces roundish black spots on the leaves which fall prematurely. The remedy is either to spray frequently with captan, thiram or maneb, starting in spring and continuing every seven to ten days all summer, or rather less frequently with a systemic fungicide such as benomyl, carbendazim or triforine.

Captan is also a good means of preventing scab disease of apples and pears which also starts by producing black spots or patches on leaves and fruits. Other effective chemicals are benomyl, triforine, bupirimate and thiram.

The very widespread disease of potatoes known as blight is another that starts by producing dark spots or patches on the leaves. These spread rapidly, so that all growth above ground withers and dies. By this time the disease has spread to the potatoes themselves, which develop brown patches of decay. The same disease attacks tomatoes and makes the fruits rot. One of the best preventives is a copper fungicide such as Bordeaux mixture, but it must be sprayed over all the leaves and stems before infection occurs. Other possibilities are thiram and bupirimate.

Viruses Lastly there is a whole class of diseases caused by various kinds of virus. These produce many different symptoms and are amongst the most difficult of plant diseases to diagnose with accuracy. Leaves may be mottled with yellow in a quite attractive way, or they may be deformed and become twisted or very narrow. Growth may be stunted or dry brown spots and streaks may appear on stems and leaves.

There is no cure for virus diseases that can be applied in the garden and all infected plants must be destroyed, but before doing so it is wise to get the advice of an expert for sometimes symptoms very similar to those of virus disease may be caused by bad cultivation or by the careless use of a selective weedkiller.

Incurable diseases Not all diseases can be controlled as yet. In some cases the only way of preventing further damage is to remove and burn affected plants as soon as detected. Even with diseases that can be treated, it is generally advisable to remove and burn specially bad plants or portions of plants. On no account should these be placed on the compost heap or left lying about. This applies, among other diseases, to plum silver leaf, all collar and root rots, club root, aster wilts and brown rot of fruits.

DIRECTORY OF CHEMICALS

Some chemicals when applied to plants remain on the outside, on leaves and stems. These are known as contact or non-systemic chemicals in contrast to systemic chemicals, which are absorbed by the plant and enter into its sap in which they may be carried from one part of the plant to another. Systemic insecticides, fungicides and weedkillers are known. The advantages are that it is not necessary to cover the whole plant with the chemical to get a good result; that the chemical is not removed by rain; and with insecticides, that it is less likely to harm useful insects since these do not feed on the plant. Drawbacks are that systemic chemicals cannot be wiped or washed off, that some persist for a considerable time and may render a crop unusable until they have been dispersed or decomposed.

The names of chemicals given in this section are those commonly used to distinguish them and they should appear somewhere on the market pack though usually in small type and not always prominently displayed. This is because several manufacturers or distributors may be marketing the same chemical and so they prefer to use their own trade names which are then widely publicized and displayed. Even the assistants in garden shops and centres can find this confusing and some keep check lists of the chemicals with the various trade names under which they may appear on their shelves. Unfortunately it would be of little use to print such a check list here since there are so many brands and some of the brand names may change, drop out, or the list may be added to.

Bioresmethrin A synthetic pyrethroid insecticide

which is more effective than natural pyrethrum extract in the control of a wide range of pests including aphids, whiteflies, leaf hoppers, thrips, beetles and small caterpillars. It is available as an aerosol for immediate use and also as a liquid for dilution according to manufacturer's instructions and application as a spray.

Bordeaux mixture An excellent fungicide against potato disease. It can be purchased as a powder ready for solution according to label instructions or it can be prepared with 9 oz of copper sulphate, 6 oz of quicklime and 5 gals of water. Dissolve the copper sulphate in 4 gal water. Put the quicklime in another vessel and slake it by adding water, a little at a time. Make up to 1 gal with water; add to the copper sulphate solution slowly and stir well. Use at once. Wooden or enamelled vessels should be used for mixing. It is advisable to test the strong solution with litmus paper before using. If blue paper turns pink, more lime should be added till there is no such reaction.

Bromophos A soil insecticide for the control of cutworms, leatherjackets, wireworms and millepedes. It does not have the tainting problems of HCH. It is available as a dust to be forked or raked into the soil.

Bupirimate A fungicide useful for the control of several diseases including potato blight, apple and pear scab, rose black spot and mildews. It is available as a liquid, sometimes in combination with triforine, for dilution according to manufacturer's instructions and application as a spray. Edible crops can be harvested one day after application.

Calomel This is the commercial name for mercurous chloride. It is usually supplied as a ready-prepared dust containing 4% calomel. It is used to kill the larvae of the cabbage root fly and onion fly, and is scattered for about 2 in on both sides of each row of seedlings at the rate of 1 lb to 60 yard, or round individual plants at about 1 oz to ten plants. The most effective time for treating brassicas is when they have made the second or third leaf; for onions when the seedlings are $1\frac{1}{2}$ in high. Second applications may be given ten to fourteen days later. May and June are danger periods. Calomel dust, well watered in, also controls many lawn diseases.

Calomel is also used to check club root, for which purpose a little of the dust is sprinkled into each hole prepared for a brassica plant or, alternatively, the roots of the plants are dipped into a thin paste prepared by mixing calomel dust with water. It can also be raked into the seed bed prior to sowing.

To control onion white rot 4% calomel is dusted along the seed drills at 1 lb to 60 yard. Calomel can also be used as a dip for diseased gladiolus corms. Add 1 oz of pure calomel to 1 gal of water and immerse corms for five to ten minutes, keeping the mixture stirred so that the calomel does not settle.

Captan A synthetic chemical used as a fungicide. It is particularly recommended for the control of apple and pear scab as it does not scorch leaves or russet or crack fruits; it is also used to control rose black spot. It is purchased as a powder which must be mixed in water according to the manufacturer's instructions and kept stirred while it is applied as a spray. Its effect does not last long and so it may be necessary to spray every ten to fourteen days from April to August to secure complete control. Captan is also used in seed dressings to protect seedlings from damping off and other soil-borne diseases. Captan is harmful to fish.

Carbaryl A synthetic insecticide effective against a fairly wide range of pests including caterpillars, codling moths, cutworms, leatherjackets, capsid bugs, flea beetles, weevils, scale insects, whiteflies, thrips, pear leaf blister mite, earwigs and woodlice. It is available as a wettable powder for mixing with water according to manufacturer's instructions. The mixture should be continually agitated while the spray is being applied. It is also available as a dust ready for use and this is commonly called sevin dust. Carbaryl is harmful to bees and fish. It is moderately persistent and should not be used with alkaline mixtures such as Bordeaux or lime sulphur. When used on edible crops at least one week must elapse before they are harvested.

Carbendazim A systemic fungicide related to benomyl and with very similar uses in the garden. It is specially recommended for control of mildews and rose black spot and has also proved effective against botrytis, raspberry cane spot and tomato leaf mould. It is available as a wettable powder to be stirred into water according to the instructions on the label and kept agitated while being applied as a spray.

Cheshunt Compound A soil fungicide used for the

prevention or check of damping-off disease, collar rot, and other soil-borne diseases. The formula for mixing is as follows.

Mix together thoroughly two parts of finely ground copper sulphate with eleven parts of ammonium carbonate (fresh) and store in a stoppered glass jar for at least twenty-four hours. Dissolve 1 oz of the dry mixture in a little hot water and add to 2 gal of water. The solution should be used at once. It may be watered freely on the soil in which plants, or even seedlings, are growing. This preparation can also be purchased ready for mixing with water.

Chlordane This is a synthetic chemical used for the control of worms and leatherjackets in lawns. It is very persistent and will remain effective for at least a year. It is supplied as a liquid to be mixed with water, and can be applied with a watering-can, or sprayer; it must penetrate the turf thoroughly. The best times to apply it are the spring or autumn. It is poisonous to warm-blooded animals and should not be used on seedling grass or turf less than three months old. Livestock should not be allowed on treated turf for two weeks.

Copper Various formulations of copper compounds, including copper oxide and copper oxychloride, are sold as 'copper fungicide' or under trade names. They may be employed for any of the purposes for which other copper sprays, such as Bordeaux mixtures, might be used. The manufacturer's instructions regarding strength and application must be followed.

Cresylic acid A powerful soil sterilizer for use against many insects and fungi. One part of 97 to 99% purity cresylic acid is diluted with 100 parts of water, 1 gal cresylic acid to 100 gal water, 1 pt to 100 pt, etc. This is applied with a watering can; 7 gal is sufficient for about 1 sq yd of soil. Treated soil should be covered with polythene sheeting, tarpaulins or wet sacks for a day or so to trap fumes, after which it should be uncovered and left for from three to five weeks before use.

Derris An insecticide that is effective against many pests including aphids, leaf hoppers, thrips, caterpillars of many kinds, apple-blossom weevil, pea and bean weevil, raspberry beetle, gooseberry sawfly, flea beetles and red spider mites. Though relatively harmless to human beings, warm-blooded creatures and bees, it is recommended that at least one day

elapse between use on edible crops and harvesting. It is very poisonous to fishes.

Derris is available as a dust, ready for immediate use, and as a liquid to be diluted with water and used as a spray according to manufacturer's instructions. The effectiveness of derris depends on the percentage of rotenone it contains and this may diminish with age.

Diazinon An insecticide used primarily to kill aphids, capsid bugs, leaf miners, thrips, red spider mites, mealy bugs, scale insects, springtails and mushroom flies. It is available as a liquid for dilution with water in granular form and as a wettable powder. Edible crops should not be harvested for two weeks after treatment.

Dichlofluanid A fungicide used primarily to control botrytis (grey mould) on strawberries, currants and black spot on roses. It should not be used on strawberries grown under glass or polythene. At least two weeks must elapse between use on edible crops and harvesting. It is harmful to fish. Dichlofluanid is available as a wettable powder to be stirred into water as recommended by the manufacturers and kept agitated while being applied as a spray.

Dimethoate A systemic insecticide used primarily to control aphids, apple and pear sucker, plum sawfly, woolly aphid and red spider mites. It is available as a liquid to be diluted with water according to manufacturer's instructions. Edible crops treated with dimethoate should not be harvested for at least one week. Dimethoate should not be used on chrysanthemums.

Dinocap A fungicide used primarily to control powdery mildews on many plants, though it will also help to control red spider mites. It is available as a liquid for dilution with water or as a wettable powder to be kept agitated when mixed with water and applied as a spray.

Edible crops treated with dinocap should not be harvested for at least one week. It is harmful to fish.

DNOC (dinitro-ortho-cresol) This insecticide has been added to petroleum oil in certain proprietary preparations to produce a winter wash for fruit trees which proves effective against the overwintering stages (including the eggs) of capsid bugs, apple sucker, aphids, winter moth, caterpillar, tortrix moth, raspberry moth, scale insects, apple-blossom weevil and red spider mites. The wash is applied as a heavy spray while the trees are dormant (December to late February). The usual formula is 2½ to 3 pints of combined petroleum and dinitro-ortho-cresol to 5 gal of water, but manufacturer's instructions should be consulted wherever possible. It is poisonous to warm-blooded animals, including man, and to fish. Rubber gloves, protective clothing and a face shield should be worn when mixing and applying this chemical.

Fenitrothion An insecticide effective in the control of numerous pests including aphids, capsids, thrips, codling moth, sawflies, caterpillars and weevils. It is available as a liquid for dilution according to manufacturer's instructions and application as a spray. It is harmful to bees, fish, birds and mammals. Most edible crops should not be used for a fortnight after application.

Formalin (formaldehyde) A powerful soil sterilizer. Formalin is the preparation used horticulturally and it contains 38–40% pure formaldehyde. To prepare this for use, all that is necessary is to mix it with forty-nine times its own bulk of water (1 pt in 49 pt; 1 gal in 49 gal etc.). Ordinarily, 75 gal of dilute formalin is sufficient to treat 1 ton of soil, or approximately 2 gal per bushel of soil. Where possible remove the soil to a hard floor, spread it out thinly and thoroughly saturate with the solution. Throw into a heap and cover with polythene sheeting or tarpaulins to trap the fumes. After forty-eight hours remove the covering and spread the soil out to dry. It must not be used for plants until it ceases to smell of formaldehyde, usually in about three or four weeks.

Formothion A systemic insecticide which kills aphids, capsid bugs, leaf hopper, scale insects, mealy bugs and red spider mites. Edible crops should not be harvested within a week of the use of formothion. It is available as a liquid to be diluted with water according to manufacturer's instructions. Chrysanthemums, nasturtiums, African marigolds and possibly some other plants may be damaged, but it is completely safe on roses. It is harmful to fish and bees.

HCH An insecticide obtained in proprietary forms for wet or dry application and also in smoke generators for fumigating under glass, and all these should be used strictly in accordance with manufacturer's instructions.

Dusts are suitable for use against ants, earwigs, flea beetles, leatherjackets, mushroom flies, springtails and wireworms. Sprays can be used against any of these, also aphids, apple suckers, cabbage root fly, capsid bugs, raspberry cane midge, sawflies, symphalids, thrips and woolly aphid.

HCH has a tainting effect and should not be used on soft fruits after the fruit has formed, nor as a soil insecticide for potatoes. It is better to treat carrot seed than the soil in which the carrots are to be grown.

Edible crops should not be harvested for two weeks after use of HCH dusts or sprays or for two days after use of HCH smokes.

Lime sulphur A fungicide once much used for fruit trees but now largely replaced by other chemicals such as benomyl and thiophanate-methyl. It is liable to damage the foliage and fruits of pears and certain varieties of apple. It must be purchased as a manufactured liquid to be used according to the instructions on the label.

Malathion An insecticide effective against many pests including aphids, leaf hoppers, thrips, suckers, scale insects, mealy bugs, leaf miners, whiteflies, mushroom flies, gooseberry sawfly, raspberry beetle, pollen beetles and red spider mites. It is poisonous to bees and fish. Four days should elapse between use of malathion and harvesting of edible crops.

Malathion is available as an aerosol and a dust, both for immediate use and as a liquid for dilution with water and application as a spray according to manufacturer's instructions. It should not be used on antirrhinums, crassulas, ferns, fuchsias, gerberas, petunias, pileas, sweet peas or zinnias.

Maneb A synthetic fungicide which is particularly good for the control of downy mildews, rose black spot, potato blight, tomato leaf mould and tomato stem rot (didymella). At least one week should elapse between its use on outdoor edible crops and harvesting and two days between use and harvesting of edible greenhouse crops. It is available as a wettable powder to be stirred into water at the rates directed by the manufacturer and agitated while being applied as a spray.

Menazon A systemic insecticide for use against aphids of all kinds including woolly aphid. It is poisonous to bees. Edible crops sprayed with menazon should not be harvested in under three weeks. Menazon is available as a liquid for dilution with water according to instructions on the label and is applied as a spray.

Metaldehyde Used as a poison bait for slugs and snails at the rate of 1 oz of finely powdered metaldehyde to 3 lb of bran. Mix well with sufficient water to make a crumbly mash. Place in small heaps beneath slates or boards. Metaldehyde in specially prepared forms is also available both as pellets for immediate use and in liquid form for mixing with water and application from a watering-can fitted with a rose. It is harmful to fish, game, birds and animals.

Methiocarb A chemical used to kill slugs and snails and is more efficient than metaldehyde under damp conditions. It is available, ready for use, as granules to be sprinkled around plants liable to be attacked, or wherever slugs or snails are likely to be. It is harmful to fish, and poultry should be kept off treated ground for at least seven days.

Mowrah meal This is obtained from the bean of a tropical tree and is used for destroying worms on lawns. The lawn should be dressed at the rate of 4 to 8 oz per square yard and then watered copiously. The most effective times for treatment are from February to May and August to October, in damp, mild weather when worms are close to the surface. The worms come out and must then be swept up.

Naphthalene Flaked or powdered naphthalene can be used as a soil insecticide to kill or drive out wireworms, millepedes and cutworms, as well as the maggots of the carrot fly, cabbage root fly and onion fly. The naphthalene is scattered over the surface at 2 to 6 oz per square yard and forked in or, for fly maggots, is dusted along the rows of young plants in May and June.

Marble-like balls of naphthalene usually sold as 'moth balls', are also a useful deterrent against moles which do not like the smell emitted by the balls. For this purpose they should be dropped into dibber holes 3 or 4 in deep and 2 or 3 in apart all round the area to be protected. They normally retain their effectiveness for several years.

Permethrin A pyrethroid insecticide of the same type as bioresmethrin but more powerful and useful in the control of the same pests. It is available as a liquid for dilution according to the instructions on the label. It is applied as a spray.

Petroleum oil (white oil) Proprietary insecticides manufactured from high-grade petroleum oils. Two grades are obtainable, one for winter, the other for summer application. In winter it is used chiefly to control capsid bug eggs and red spider mite winter eggs on fruit trees; in summer to control red spider mites, thrips, scale insects, and white fly on all plants. Summer petroleum is used on a wide variety of plants, particularly glasshouse plants, but may damage carnations, smilax and asparagus fern. Manufacturer's instructions regarding preparation and application must be followed.

Pirimicarb An insecticide peculiar in being an extremely effective and rapid aphid killer but having little or no effect on other insects including bees and useful predators. Most edible crops should not be harvested less than fourteen days after application. It is available as a liquid to be diluted according to label instructions and applied as a spray and also as an aerosol for immediate use.

Pirimiphos-methyl An insecticide effective against a wide range of pests including ants, earwigs, aphids, beetles, weevils, caterpillars, cabbage root fly, carrot fly, onion fly, sawflies, codling moth, leatherjackets, wireworms and whiteflies. It is harmful to bees and fish. Edible crops should not be harvested under seven days after application. It is available as a liquid for dilution according to manufacturer's instructions and application as a spray.

Pyrethrum An insecticide prepared from the flower heads of certain tropical plants. It is not very poisonous to warm-blooded animals, including man, but acts very rapidly on many insects, including aphids, capsid bugs, leaf hoppers and thrips, giving a knockdown effect but not always a complete kill, for which reason it is often combined with slower but more certain insecticides. Pyrethrum is available as a dust ready for use or as a liquid to be diluted with water and applied as a spray according to manufacturer's instructions.

Quintozene A fungicide primarily used for the control of soil-borne diseases such as damping off, wire stem, foot rot, root rot and grey bulb rot, and also of tulip fire and lawn diseases such as dollar spot, corticium (red thread) and fusarium patch (snow mould). It is supplied as a dust ready for use and may be worked into the soil, dusted on plants or over bulbs according to manufacturer's instructions. It is also available as a wettable powder to be stirred into water and kept agitated while being sprayed, watered in or used as a dip. It should not be used on soil intended for cucumbers, marrows or melons.

Resmethrin A pyrethroid insecticide of similar type to bioresmethrin and with a similar range of usefulness. It is available as an aerosol for immediate use or as a liquid to be diluted according to label instructions and applied as a spray.

Sulphate of iron Used to control some soil-borne diseases, notably fairy rings on lawns. The method is to spike the affected area fairly closely to a depth of 4 in and then to apply a solution of sulphate of iron, mixed with water at the rate of 4 oz per gal. The solution is applied freely and can be repeated in six week's time if necessary.

Sulphur A fungicide particularly useful against mildews and moulds, and also as a deterrent of red spider mites. It is available as a fine powder, often known as 'flowers of sulphur', for use direct or in various colloidal or wettable formulations to be mixed with water and applied as a spray according to manufacturer's instructions. Flowers of sulphur for garden use is often coloured green so that it does not look unsightly on foliage.

Tar oil wash Proprietary sprays made from tar distillate and used to clear fruit trees of caterpillar and aphid eggs, scale insects, lichen and moss. These can only be applied with safety while trees are completely dormant and are usually applied in late December or early January. Manufacturer's instructions should be obtained where possible. As tar oil scorches foliage, care must be taken when applying it to trees underplanted with green crops.

Tecnazene (TCNB) A fungicide used to control dry rot in potatoes, to check the premature sprouting of stored potatoes and to control grey mould (botrytis) on chrysanthemums, lettuces, tomatoes and other plants grown under glass. It is applied to potatoes as a dust, purchased ready for use at the rate of $\frac{1}{2}$ lb per 1 cwt. The potatoes must be covered immediately with soil, straw, polythene sheets or tarpaulins. To control grey mould (botrytis) tecnazene is obtained in a smoke generator to be ignited in the greenhouse according to manufacturer's instructions.

Thiophanate-methyl A systemic fungicide for the control of various diseases including grey mould (botrytis), mildews and apple and pear scab. It is available as a wettable powder to be stirred into water according to label instructions and kept agitated while being applied as a spray.

Thiram A fungicide effective in controlling a wide range of diseases including rose black spot, grey mould (botrytis), tulip fire, some rusts, apple and pear scab, downy mildew, raspberry cane spot and tomato leaf mould, as well as some soil-borne diseases such as damping off and pea and bean foot rot. It is available as a dust for treatment of seeds before they are sown and also as wettable powders to be stirred into water and kept agitated while being applied as a spray. Manufacturer's instructions must be followed. Thiram should not be used on fruit intended for canning or freezing because of a tendency to taint and also to affect the lacquer used inside tins.

Trichlorphon A synthetic insecticide which is also very effective in killing flies and fly larvae, leaf miners, caterpillars, cutworms, earwigs and ants. A minimum period of two days should be allowed between use and harvesting of edible crops. It is applied as a spray prepared according to manufacturer's instructions. Trichlorphon is harmful to fish.

Triforine A systemic fungicide used in spray form. It is an effective control of mildew, rust, black spot on roses and scab on apple and pear trees.

Zineb A fungicide effective in giving protection against many plant diseases, including potato blight, tomato leaf mould, various mildews and rusts, black currant and celery leaf spot, grey mould (botrytis) and tulip fire. Outdoor edible crops should not be harvested under one week after application of zineb, glasshouse crops not under two days. It is available as a dust for direct application, or as a wettable powder to be stirred into water, as directed by the makers, and kept agitated while being applied as a spray.

Herbicides

All weeds can be killed in time by digging and hoeing. Frequently these are the best means, though laborious. Deep-rooted weeds if dug out to a depth of 18 to 24 in and top growth prevented for one whole spring and summer by hoeing are not likely to give further trouble. Annual and biennial weeds such as groundsel, chickweed, and common purple thistle can be killed quickly by hoeing, but only if this is done before they ripen seeds. Most surface-rooting weeds, such as creeping buttercup, nettles, and couch grass, can be killed by burying them 18 in deep.

Types of herbicide Some chemicals kill almost all kinds of plants and are called total herbicides. Some kill particular types of plant but are more or less harmless to others and these are called selective herbicides. Some kill plants by being scattered or sprayed over them, some are applied to the soil and some are effective applied in either of these ways. Herbicides which kill only the part of the plant they touch are known as contact herbicides in contrast to systemic herbicides, which enter the plant either by leaves or roots and are carried round in the sap. Herbicides which remain active in the soil for a considerable time, preventing the growth of seedlings or small plants, are known as residual herbicides.

Scientists prefer the term 'herbicide', meaning plant killer, to 'weedkiller' since no chemical can distinguish between a garden plant and a weed. The user, by selection of an appropriate chemical and choice of the right method and time for application, ensures that weeds, not garden plants, are killed.

Application of herbicides Both dry and liquid chemicals are available. Some of the forms are applied direct to weeds, others are dissolved in water and applied as sprays or from sprinklers. Dry herbicides may be spread by hand but care is needed to ensure even distribution and correct dosage. Alternatively the various mechanical fertilizer distributors may be used to spread herbicides. Some manufacturers prepare lawn fertilizers blended with chemicals to kill lawn weeds.

Liquid herbicides, after dilution with water, may be sprayed with any garden spraying equipment but there is often danger of spray drifting where it is not wanted unless an effective hood is fitted around the spray nozzle. Alternatively liquid herbicides can be applied from a watering-can or special applicator fitted with a fine rose or sprinkler bar, from which the liquid can be delivered almost in contact with the weeds or soil. Sprinkle bars of different widths are available to suit particular requirements; a very narrow (3-in) bar for applying herbicides between garden plants or in awkward places and a wide (18-in) bar for covering lawns or large vacant areas.

All equipment should be well washed after use. It is best to keep equipment solely for application of herbicides, thus reducing the risk of the chemicals getting on to garden plants.

DIRECTORY OF HERBICIDES

Calomel (mercurous chloride) Used either alone or in combination with sulphate of iron as a moss killer, particularly on lawns. For this purpose it may be supplied as a liquid for spraying or sprinkling or as a powder for application direct according to manufacturer's instructions. It is rather slow in action but persistent, and is most effective in early autumn. It is harmful to fish.

2,4-D A selective weedkiller which will kill a good many weeds in lawns without injury to the grass. It is often mixed with other herbicides, such as mecoprop, to widen its band of efficacy. It is most effective if applied when grass and weeds are growing actively. Lawns should not be cut for a few days after application to give the chemical time to act. It is harmful to most garden plants other than grass and also to fish, so care should be taken to prevent drift. It is not persistent in the soil. It is available in various forms to be used according to manufacturer's instructions. It is also very effective in killing bindweed.

Dalapon A systemic selective herbicide which will kill grass, including couch grass, also reeds, sedges and other monocotyledons but is much less toxic to dicotyledons. It is particularly useful for killing grass in orchards and around bush fruits. It should not be used near the apple Cox's Orange Pippin in winter. Sensitive plants should not be planted on treated ground under six weeks. Dalapon is sold as a powder to be dissolved in water according to manufacturer's instructions and applied as a spray or sprinkled onto the weeds.

Dicamba A systemic selective herbicide used either alone or in combination with other herbicides such as MCPA for the control of weeds in lawns. It is supplied as a liquid to be diluted with water and applied as a spray or sprinkled onto the lawn or weeds. It is harmful to most plants, other than grass, and also to fish.

Dichlobenil A total residual herbicide which can be used to keep paths and drives clean for many months or in carefully limited doses can also be used to prevent growth of seedlings and small weeds around established shrubs, trees, blackcurrants and goose-berries. It is purchased in granular form for application direct according to manufacturer's instructions.

Glyphosate A systemic herbicide which will kill most plants. It is available as a liquid for dilution with water according to manufacturer's instructions. Apply as a spray or sprinkle onto the leaves of the plants to be killed. It is also available as a soft jelly which can be painted onto the leaves of weeds. Glyphosate is most effective when applied to plants in active growth, especially to young leaves. It is slow in action but will kill the roots as well as the leaves and stems of even deep rooting weeds such as bind-weed, ground elder and docks.

Ioxynil A systemic selective weedkiller primarily used to kill weeds in young seedling lawns. It must be used seven to ten days after the germination of the grass seed when each seedling grass plant has approximately two leaves. It is purchased as a powder to be dissolved in water according to manufacturer's instructions and applied as a spray or sprinkle.

MCPA A systemic selective herbicide used mainly in gardens for the control of weeds on lawns. For this purpose it may be used alone or in combination with other selective herbicides such as 2,4-D or dicamba. Both it and these mixtures are used as 2,4-D.

Mecoprop A systemic selective herbicide chiefly used in gardens for the control of weeds in lawns. It is more effective than either 2,4-D or MCPA in killing clover and is often offered in mixture with 2,4-D to

provide a weedkiller with a wide band of effective-ness. Method of use is the same as for 2,4-D.

Paraquat A total contact herbicide which is in-activated by contact with the soil. It is not itself poisonous to plants but is changed into a poisonous substance in the plant leaf by photosynthesis. Light is therefore essential for its action which is most rapid in warm, bright weather. It is available as granules to be dissolved in water according to manufacturer's instructions and applied as a spray or sprinkled directly onto the leaves of the plants to be killed. Pure paraquat is extremely poisonous to warm-blooded animals including man.

Simazine A residual herbicide which in heavy doses will inhibit the growth of all plants and can be used to keep paths and drives clear of weeds for long periods. In smaller, carefully controlled doses it can be used selectively to prevent growth of weeds in rose beds, round ornamental trees and shrubs, in orchards, and around bush and cane fruits. It is available as a powder for dissolving in water and application as a spray or sprinkle direct to the soil according to manufacturer's instructions. It moves about very little in the soil.

Sodium chlorate A total herbicide which is both translocated in the plant and also effective in the soil. It is useful for clearing waste land and for keeping paths and drives clear of weeds. Drawbacks are its readiness to move about in the soil where it may easily be carried to places where it was not intended; the difficulty of knowing just how long it will remain effective, since it is easily washed out by rain yet may be retained for a long time in heavy soils or in dry weather; and its inflammability. To counter this last danger sodium chlorate is often mixed with a fire depressant. It is applied as a powder (or granules) for dry use or used in solution in water and applied as a spray or sprinkle either to the weeds or to the soil. Clothing wetted with sodium chlorate may become highly inflammable.

Sulphate of iron This is sometimes used as a moss killer on lawns and elsewhere, either by itself at 2 to 4 oz per gal, or more usually in combination with other chemicals such as sulphate of ammonia to make lawn sand, which can be purchased ready for use according to the manufacturer's instructions.

Index

Acknowledgements

Line and tone illustrations by Ron Hayward.

PHOTOGRAPHS

Pat Brindley 54, 55 (bottom), 66, 71 (top left and right), 74–5, 79, 83, 94, 96, 111 (top left and top right), 119, 122, 135, 139 (bottom), 151 (top), 171 (top right), 207 (left); Robert Corbin 146; W.F. Davidson, 10–11, 22–3, 38–9, 98–9, 198–9; Paul Freytag – Zefa 142–3; Jerry Harpur 90 (designer Glazenwood, Essex), 102 (designer Valery Stevenson), 110, 111 (bottom –

designer Valery Stevenson), 123 (left), 123 (above right and below right – designer Valery Stevenson, 127 (designer Victor Shanley, Clifton Nurseries) 128 (designer Victor Shanley, Clifton Nurseries), 139 (top left – designer Peter Rogers, top right – designer Valery Stevenson), 150 (left – designer Paul Miles, right – designer Glazenwood, Essex), 158, 175 (designer Victor Shanley, Clifton Nurseries); The Hamlyn Group 27, 58–9, 159, 171 (bottom right), 191 (top left); Peter Loughran 114–5,

130–1; Robert Pearson 47; The Harry Smith Horticultural Photographic Collection 6, 15, 18, 19, 30, 31 (top, centre right and bottom left), 35, 55 (top), 70, 71 (bottom left), 86, 91, 106, 107, 118, 151 (bottom), 154, 155, 166, 167, 170, 171 (centre right), 182, 190, 191 (top right and bottom), 206, 207 (top right and bottom right); Tony Stone Associates 178–9; Michael Warren 31 (bottom right), 162–3, 171 (left), 187, 203.